This book was given to the library
by the DUC Library Program
of Art Resources Transfer, Inc.
New York City

in honor of

Laurie Simmons

for her unique voice as an artist
and for her important
and ongoing contributions to
the visual arts community.

MODULATIONS

MODULATIONS

A HISTORY OF ELECTRONIC MUSIC:
THROBBING WORDS ON SOUND

EDITED BY PETER SHAPIRO

PROJECT DIRECTOR IARA LEE

CONTENTS

Edited by: Peter Shapiro
Project Director: Iara Lee
Graphic Design: Alan Hill
Production Managers: Mark Lukowitsky, Rob Marane, Craig Willis
Production Coordinator: Giles Miller

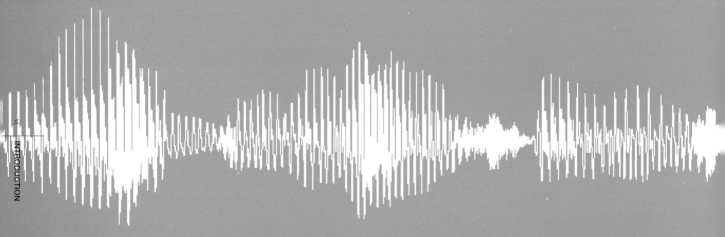

Published in 2000 by:
Caipirinha Productions, Inc.
510 LaGaurdia Place #5, New York NY 10012
caipirinha@caipirinha.com www.caipirinha.com

ISBN 1-891024-06-X

Printed in Hong Kong

Manufactured Through Asia Pacific Offset

in association with:
D.A.P./Distributed Art Publishers, Inc.
155 Sixth Ave. 2nd Floor, New York NY 10013
Tel: 212-627-1999 Fax: 212-627-9484
dap@dapinc.com www.artbook.com

F O R E W O R D

Following screenings of *Modulations*, I would often hear people say how they felt that the film was just the beginning of a journey into this forever expanding electronic music culture.

All projects at Caipirinha Productions seem to have a snowball effect. What begins as curiosity eventually becomes an obsession. Our desire to expose this culture to others, as well as to learn more ourselves, has pushed us not only to produce a film, but also a cd series and now a book.

Technology is not only the subject of our projects, but also a powerful tool, that allows us to be truly synergistic with other art forms. Why must we limit ourselves to only one medium? Through mixed-media projects, we hope to expose and excite new minds. The idea is to continuously celebrate the hybrids of culture, to take on new adventures, and to break out from pre-conceived notions of melody music making. Why not mix analog with digital, or acoustic instruments with electronics, in the hope of enhancing creativity?

By using the cut-and-paste philosophy, we've pieced together some of the history behind the evolution of this music from its early pioneers through today's bedroom musicians. The book is composed of chapters devoted to different styles of electronic music and accompanied by quotes and interviews conducted for the film.

I would like to thank all the writers, researchers, photographers, and contributors who have made this project possible. Also, my gratitude and respect to the artists and record companies that have been so cooperative and supportive.

Like the film, this book took a great amount of devotion, perseverance, and endurance. This is the product of our efforts, but it is by no means a complete one. This culture is forever changing, evolving, mutating . . .

— Iara Lee and the Caipirinha Productions Crew

It is time to reassess what has happened in the century and to look at it with a longer lens. **MIXMASTER MORRIS** There is a great struggle going on at the moment about what we do with our humanness, what we do with our virtual selves. When do we give up our humanness and simply accept the machines? **DAVID TOOP** There are no UFOs. Machine music is the only way forward. **JUAN ATKINS** a.k.a. MODEL 500

INTRODUCTION

BY PETER SHAPIRO

Although Thomas Alva Edison's phonograph was a handcranked mechanical device made of cogs and gears rather than an electronic box of wires and capacitors (electronic recording didn't begin until the mid-1920s), his first recording of "Mary Had a Little Lamb" in 1877 was the dawn of electronic music. The partially deaf Edison originally imagined the phonograph simply as a dictating machine: It was advertised as "the ideal amanuensis" when it was first put on the market. The user would speak into the machine's horn while a needle engraved the patterns of the soundwaves into grooves on a cylinder covered with tin foil that could then be played back. Though Edison failed to capitalize on the commercial potential of his invention, this strange new device that captured the human voice became the toast of the society set in parlors across Europe. Entranced by the sound of their own voices, the singers of the day (always the most egotistical of musicians) were captivated by the phonograph and instigated its use as a musical reproduction device.

The phonograph created popular music not only in the sense that it allowed music to become a mass commodity, but also in the sense that it created twentieth century music's fundamental paradigm. The history of music in the millennium's final hundred years has largely been the history of technology: The invention of the ordinary volume microphone that allowed Bing Crosby and Frank Sinatra to croon softly on top of a big band; the development of the 33 RPM record that allowed jazz musicians to expand their compositions beyond the four minutes allowed by 78 and 45 rpm discs; country session musician Grady Martin discovering the pleasures of an overdriven guitar amplifier on Marty Robbins' 1961 hit "Don't Worry"; and the junglists' discovery that the time-stretch function of the sampler was a musical effect in and of itself. The excitement generated by pop music has often been the thrill of exploration and the sense of possibility provided by technology's shock of the new.

However, the exploitation of technology is often disguised by claims of authenticity and naturalism — camouflage designed to preserve and protect the myth of artistic inspiration. From the Rolling Stones to James Brown, even the "earthiest" musicians have kept it real by surreptitiously dabbling in the black magic of the recording studio. The musicians featured in *Modulations*, on the other hand, make no bones about their relationship to machines; they don't masquerade in the cloak of roots or tradition. They recognize that the drum machine and sampler are no less organic than an acoustic guitar and a harmonica. Following the dictum of *musique concrète* pioneer Pierre Schaeffer — "It is by ruler and compass that the Greeks discovered geometry; musicians might do well to follow their example" — electronic musicians have jimmied open the bars and staffs that have imprisoned western music for centuries and created their own multi-dimensional configurations of sound. Tuning into the noise of the city, hot-wiring the hearts of their machines, diving headfirst into mysterious realms, reinstating lost rituals and imagining new identities, these musicians have opened their minds to the possibility that the supposedly dehumanizing machine might actually make us more human.

The phonograph was perhaps the first machine to truly live up to the Luddites' fears by imprisoning a fundamental aspect of human identity within its cogs and gears, but the history of music and technology has not been dominated simply by the logic of the machine. Maybe the first technological advance to become truly practical only when it was used in a way for which it was not originally designed, the phonograph and its subsequent use and misuse has taught us that the human-tech interface is not all one-way traffic.

A century after its invention, a Bronx teenager once again changed the way we approach the phonograph. Practicing his mixing skills on two turntables in his bedroom, Theodore Livingston (soon to be called Grand Wizard Theodore) was interrupted by his mother who wanted him to turn the music down. As he turned around to say something like, "Aww Mom, get off my back," he accidentally rubbed one of the records across the stylus and serendipitously invented scratching. As hip-hop's signature flourish, the technique of scratching (not to mention subsequent developments like transforming and beat juggling) has shown that, despite Edison's best intentions, the phonograph is really a percussion instrument and not simply a playback device.

Even more malleable than the vinyl disc, and just as crucial to the development of music in the twentieth century, was magnetic tape. Although the process of converting soundwaves to electronic signals and imprinting them on to tape was invented in the 1930s, recording tape machines did not come onto the market until after World War II. With a greater signal-to-noise ratio, the possibility of controlling volume, and the potential for mixing and filtering, magnetic tape quickly replaced recording straight to disc as the standard medium of sound reproduction.

Just like the vinyl record, though, it was the fact that tape could be spliced and its information rearranged that really captured the imagination of more inventive musicians and composers. After hours of painstaking tape editing with a razor blade, a broadcasting engineer for *Radiodiffusion-Télévision Française* named Pierre Schaeffer constructed two pieces of music out of the noises of trains (*Étude aux Chemins de Fer*) and saucepans (*Études aux Casseroles*) that were broadcast on French radio in 1948. He called his collages *musique concrète*, but in the ensuing years, this process of reassembling fragments of sound has been called dub, disco, hip-hop, house, drum and bass, trip-hop, electronica – heck, even rock 'n' roll.

While there might be something of Marshall McLuhan's famous pronouncement that "the medium is the message" in all of this, it is not merely the fact that it is electronic that makes electronic music interesting. By taking trips to the moon on gossamer wings and submerging 20,000 leagues under the sea, electronic music represents what journalist Kodwo Eshun calls "sonic fiction." After all, why keep it real when you can surf on sine waves? *Modulations* is about this ecstatic freefall into the unknown in the era of electronic and digital technologies – an age in which the boundaries between human and machine are becoming increasingly blurred, a time in which the rhythms of machines are beginning to sound like what Detroit techno producer Derrick May calls the "Strings of Life."

Italian futurist Luigi Russolo issues his manifesto "The Art of Noises," which calls for futurist musicians to "substitute for the limited variety of tones posessed by orchestral instruments today the infinite variety of tones of noises, reproduced with appropri-ate mechanisms" and states that "we find far more enjoyment in the combination of the noises of trams, backfiring motors, car-riages, and bawling crowds than in rehearsing, for example, the *Eroica* or the *Pastoral*." Russolo also creates his intonarumori, or noise intoner.

1913

Canadian scientist Thaddeus Cahill invents the telharmonium, the first electronic instrument. The only problem is that it is 60 feet wide, 20 feet tall and weighs 200 tons. American inventor Lee DeForest invents the triode, a vacuum tube that allows the transmission of sound through electrical signals.

1906

George William Guest and Horace Merriman record the burial service of the Unknown Warrior at London's Westminster Abbey—the first recording made with an ordinary volume microphone. Meanwhile, in Paris, Léon Thérémin develops the theremin, the first practical electronic instrument.

1920

Alexander Graham Bell invents the telephone, which converts sounds into electronic signals.

1876

1877
Thomas Edison invents the phono-graph, heralding the age of mechanical reproduction.

1907
Inspired by the telharmonium, Italian composer Ferruccio Busoni writes *Sketch for a New Aesthetic of Music*, which envis-ages a future of new scales and an entirely electronic music.

1915
Lee DeForest invents the oscillator, which produces tones from electronic signals and is the basis of all electronic tone-gen-erating instruments.

1926
George Antheil's *Ballet Mécanique*, scored for pianos, xylophones, doorbells, and airplane propellers, causes a sensation in Paris.

Maurice Martenot invents the ondes martenot, which uses a keyboard, ribbons and knobs to produce electronic tones.

1928

John Cage creates his *Imaginary Landscape No. 1*, a composition for recordings of pure frequency tones played on variable-speed turntables.

1939

Bell Labs develops the vocoder, a device that electronically transforms the human voice, and bequeaths hits to Joe Walsh, Peter Frampton, and Zapp.

1948

On "How High the Moon?" Les Paul pioneers the art of overdubbing and speeds up the tape of his guitar solo, causing a whole generation of budding guitarists to contract carpal tunnel syndrome by trying to copy his solo.

1951

1935

Laurens Hammond creates the electric Hammond organ, and the Nazis develop the tape recorder as a propaganda tool.

1946

The atomic test at the Bikini atoll in the South Pacific is broadcast on radio in the United States—the ultimate realization of Russolo's pronouncements.

1949

Pierre Schaeffer creates his *Symphonie Pour un Homme Seul* - the first fully realized *musique concrète* piece and the first piece of music to take advantage of the possibilities of magnetic recording tape.

1954

Guitar Slim and Johnny "Guitar" Watson introduce the world to the pleasures of guitar distortion with their records *The Things That I Used to Do* and *Space Guitar*.

After a decade of experi-
mentation, RCA engineers
Harry Olsen and Herbert
Belar introduce the RCA
Sound Synthesizer.

1956

Session guitarist Grady Martin
unintentionally develops the Fuzz
Box effects pedal with his busted-
amp solo on country singer Marty
Robbins' "Don't Worry."

1961

The first completely
synthesized record, Walter
(Wendy) Carlos' *Switched
on Bach*, is released and
quickly becomes the
biggest selling classical
LP of alltime.

1968

1958
At the World's Fair in Brussels,
Edgard Varèse premiers his
collage of electronic noise
and airplane sounds, *Poème
Électronique*, alongside Iannis
Xenakis' *Concret PH*, a score
for burning charcoal.

1967
Morton Subotnick records
Silver Apples of the Moon
using Donald Buchla's
touch-pad synthesizer.

1971
Little Roy's "Hard Fighter"
includes "Voo-doo" – an instrumental version that features dropout and echo – on the flip, which
becomes the first dub record.

The holy trinity of synthesizer records is released: Donna Summer's "I Feel Love", Parliament's "Flashlight," and Kraftwerk's *Trans-Europe Express*.

1977

Kraftwerk releases *Computer World* and invent Techno, while Grandmaster Flash has a most excellent adventure on the wheels of steel, and proves that the turntable is a percussion instrument and not a playback device.

1981

Jesse Saunders releases "On and On," generally regarded as the first Chicago House record.

1983

Producer and remixer Marley Marl makes the sampler the electric guitar of the next fifty years on his mix of Eric B & Rakim's "Eric B For President".

1986

1978
The first polyphonic synthesizer, the Sequential Circuits Prophet 5, comes on the market.

1982
Afrika Bambaataa, Arthur Baker, and John Robie give Kraftwerk afros and shell-toed Adidases with fat laces on *Planet Rock*. Yamaha's DX-7 synthesizer rocks the planet even more by intro-ducing digital technology to the music world. Meanwhile, Japanese synthesizer company Roland releases the incomparable TR-808 drum machine and the ill-conceived TB-303 bassline machine, which would become notable only because of the ingenuity of musicians in Chicago.

1985
Juan Atkins releases "No UFOs" and creates the blue-print for Techno, while MC ADE's proto-Miami Bass records, "Bass Mechanic" and "Bass Rock Express," make booties bounce in Florida.

1992
Goldie's "Terminator" introduces the technique of timestretching to hardcore Techno and lays the foundation for Jungle.

1

As soon as you have electronic music, by definition, you're operating to create new worlds of sound. These producers don't want to change the world. They don't want to create love songs. They don't want to sing about revolution. They don't want to get angry. They want to be scientists of sound. They want to explore new universes of sound. **KODWO ESHUN** I would say that Stockhausen is the closest thing to hip-hop in its original form. The whole idea of taking something and shaping it and forming it and translating it into a form of expression. **DXT**

PIONEERS

ROLL TAPE: PIONEER SPIRITS IN *MUSIQUE CONCRÈTE*

BY ROB YOUNG

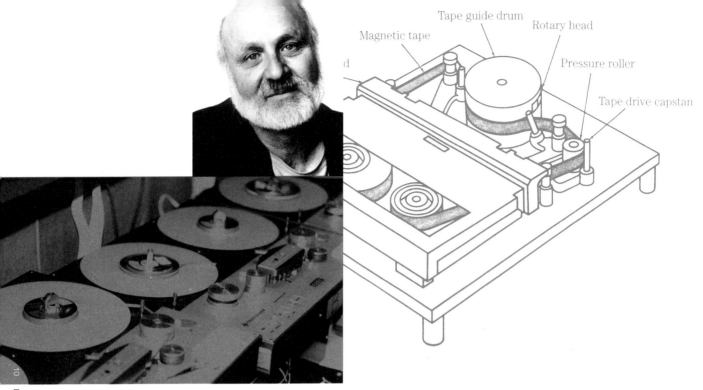

Magnetic tape
d
Tape guide drum
Rotary head
Pressure roller
Tape drive capstan

Discography:			
	PIERRE SCHAEFFER	*Complete Works*	INA/GRM
	PIERRE HENRY	*L'Homme À La Caméra, Fragments Pour Artaud, Le Voyage*	Mantra
	KARLHEINZ STOCKHAUSEN	*Hymnen, Kontakte, Telemusik*	StockhausenVerlag
	DAVID TUDOR	*Rainforest*	Lovely Music
	IANNIS XENAKIS	*Electronic Music*	EMF
	LUC FERRARI	*Acousmatrix 3*	INA/GRM
	VITTORIO GELMETTI	*Musiche Elettroniche*	Nepless
	BBC RADIOPHONIC WORKSHOP	*Tomb of the Cybermen*	Via Satellite
	RUNE LINDBLAD	*Death of the Moon*	Pogus
	TOD DOCKSTADER	*Quatermass*	Starkland

In 1997, the French division of the classical label Philips released a cd called *Métamorphose: Messe Pour Le Temps Présent*. Issued alongside a conventional rerelease of the original Messe, a 1967 dance piece by composer Pierre Henry and Michel Colombier with choreography by Maurice Béjart, the "métamorphoses" were remixes by dance music producers including William Orbit, Coldcut, Fatboy Slim, Dimitri From Paris, and 4 Hero's alter ego Tek 9. This was not the only time Henry's music would interface with pop's *modus operandi:* In 1969, he collaborated on *Ceremony* with proto-progressive rockers Spooky Tooth. But with *Métamorphose*, a circle appeared to be closing.

Most of the remixers inevitably picked out the most listener-friendly section of the *Messe*, "Psyché Rock", a kooky, upbeat pop-psychedelic cocktail of flutes, beatnik rhythms, "electronic jerks" chopped out on guitar, and swooping, synthesized photon beams. Alongside another slice of kitsch electronica, Jean Jacques Perrey's Moogbass-heavy "EVA," "Psyché Rock" was—perhaps because of its superficial cuteness—repositioned as a cornerstone in the history of collage music, and by implication, became an ancestor of sampled musics everywhere.

At around the same time, another father of electronic music, Karlheinz Stockhausen, was publicly (on BBC Radio and in *The Wire* magazine) involved in an exchange of views with younger techno/electronica artists such as Aphex Twin and Scanner. In America, Paul D. Miller (a.k.a. DJ Spooky) cued up quadraphonic tape on a recording of Iannis Xenakis' caustic electro-acoustic work *Kraanerg* (released on a label better known for its streetwise hip-hop stylings).

In these small ways, debts were being recognized between one generation of dance music creators and another, however different the forms of music in question. Nonetheless, Monsieur Henry must have been miffed that his least typical work had been singled out for resurrection when he commented, in typically rebarbative mood, in a *Wire* interview at the time: "It so

happens that the original version is doing as well, if not better, than the remixes."

This incident took place one year short of the fiftieth anniversary of the first dabblings with magnetic tape composition in a French electronic music studio, dabblings that would become formalized into a process dubbed *musique concrète*. The postwar history of electronic music begins with a singular man, Pierre Schaeffer, whose late-forties tapeworks such as *Symphonie des Bruits* opened the spectrum of available sound to include dissonance, jump-cut rhythms and the blare of gritted noise. The landmark piece from this first phase is a further expression of singularity, *Symphonie Pour un Homme Seul* (*Symphony For a Man Alone*, 1950). Although it currently exists on record only as part of a boxed cd set comprising Schaeffer's complete works,

it was in fact a joint composition made by him and Pierre Henry while they were both employees at the studios of the national broadcasting company, Radio France.

At this distance, it's easy to forget the revolutionary importance of their long, after-hours splicing sessions. Almost three-quarters of a century previously, two American inventors had redefined the way people listened to and communicated with each other. In 1876, Alexander Graham Bell converted sound into an electronic signal and worked out how to decode it again with the telephone; the following year, Thomas Edison invented the recording machinery that could preserve those sounds for the future. Yet the machinery was rarely used as a creative tool in itself. (John Cage, as ever, provides the rare exception: His 1939 *Imaginary Landscape No.1* was "scored" for three turntables spin-

ning test-tone records at different speeds.)

By the end of the forties, the gramophone was as much a part of the home as the wireless radio. The sonic space they produced was regarded as objectively and acoustically "truthful" rather than a virtual site where sonic phantasms could swim and play. In America, paradoxically, one of the most radical musical eruptions—bebop—occurred during the absence of recording. The two recording bans of 1942-1944 and 1945-1948 that had arisen from a dispute between the American Federation of Musicians (AMF) and major record labels meant that Charlie Parker was only spottily captured at the point where he was wrestling the blues out of their traditional, hardened shape. Only twenty years later, with George Russell's *Electronic Sonata for Souls Loved by Nature* and Miles Davis' *In a Silent Way*, would jazz make its own quantum leap into the smoke and mirrors realm of studio alchemy.

Meanwhile, academic classical music—the tradition out of which Pierres Henry and Schaeffer had emerged—was, and largely remains, stubbornly resistant to the flexibility of the recorded medium. (Even in the late nineties, the emphasis is on transparency and seamlessness, with "4D" digital recording used as a selling point and hundreds of digital edits per minute on even the largest orchestral sessions.) The musical landscape of the mid-twentieth century is peopled with heroic individuals: driven divas (Maria Callas, Victoria De Los Angeles); tempestuous or idiosyncratic conductors (Arturo Toscanini, Thomas Beecham, Wilhelm Furtwängler); and passionate pianists (Sviatoslav Richter, Vladimir Horowitz). As Romanticism played out its final act, the

mercurial relationship between composed score and bold, freewheeling interpretation was preserved as the focus of music appreciation.

Schaeffer and Henry's constructive transgression was to act on the knowledge that tape materialized music into a solid, concrete object. In its plastic form, music could be interfered with—reversed, sped up, or slowed down, measured in inches, laid out on a slab, and dissected at will. The artistic moment no longer occurred in the written manuscript, nor with the physicality of performance, but became distributed within the manipulation of stock and found sounds, a process resembling film editing. With source material grabbed from railway stations, dockside clanging, street shouts, creaking doors, sighs, cries and whispers, the new approach sought to amplify the ambience of contemporary life. When *concrète* music

was played in public, new techniques and technologies had to be used: sound diffusion (Jacques Pouillon designed his *pupitre d'espace*–space desk–to spread sound into every corner of a concert hall); time-bending distortions (the *phonogène* allowed the user to vary the speed and pitch at which the tape played back); and extraneously applied sound modulations (the morphophone, another invention commissioned by Schaeffer, featured multiple tape heads that could generate primitive delay and echo effects). All of these functions have since been improved, enhanced, and incorporated into so many areas of contemporary music production—from rock's amplification systems to the sampler's time-stretch facility and the digital delay pedal—that music without them is unthinkable.

Personal differences between Schaeffer and Henry

eventually yawned into a rift. Schaeffer embodied a cool approach to studio-bound discoveries, hoping to gently work up a stately theory of sound. Henry, at the time, was a Dionysian firebrand, writing manifestoes that called for "all music to be destroyed" and placing a visionary topspin on the creations that were emerging from their rechristened *Groupe de Recherche de Musique Concrète* (GRM) studio. The GRM was accumulating internationally: avant-garde composers such as Pièrre Boulez, Karlheinz Stockhausen, Olivier Messiaen, Darius Milhaud, and Edgard Varèse were making pilgrimages to the GRM studio in order to produce sounds they were unable to achieve anywhere else. Between 1958 and 1959, Henry broke away from Schaeffer—later claiming that Schaeffer had found his single-minded approach to the new music dangerous—and founded his own self-financed Studio Apsome. Here he recorded many film soundtracks, publicity tapes, and dances; he also promoted multimedia events where his own music would be performed theatrically with choreographed light shows.

At the end of the nineties, the innovations that began with GRM's founders have been fully integrated into the everyday working practice of almost all musicians working across the entire musical spectrum. The breakbeat, created entirely from the manipulation of records on turntables or from recorded segments spliced together manually or digitally, is the epitome of *musique concrète*. At the same time, many original *concrète* works are undergoing a minor renaissance as the cd era ploughs through the archives; their influence has been acknowledged by current electronica artists such as Aphex Twin, Autechre, Mouse On Mars, and Pan sonic. Relatively affordable miniature samplers, allowing infinitely greater fingertip control over the shape of a sound than any of Pouillon's varispeed tape machines, now come pocket-sized and are widely available.

Although *musique concrète* and its underpinning strategies are more accessible now than at any time previously, electronic music is still treated as a second-class citizen by a classical establishment bent on privileging

those who compose for acoustic instruments. Although the activities of, say, painters, whose creations are painstakingly labored over alone in a cloistered studio have produced some of the most widely celebrated—not to mention bankable—artworks of the century, musicians who isolate themselves in a roomful of electronic toys are often mistrusted, derided, and accused of elitism. Mainstream aesthetics demands that music be a socialized, real-time pursuit, whether in an orchestra or in a rock band. With "classical" electronic compositions, the work is the recording.

Musique concrète mocks this desire for sonic "clarity," substituting an ideological clarity of its own. Gathering up the threads laid down by Luigi Russolo's *Art of Noises* manifesto (1913), in which the Italian futurist envisaged a mechanical form of music that reflected "the musical soul of crowds, great industrial complexes, transatlantic liners, trains, tanks, automobiles, and aeroplanes...the domination of the machine and the victorious reign of electricity," Pierre Henry announced the arrival of a music suitable for the accelerated information flows of the twentieth century. In his *Variations for a Door and a Sigh* (1963), the tape-splicing existential artist uses the microphone as a forensic probe to penetrate the "doorness" of a door. Where modernism had spent the first half-century collaging echoes from the past, this was an attempt to grasp enlightenment from the fractured materials of the immediate present, peering closely at what the snipped-up tape loops revealed like a Chinese seer examining the splinters in an ox's shoulder blade. For Henry, writing in 1950, *musique concrète* meant a humanist descent from the absolute to the material realm: from "the sacred" to "a relationship with cries, laughter, sex, death. Everything that puts us in touch with the cosmic, that is to say, with the living materiality of planets on fire."

JOHN CAGE WITH TOSHIRO MAYUZUMI

Like almost all singularities that are seen in hindsight as innovations, this pioneering movement was not occurring in isolation. In the same year that the two Pierres were chopping out their symphony for a man alone, the first "vocoder"—an electronic device designed to alter the sound of the voice—was brought from America to the Institute of Phonetics in Bonn, Germany. Its cybernetic transformations of the instrument always held to be the most natural in the world so impressed Robert Beyer, a producer from the Cologne-based radio station *Westdeutscher Rundfunk* (WDR), that he went on, in 1951, to build a studio dedicated to the development of electronic music techniques. Enter Karlheinz Stockhausen.

At the turn of the twentieth century, tonal music had reached its limits in the broiling orchestral soups of Gustav Mahler and Richard Wagner. A way out of the impasse—serialism or twelve-tone composition—evolved among the practitioners of the Second Viennese School, Arnold Schoenberg, Alban Berg, and Anton Webern. Mathematical organization, rather than the vagaries of emotional resonance, lay behind the formal organization of the serialists' twelve-note rows, which acted as harmonic cells that could be combined, shuffled, transposed, pitch-shifted up or down the stave, turned backwards, stood on their head, or all of these transformations at once.

By the fifties, serialism was already a basic practice in classical music's avant-garde, and Stockhausen had been a rigorous student of the technique. Initially, he used the WDR studio as a test bed for his conception of applying serialist structuring to sine waves generated on electronic oscillators. His early efforts in this mode were the slightly arid *Studien I & II*, but in 1956, Stockhausen recorded *Gesang Der Jünglinge* (Song of the Children), which incorporated tape segments of a boy soprano reading biblical passages from the Book of Daniel. Stretching the voice out into long, gummy strings, Stockhausen folded them into a shifting envelope of electronic sounds to form what he called "a mutual sound-continuum." With the music running on tape loops, the sense of human effort prevalent whenever real instrumentalists or vocalists are involved was removed. You feel that the song could go on forever.

Stockhausen bestrides the parallel developments of instrumental and electronic music in the postwar years. Often ridiculed for control freakery and downright eccentricity (his claims of having descended from the star Sirius being his grandest *Dummheit*), his interests in the music of non-Western cultures surfaced in *Hymnen* (1967), which fused assorted national anthems into a morphing sequence; and *Telemusik* (1966), an integration of Japanese gagaku court music and the Balinese gamelan. This predated the interest shown in ancient oriental musics by Brian Eno, Jon Hassell, and a gallery of contemporary ambient musicians. The word "integration" describes Stockhausen's prime contribution to the evolution of electronic composition. Through a conceptual and technical process he described as "intermodulation," he moved tape music from disjointed collage into a newly swirling pool of sound in which references and sounds could cross-connect and dissolve into a controlled fluidity in the mix. *Telemusik* summed it up, compressing cultural, spatial and temporal distance into magnetic particles and feeding them into the microworld between the speakers.

Electronic music was reared in an age of accumulating networks and has been marked throughout the postwar decades by its relentless, rapid, global spread. Recording facilities in cities all over the world—in commercial and broadcasting contexts as well as in academic research centers—led to outgrowths of serious electronic

music throughout the early fifties. In Milan, Italy Luciano Berio wove together strands of tape featuring the speech of Cathy Berberian into his *Thema-Omaggio à James Joyce*. In New York, John Cage and longstanding collaborator David Tudor, in conjunction with Forbidden Planet soundtrackists Louis and Bebe Barron, began the full-scale anatomization of the electronic sound palette known as the *Project for Music for Magnetic Tape* that survives as the tape-spliced, I Ching-directed *Williams Mix*. Tokyo's NHK studio equipped Cage associate Toshi Ichiyanagi, one of a growing number of Japanese electronic experimenters, with the means to study the interactions of microphone and tape. At the same time, in Tokyo, Toru Takemitsu was tracing out the windswept, filtered blasts of white noise that would gust across his film score *Kwaidan*, with the aid of a prototype light-pen.

Elsewhere in New York, as Cage and Tudor were snipping up lengths of reel-to-reel tape for *Williams Mix*, Columbia University agreed to house the room-sized synthesizers of Otto Luening and Vladimir Ussachevsky, laying the foundations of the Columbia-Princeton Electronic Music Center after the synth's Princeton exponent, Milton Babbitt, brokered a merger of the two college departments. The Center quickly became a test bed for the RCA Mark II Electronic Synthesizer. It was visited by such figures as Berio and Charles Wuorinen (a dyed-in-the-wool American serialist who'd churned out dozens of orchestral and chamber works, and whose head was sufficiently rewired by the experience to generate the 1969 computer work *Time's Encomium*). It's especially in the unbending mathematical rigor of Babbitt, though, that it's possible to pinpoint the ancestry of the lab-coated "sci-

KARLHEINZ STOCKHAUSEN

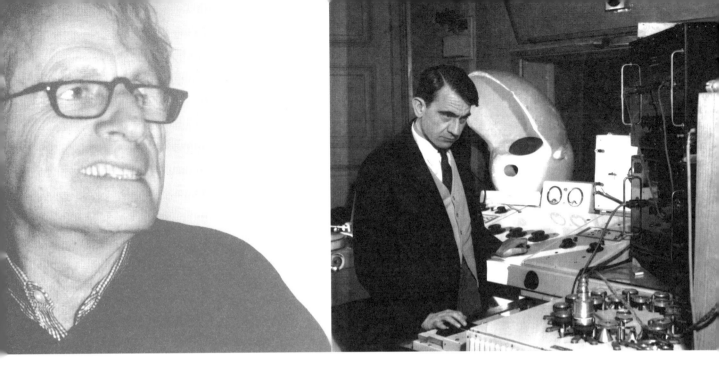

ence" element of electronic music that's survived as a characterization of late-twentieth-century techno boffindom. It didn't ease the creeping sense that electronic composition was becoming a hermetic art—a closed loop restricted to sonic dialogues between initiates—when Babbitt published an article entitled "Who Cares If You Listen?" But it wasn't just these odd, molelike creatures you occasionally saw pictured in front of their pocked patchboards. More glamorous and easily marketable forms of revolution were simultaneously springing up in other sectors—rock 'n' roll, jazz, pop and all its hybrids—all centered on live art, real-time performance, emotional, psychosexual theatre. Sound stored electronically—on tape, digitally encoded, engraved in vinyl—was a substance that could be pinned down in the lab like a frog under the scalpel and was accordingly received in the

public domain with the kind of support usually reserved for the activities of vivisectionists.

Ways were found to introduce an electronic music removed from the confinement of the concert hall to a wider public. In 1958, architect Le Corbusier embarked on the installation of a spatialized whorl of "sound, light, color, rhythm"—a multimedia *poème électronique*"—in the Philips Corporation's pavilion at the Brussels World's Fair Expo. Both veteran avant-garde composer Edgard Varèse and Le Corbusier's architectural assistant, Iannis Xenakis, ran tape loops of fizzling metallic rain through a distributed network of 425 speakers; the sound was then directed into clusters by the respective composers. Heard by approximately two million visitors passing through the Expo, this was perhaps the pinnacle of *musique concrète's* achievement. Never a spectacular success in the

IANNIS XENAKIS

PIERRE SCHAEFFER

restrained seating of concert halls, the music's physical malleability and mobility allowed it to come alive in new, wired-for-sound public thoroughfares. Electronic music of this kind did not, of course, get much more mileage out of soundtracking public space—no shopping mall today rings with the sound of *Concret pH* or *Poème Électronique*. Instead, the products of the Muzak Corporation are piped into the workplace, while the less tonal aspects of electronic music disappeared from public view into fund-hungry research laboratories such as Paris's IRCAM (Institute for Research and Co-ordination of Acoustics and Music), Boston's MIT, and Amsterdam's STEIM (Studio for Electro-Instrumental Music).

Still, the music slowly leaked into the pop domain. In the second half of the 1960s, the Beatles (or the art-conscious John Lennon, anyway) included a pseudo-academic *concrète* piece, "Revolution Number 9," on their 1968 *White Album*; the Grateful Dead's *Anthem of the Sun* relied on a conscious collaging of treated tape fragments culled from different live performances; and an obscure but latently influential New York art-rock group named themselves the Silver Apples after Morton Subotnick's composition for Buchla synthesizer, *Silver Apples of the Moon*. Frank Zappa, forever indebted to Varèse's pioneering works, dropped references to his hero at any opportunity; Miles Davis and Herbie Hancock both cited Stockhausen as a key catalyst in helping them melt jazz down into the liquefied astro-funk of *On the Corner* and *Sextant*; in Germany, two pupils of the Cologne Tonmeister—Holger Czukay and Irmin Schmidt—took what they'd learned into the founding of their group Can, arguably the first German outfit to slip the shackles of American rock 'n' roll and set the controls for the playfully motorik heart of central European sensibility. And from 1963 on into the mid-seventies, a slice of classic *musique concrète* scared the pants off millions of British

households every Saturday night courtesy of the BBC Radiophonic Workshop as Ron Grainer and Delia Derbyshire's scything soundtrack for sci-fi series *Dr. Who* heralded a weekly galaxy of time travel and low-budget alien exotica.

Poorly served on record for almost two decades, there have been signs of renewed interest in the beginnings of electronic music now that the sonic cut-up has become media cliché instead of avant-garde staple. For a generation of DJs and low-budget bedroom operatives, the hit-and-miss trials of the likes of Henry and Schaeffer (who had only their enthusiasm and sense of purpose to compensate for the limitations of a tape technology not equipped to handle the rate at which the ideas were flowing) offer a bond across time. Adventurous labels such as Pogus, Nepless, Alga Marghen, Starkland and Rune Grammofon are recovering a vast archive of forgotten tape works from vaults in Norway, Sweden, Italy, and the United States. Stockhausen himself bought his own back catalogue from the huge German company Deutsche Grammophon that didn't share the enthusiasm of the significant numbers of listeners who now besiege the composer with CD orders. In Stockhausen's gesture is encapsulated the enduring spirit that *musique concrète* engendered. Tape and computer music, turntablism, techno, do-it-yourself record manufacture and distribution—all these seizures of the means of (re-) production add up to a cataclysmic system-hack made all the more devastating by its invisibility. 🐾

Lots of things about Cage are very inspiring. To me, the books are even more inspiring than the music. Cage's music is more fun to read about than listen to sometimes. But his playfulness is very apparent; even when he was seventy, receiving all these honorary doctorates, he would turn up with these dellyboppers on for the doctorate ceremony because he was just a big kid at heart, and again Cage was in the inventive tradition – his father was an inventor, wasn't he? He always invented things because they didn't exist and, to me, that's the right attitude, instead of working with what you are given. **MIXMASTER MORRIS** Jean-Jacques Perrey and I have been starting to think about doing a performance somewhere. He insists on doing his music by cutting tape and splicing it together. On the computer, this is probably the simplest thing you can do. But getting the razor blades and getting the splicing block and running the tape through the heads – this man still does this. And to embrace this idea, we would make the longest tape loop and string it around the auditorium and maybe have a thirty minute tape loop and perform along with it. **MONEY MARK**

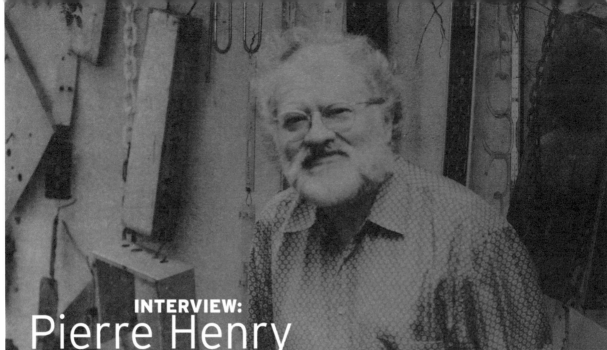

INTERVIEW:
Pierre Henry

Musique concrète is not a music of today or yesterday. It comes from a long way off. Many composers, artists, writers, and painters imagined that one day music would transform itself into a vast opera of new, unprecedented sounds – sounds that have never been imagined. As a child, my head was filled with new sounds, sounds that couldn't be interpreted. That is the peculiarity of *musique concrète*. It doesn't come from interpretation or performance. Its essence is imagination. This imagination is linked to a technique: It's the fabrication of music. Fabrication, but also the conception and composition. It is thought, imagined and engraved in memory. It's a music of memory. *Musique concrète* is based on nothing. It's a dust of sound, a comma of sound. In *Spiral*, the sound came from some sort of amplified respiration that repeated itself endlessly. This music cannot be played with acoustic instruments, but rather with electronic tools. I didn't have any opposition to atonal or serial music. The idea was to find a new form of music, a new writing style instead of just imitating and being stuck in a trend. We wanted to bring out a new music. It was meant to be a revolution. We are different from other musicians, but we are not opposed to any music. Variation is the principle of *musique concrète*. A cell becomes another, and then there are combinations, associations, and many possibilities of intermixing, of polyphony. Current music is extremely polyphonic. It's like a grand orchestra, but it's done track by track. A composer is inevitably revolutionary. I wrote about destroying music in order to alter, little by little, the act of listening. Contrary to groups of painters or writers, the musician is like a monk. He has to stay in his studio and work. Musicians don't have time to be revolutionary. *Musique concrète* proceeds from photography, from cinema. We've been recently talking a lot about techno music. I think it's unfortunate that it is for the moment too much connected to the place it is listened to. It's too dependent on the loudness, which allows the bass to be powerful. It's a music far too much connected to physiological reactions and not enough to mental reactions. It has no sensitivity; it's not surprising enough, and it lacks poetry. I feel music should keep its share of poetry. There are many things we can do with digital sound. All sounds become original sounds, the sound of the beginning. That's interesting, but there is a betrayal in the sense that digital sound is not as good as analog sound. It has less strength, less impact, less presence. Therefore it's necessary to mix analog — that is, old equipment — with new equipment. We can't get rid of the old equipment. We still need to have the future connected to the past. That's what life is, this mixture of the slightly archeological laws of the past with the foresight of the future. Drifting is necessary once in a while. I often play everything together and then listen. Sometimes a strange phenomenon occurs. We need to catch it. That which is intuitive, instinctive, imaginary comes from fate, because fate is nature. It's always the same. There's thought and fate, the control of fate by thought, and the simulation of thought by fate. I can't really say that I felt close to Italian futurists. I thought of them as fascists and not as artists. Of course, it was glorifying for them to say we could make noise, but there always has been noise. Even classical composers would add a cannon shot in their work. Noise becomes a musical note when altered. Real noise is very interesting. A drama should be told with noise. In film, for example, I enjoy noise. I dislike music in film. I would like to conceive a score like a film, with noises, voices. During the evolution of technique, engineers wanted to bring out finished products, to standardize manufactured products. What was interesting in electro-acoustic music was to search, to find new ways, new possibilities. Having specialized, standardized tools isn't usually very inspiring. Current music is constantly invented over and over again — it has become like the sound of the sea, constantly renewed, but always the same. That's why I fear that sound will be the same everywhere, on the radio, in films. It's easy now for youngsters — they can get for only a few thousand francs, a box, an amp, equipment that makes sounds. I prefer music that stays inside of us, that allows us to dream, to imagine, and even perhaps to love. The music I'm referring to is one of communication. It's a language more than an art. Now it's no longer a language. It's some sort of constantly present tam-tam. I'm not convinced by current music, the way it is done. But there are some possibilities. Its form is similar to the beginning of music in the Middle Ages in France, where it was not only just a form, but it was also very boring. I don't particularly like cave music. Music of yesterday was linear and white. When Renoir spoke of white, he meant with no colors. Music of today has no colors. That's why I try to add spatial effects and colors in my music. At first I was against stereo. I didn't like it. I like mono sound, the sound of one dimension. In that dimension, there is a past, a present, and movement between the two. I didn't like the panoramic aspect of sound. I like the sound to be enlarged and elaborated, like under a microscope. The first concerts I did were in mono. First the sound came through one track. Then there were tape recorders with two tracks, stereo, that inevitably had a center. There was still mono in stereo. I thought of it as being too artificial. I then imagined concerts using a lot of mono. My next piece for the radio will be on sixteen tracks. Those sixteen tracks will each go directly in a speaker. ❧

2

Around the late forties the atom was split. Everything was forever changed when we discovered the world could be cut up and that sound could be cut up. We discovered that everything that had to do with culture could be cut up and reassembled in ways that didn't exist before. That will be seen as one of the most radical and important things that happened in this century. **GENESIS P. ORRIDGE** According to Descartes, the way you solve a problem is by breaking it into little pieces, so we developed a culture in the West that is particularly good at breaking problems into tiny little bits and pieces. What we're not good at is putting these pieces back together again. **ALVIN TOFFLER**

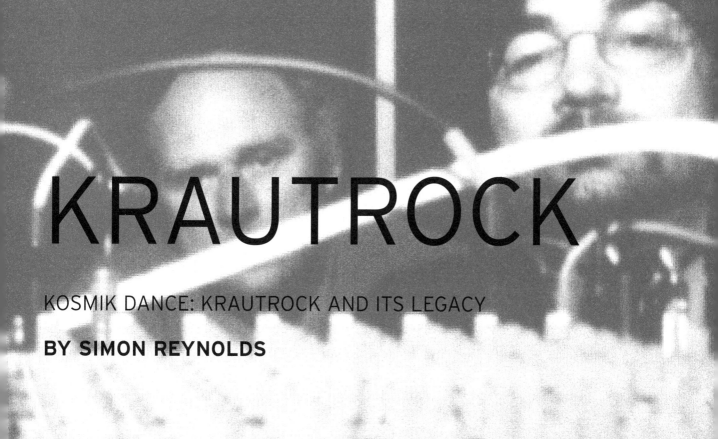

KRAUTROCK

KOSMIK DANCE: KRAUTROCK AND ITS LEGACY

BY SIMON REYNOLDS

Discography:	CAN	Tago Mago	Spoon, 1971
		Future Days	Spoon, 1973
		Soon Over Babaluma	Spoon, 1974
	NEU!	Neu!	Germanofon
		Neu! 2	Germanofon
		Neu! 75	Germanofon
	FAUST	Faust	Polydor, 1971
		So Far	Polydor, 197
		The Faust Tapes	ReR, 1973
		Faust IV	Virgin, 1973
	CLUSTER	Cluster II	Tempel
	KRAFTWERK	Kraftwerk 2	Germanofon 1972
	AMON DUUL II	Yeti	Liberty/UA
	POPOL VUH	In Den Garten Pharaos'	Pilz
	ASH RA TEMPEL	Join Inn	Ohr; reissued on Purple Pyramid
	COSMIC JOKERS	Planeten Sit-In	Spalax
	HARMONIA	Musik Von Harmonia	Germanofon

Immerse yourself in Krautrock – and this is immersive, engulfing music par excellence – and you'll find a paradox at the music's heart: a combination of absolute freedom and absolute discipline. Krautrock is where the overreaching ambition and untethered freakitude of late-sixties acid rock is checked and focused by a proto-punk minimalism. Krautrock bands like Can, Neu!, and Faust unleashed music of immense scale that miraculously avoided prog-rocks bombastics and cult of virtuosity for virtuosity's-sake. Where progressive rock boasted, "Look at me, look how fast my fingers can go," Krautrock beseeched, "Look! Look how VAST we can go." Or as Can's Michael Karoli put it: "We weren't into impressing people, just caressing them."

Alongside Tim Buckley's *Starsailor*, Miles Davis circa *On the Corner*, and Yoko Ono circa *Fly*, Krautrock was true fusion, merging psychedelic rock with funk groove, jazz improvisation, Stockhausen-style avant-electronics, and ethnic flava in a way that avoided the self-congratulatory, dilettante eclecticism that marred even the best of the seventies' jazz-rock bands. Krautrock's primary impetus, and urgency, came from late-sixties rock: Velvet Underground's mesmerizing mantras, Hendrix's pyrotechnique, Syd Barrett-era Pink Floyd's chromatic chaos, plus dashes of West Coast folkadelic rock and the studiocentric experiments of Brian Wilson and the later Beatles. Equally significant is what they didn't draw on – namely the blues-bore purism sired by Cream and the Stones.

Tweaking this Anglo-American legacy, the German bands added a vital distance (coming to rock 'n' roll as an alien import, they were able to make it even more alien), and they infused it with a German character that's instantly audible but hard to tag. A combination of Dada, LSD, and Zen resulted in a dry absurdist humor that could range from zany tomfoolery to a sort of sublime nonchalance, a light-headed but never light-hearted ease of spirit. Although they occasionally dipped their toes into psychedelia's dark side (the madness that claimed psychonauts such as Syd Barrett, Roky Erikson, or Moby Grape's Skip Spence), what's striking about most Krautrock is how affirmative it is, even at its most demented. This peculiar, serene joy and aura of pantheistic celebration is nowhere more evident than in the peak work of Can, Faust, and Neu!

If the triumvirate of Can/Faust/Neu! has gotten clichéd as a hip reference point, it's for good reason. Despite being quite dissimilar and lacking any kind of fra-ternal, comradely feelings towards each other, Can, Faust, and Neu! are the unassailable center of Krautrock's pantheon – its Dante/Shakespeare/Milton, or Beatles/Stones/Dylan, if you will.

Can's core was a quartet of lapsed avant-garde and free-jazz musicians (bassist Holger Czukay, guitarist Michael Karoli, keyboardist Irmin Schmidt, and drummer Jaki Leibezeit) who – blown away by the Velvet Underground and the Beatles' "I Am the Walrus" - decided rock was where it was at. Can was the most funky and improvisational of the Krautrock bands. Recording in their own studio in a Cologne castle, they jammed all day, then edited the juiciest chunks of improv into coherent compositions. This was similar to the methodology used by Miles Davis and producer Teo Macero on classic jazz-rock albums such as *Bitches*

Brew, *Jack Johnson*, and *On the Corner*. As Can's resident Macero, Czukay deployed two-track recording and a handful of mikes to achieve wonders of proto-ambient spatiality, shaming today's lo-fi bands.

Can's early sound–spartan, crisp and dry trance-rock, like the Velvet Underground circa *White Light White Heat* but with a smokin' rhythm section and black American vocalist Malcolm Mooney–peaked with the fifteen minute mindquake of "Mother Sky." As the influence of James Brownian motion kicked in, Can began to fuse "head" and "booty," atmosphere and groove, like nobody else save Miles Davis. After the shamanic avant-funk of *Tago Mago* and the brittle angst-funk of *Ege Bamyasi*–both featuring their psycho-surreal second singer Damo Suzuk–Can's music plunged into the sunshine with *Future Days*, *Soon over Babaluma*, and

Landed, their mid-seventies "Gaia trilogy." A kind of mystic materialism quivers and pulses inside these ethno-funkadelic groove-scapes and ambient oases, from the moon serenade "Come Sta, La Luna" to the fractal funk and chaos theorems of "Chain Reaction /Quantum Physics." This is music that wordlessly but eloquently rejoices in Mother Nature's bounty and beauty.

The pan-global panoramic trance-dance of Talking Heads' Remain in Light owed a lot to *Soon over Babaluma*, and yet more sincere flattery came in the form of David Byrne and Remain producer Brian Eno's *My Life in the Bush of Ghosts* (1981). Its use of ethnic vocal samples was unfavorably compared with Czukay's contemporaneous *Movies*, whose "Persian Love" recontextualized an Iranian ballad: In actual fact, Czuckay had got there twelve years earlier with *Canaxis*, which used

a Vietnamese boatwoman's song!

Despite an almost utter absence of input from black music, Neu! was probably the closest to Can in their sheer hypno-groove power and shared belief that "restriction is the mother of invention" (Holger Czukay's minimal-is-maximal credo). Devoid of funk or swing, Neu! was all about compulsive propulsion. Klaus Dinger was an astoundingly inventive, endlessly listenable drummer who worked magic within the confines of a rudimentary four-to-the-floor rock beat. Together with guitarist Michael Rother, he invented motorik, a metronomic, pulsating rhythm that instills a sublime sensation of restrained exhilaration, that's like gliding cruise control down a freeway into a future dazzling with promise. That "dazzle" comes from Rother's awesomely original guitar work, all chiming radiance and long streaks and smears of tone color. Like the New York band Television a few years later, Neu! bridged Byrdsy psychedelia and punk. They also wove ambient texture-scapes (e.g. the ocean-side idyll "Leb' Wohl") and experimented with weird noise (after blowing their recording budget, they filled the second side of *Neu! 2* with sped-up and slowed-down versions of an earlier single!). But it's *motorik* excursions like "Hallogallo," "Fur Immer," and "Isi" that constitute Neu!'s great legacy, one that's only now being fully exploited by admirers like Stereolab and Trans-Am.

Faust similarly combined a proto-punk mess-thetic with acid rock's galactic grandeur. But instead of Neu!'s streamlined symmetry, Faust oscillated wildly between filthy, fucked-up noise and gorgeous, pastoral melody, between yowling antics and exquisitely sculpted *sonic objets d'art*. Above all, they were maestros of incongruity, their albums riddled with jarring juxtapositions and startling jump cuts. Heterogeneity was their antiessence. This cut-up Dada side of Faust was explored to the hilt on *The Faust Tapes*, a collage album of some

twenty-six segments. It's a methodology they revisited on their late-nineties comeback *Rien*, which was assembled by producer Jim O'Rourke using live tapes of the band's reunion tour of America. Parallel to the in-vogue cut-up techniques of William Burroughs, Faust's collage aesthetic impacted the burgeoning "industrial" scene of the early-eighties (Cabaret Voltaire, Zoviet France, This Heat, Nurse With Wound, etc.). But for all Faust's avant-garde extremities, they were also great songwriters, scattering such gems as the bittersweet psychedelic love song "Jennifer" and the wistful acid blues of "It's a Bit of a Pain" amid the zany chaos.

Once you've immersed yourself in the best, what about the rest? Ash Ra Tempel took The Stooges' downered wah-wah rock ("We Will Fall," "Ann," "Dirt") way way out into the mystic. Guitarist Manuel Gottsching's subsequent solo records have their moments, but veer too often into beatific New Age wispiness. An exception is Gottsching's gorgeous and astonishingly prophetic *E2-E4* (1984), an album-length electronic track that paved the way for the ambient-techno watercolors of Carl Craig, The Black Dog, and The Orb, and even became a Balearic rave anthem when remade by Sueño Latino. Another, less acknowledged precursor to nineties techno – especially the metronomic and Teutonic sound of trance – was Tangerine Dream, which evolved from the transcendental guitar tumult of their first four albums to a synth-dominated, hypnotic style not far from the silvered rush of English neo-hippie outfit Hawkwind.

Amon Duul II was the most baroque and bombastic of the krucial kraut kontenders: Imagine Led Zeppelin produced by John Cale with Nico on vocals and a crate of magic mushrooms on hand. They had a fab line in lysergic song titles, too: "Halluzination Guillotine," "Dehypnotised Toothpaste," "A Short Stop at the

Transylvanian Brain Surgery." Their estranged and more politicized sister-band Amon Duul I pursued a similarly drug-burned rock, but were more primitive and sloppy. Also on the acid-soaked, kosmische tip, Popol Vuh recorded a sprawling, diverse oeuvre ranging from meditational, medievalist reveries to primordial, percussive freak-outs.

After Can/Faust/Neu!, Cluster was probably the most innovative and ahead-of-their time of the early-seventies German bands. After a spell as the purely avant-garde Kluster, the two-man soundlab of Hans-Joachim Roedelius and Dieter Moebius hit their stride with the mesmeric drone-scapes of *Cluster II* and *Cluster '71*. Later, they traded in their armory of FX pedals and guitar loops for synths, knocked out a bunch of bewitching albums in collaboration with Brian Eno, and chalked up a mammoth discography (as Cluster, but also solo and as Roedelius and Moebius) with the odd gem lurking amid much new age mush. Hooking up with Neu!'s Michael Rother, the duo also recorded as Harmonia, producing two albums worth of serene and soul-cleansing proto-electronica. Cluster's *Zuckerzeit*, the Harmonia records, and the Neu! sound were a big influence on Eno and his pal David Bowie during the latter's mid-seventies sojourn in Berlin. You can hear it in the lustrous guitar canopies of "Heroes" and the glistening, pensive synth-strumentals on side two of *Low*.

Krautrock brought into focus an idea that had been latent in rock from Bo Diddley to the Stooges to the Modern Lovers: that the rhythmic essence of rock music – what made it different from jazz – was a kind of machine-like compulsion. Pitched somewhere between

Kraftwerk's man-machine rigor and James Brown's sex-machine sweat, bands like Can and Neu! created grooves that fused the luscious warmth of flesh-and-blood funk with the cold precision of techno. There was a spiritual aspect to all this, sort of *Zen and the Art of Motorik Maintenance*: the idea that true joy in life isn't liberation from work but exertion and fixation, a trance-like state of immersion in the process itself, regardless of outcome. Holger Czukay declared: "Repetition is like a machine ... If you can get aware of the life of a machine then you are definitely a master ... [machines] have a heart and soul ... they are living beings." Taking this idea of the "soft machine" or "desiring machine" even further, Neu! created a new kind of rhythm for rock, bridging the gap between rock n' roll's syncopation and disco's four-to-the-floor metronomics. As Stereolab's Tim Gane says, "Neu!'s longer tracks are far closer to the nature of house and techno than guitar rock."

But Kraftwerk was the group that really bridged the gap between rock and electronic dance music. (In fact, Rother and Dinger were briefly members of Kraftwerk before going off to do their own thing as Neu!.) On their first three albums, Kraftwerk's creative core, Ralf Hutter and Florian Schneider, jumbled the New York minimalist school (La Monte Young, John Cage, Steve Reich, etc.) with German avant-electronics (Stockhausen). Then they staked everything on the idea that the synthesizer was the future and won. The band's pop breakthrough was "Autobahn," the twenty-four-minute title track of their fourth album, a synth-and-drum-machine symphony that evoked the Zen serenity of gliding down the freeway. The track combined Beach Boys-style harmonies with *musique concrète* sound effects–a celebration of the car as "a musical instrument," proclaimed Hutter. In edited form, the song became a global hit in 1974. But Kraftwerk's aesthetic pinnacle was 1977's *Trans-Europe Express*, an awesomely minimal slice of "*Industrielle Volkmuzik*" that did for the locomotive what "Autobahn" did for the motorcar. With its Doppler effect synths and indefatigable beats, the album's "Trans-Europe Express/Metal on Metal" segue captured the spiritual passion behind technological progress – "all the dynamism of industrial life, of modern life," as Hutter put it. Two further albums – 1978's *The Man Machine* and 1981's *Computer World* – consolidated Kraftwerk's achievement, and sealed the staggering enormity and sheer pervasive range of their legacy. In the eighties and nineties, they were renowned and revered as the godfathers of (just count 'em!) Eurodisco, new romantic synth-pop, electro, Miami bass, Detroit techno, and North of England bleep-and-bass (LFO, Sweet Exorcist, Forgemasters).

Why is the Krautrock legacy such a touchstone for contemporary musicians? Firstly, Krautrock is one of the great eras of guitar reinvention. Expanding on the innovations of Hendrix, Syd Barrett, the Velvet Underground, etc, the Krautrock bands explored the electric guitar's potential as a source of sound-in-itself. Fed through effects pedals and the mixing desk, the guitar ceased to be a riff-machine and verged on an analog synthesizer, i.e. a generator of timbre and tone color. As such, the Krauts anticipated the soundpainting and texturology that characterizes today's computer-based music, while still retaining the rhythmic thrust of rock n' roll. Simultaneously kinetic and cinematic, Krautrock is one of the golden phases in a continuum that runs through rock history: the textured groove-scape. It's a thread that runs from Hendrix, Sly Stone, Miles Davis, dub reggae, and Parliament Funkadelic, through the early-eighties avant-funk of PiL, The Pop Group, A Certain Ratio, et al., right up to the more ambient and atmospheric forms of electronic dance music (Orbital, Seefeel, Basic Channel/Chain Reaction, Mouse On Mars). Whether they're live bands jamming in the studio then editing and resequencing their improvs, or solitary computer boffins constructing digital mosaics using a mouse, a VDU, and a library of samples and synth-tones, all these artists create pulsating, vividly textured soundscapes through which the listener is gently transported. Krautrock

belongs on a continuum of psychedelic dance music based around the intensification of rock's three most radical aspects: groove, space, and timbre/texture/chromatics. "Groove" relates to repetition, to the loop, to timelessness – the dream of escaping History by getting back into the body. Conjured on the mixing board through echo, reverb, and delay, "space" induces a stoned way of listening – hallucinatory eyelid movies. Created through effects pedals, analog synths, or sampladelic treatments, "timbre" is trippy, paralleling the synaesthetic effects of drugs like LSD, where sound is tactile or immersive.

Beyond all its claims to radicalism, though, Krautrock is simply fabulous music, a dizzy kaleidoscope of crazily mixed-up and incompatible emotions and sensations (wonder, poignancy, nonchalance, tenderness, derangement), an awesome affirmation of possibility that inevitably appeals in an age when guitar-based music appears to be contracting on a weekly basis. Listeners are turning to Krautrock, not as a nostalgia-inducing memento of some wilder, more daring golden age they never lived through, but as a treasure trove of hints and clues as to what can be done right here, right now. Krautrock isn't history, but a living testament that there's still so far to go. ✤

Sampling is like sending a fax to yourself from the sonic debris of the future. If the fax is a copy of a document you're making and sending, then it's gone. You can send a fax anywhere. Same with beats at this point. To me, the sampler is kind of a time machine. It's a way of manipulating and reconfiguring pieces of the past into the present and allowing permutations of the present to really reflect where music could be going. So you're playing with past, present, future and the imperfect tense of language itself. **DJ SPOOKY** A collage, a good collage, is new, even though the elements in it may not be. **ALVIN TOFFLER** I think it would be interesting to do a record where all the samples were charted, kind of like an archaeology. So you'd have this color-coded graphic saying this kick drum came from this studio in 1963 with this kind of reverb. I think it would be a revelation to people who think of sampling as being large chunks of someone else's record with your voice on top. They'd see how much of music had become collage. **JON HASSEL**

INTERVIEW:
Holger Czukay & Irmin Schmidt

SCHMIDT: Music and technology have gone together for the last 20,000 years. Building a drum is an act of technology. If you look at the nineteenth century grand piano, it represents exactly the technology and the standard of technology of the nineteenth century. SCHMIDT: There's something Holger says: With a grand piano you have to study to play it. And a synthesizer with presets and a rhythm box, you don't have to play. You push a button and it makes music. In actuality, the most inventive way to use a synthesizer is to misuse it. That's what we've done. That's what a lot of techno musicians do now. The French call it deconstruction. CZUKAY: I saw an interview with the owner of a very famous synthesizer company. He was an old man and a Kraftwerk fan. What he liked was the idea that dilettantes are able to express themselves through these instruments. He said he had given up trying to imagine how his new instruments would be used. He said, "I do something and it goes out in the world and comes back to me as a completely different instrument." CZUKAY: The interesting thing about collage is that there are two worlds coming together that seem incompatible. For example, take an instrument from the Middle East somewhere. They have a completely different tone system that is not compatible with our harmony system. Now, you bring these two together and you find out that it's somehow convincing. It's striking. It shouldn't be, by law, but it is. SCHMIDT: Or it may not work, but it's surprising. It's very interesting. CZUKAY: Also, collage is not too expensive. SCHMIDT: There's another thing about collage, which is that it sort of governs the whole art of this century, and does it more and more, because we don't see the world anymore as one, as a unity. We see it in pieces or fragments that we have to put together. You see that in painting already in the late nineteenth century. The world goes into pieces and into fragments and all we can do is put fragments together and get a new whole out of it, but it always stays as fragments. That's how we, at this time in history, see the world. SCHMIDT: The editing process has something to do with the splitting of the atom. This is what I would say. It was incredibly powerful. You splice something and you separate something which was organic before. You kill it. Then you must have the vision to put it back together again, and it should be even better — or at the very least different. Actually, we wanted to make things better. Because editing starts when you make a mistake and you want to make a correction. This is the beginning of the process, but not the end of editing. CZUKAY: The remix thing is the state of the art of the nineties, that's for sure. It involves looking through the window of what was before and seeing a little something, and — like an insect — reconstructing it. It gives you a new vision. It's a new picture that's coming up. At the moment, for example, I'm working on remixes of the Can remixes. SCHMIDT: Sampling may be a new idea technically speaking, but conceptually, as a process, composers always have sampled. Mozart, for example, uses little patterns that everybody used. He used patterns from Haydn and built them in. They became a certain style, a certain way of harmonic succession, of how a melody goes with certain harmonies. They used samples of other music that already existed. That's what we do now except we can put in anything, not only music. We can use everything that surrounds us. The sampler is the real musical instrument of our day, allowing us to put any fragment of the acoustic world into it, and start working from there. CZUKAY: It used to be a composer would imagine the music; it would only be realized and performed later. What we do is we make the music first and then compose it. CZUKAY: I found I could impress girls with electricity. I had a big horn from a ship in front of my window — I lived on the fifth floor — and when a girl came up here, I put up that big horn and really impressed her. Then I would throw down water balloons. We haven't done that on stage yet. SCHMIDT: It took me a while to move from academic to popular music. For me, it was a process that took some time. I went to New York in January 1966 to take part in a conductors' competition. After a very short time, just by chance, I met Steve Reich and Terry Riley. These people, after only one week, seemed so much more interesting than the conductor thing. I missed a rehearsal and was sort of thrown out. I stayed for about two months in New York and that was a very influential time. It was just before the Velvet Underground. Some music here, Lamonte Young for example, was very strange and very loud and lasted days sometimes. This didn't exist in Germany. Here it was Stockhausen, very structured. It was very academic and it was at that time very scientific, in a way. I met Cage at that time, and all of a sudden I was very unsatisfied with what I was doing. Then, of course, came this time of '68 where a lot of people were unsatisfied in Europe with a lot of things. So I threw that all away, this career as a conductor, and asked Holger if he would be interested in founding a group. I found he was not only interested, he had the same idea. CZUKAY: We didn't expect to become a rock group of sorts. ❧

3

This idea of a seamless flow of music that ran all night created by a DJ, that came from disco, and that has been one of the most radical changes of music in the last thirty years. **DAVID TOOP** We are now respecting the disco era for what it stood for, because most of the records that are very popular and predominant right now are disco cut-ups of very famous riffs of disco music of the seventiess. It has just come around full circle. It's incredible. **CARL COX** Most music and beats come from the seventies. That's my belief, anyway. Because the last twenty years, we've just been sampling and getting breaks and loops, wah-wah guitars, saxophone, flute, riffs; it's all from the seventies. **LTJ BUKEM**

DISCO

PLAYING WITH A DIFFERENT SEX

BY PETER SHAPIRO

3T 4T 5T 6T 7T 8T 9T 10T

Long before John Travolta, the Bee-Gees, and Rod Stewart's "Do Ya Think I'm Sexy?" brought disco into the mainstream, it was the exclusive property of all-night party people who frequented New York's underground network of members-only loft parties, disused ware-house spaces cum dance clubs, and clandestine juice

Discography:			
	DONNA SUMMER	"I Feel Love"	Casablanca, 1977
	MARTIN CIRCUS	"Disco Circus"	Prelude, 1979
	SYLVESTER	"(You Make Me Feel) Mighty Real"	Fantasy, 1979
	SYLVESTER	"Do You Wanna Funk?"	Fantasy, 1980
	DINOSAUR L.	"Go Bang!"	Sleeping Bag, 1982
	PEECH BOYS	"Don't Make Me Wait"	West End, 1982
	THE J.B.'S	*Damn Right I Am Somebody*	People, 1974
	DEXTER WANSELL	"Life on Mars"	Philadelphia International, 1976
	PARLIAMENT	*Mothership Connection*	Casablanca, 1976
	PARLIAMENT	*Funkentelechy vs. the Placebo Syndrome*	Casablanca, 1977

SYLVESTER

DONNA SUMMER

bars. It was also almost exclusively gay. As the cultural adjunct of the emerging Gay Pride movement, disco was the embodiment of the pleasure-is-politics ethos of post-Stonewall culture. Searching for alternatives to the aggressively heterosexual rhythms of rock and funk, disco enacted marathon, nocturnal trance sessions in which poppers, strobe lights, tight trousers, and a seamless mix of hysterical diva vocals: African and Latin American polyrhythms, camp English-as-foreign-language songs from Spain and Italy and a relentless four-to-the-floor machine beat created a ritual of outlaw desire and physical abandon that existed outside the straight and narrow.

The veneer of naturalism and authenticity that people ascribed to blues-based rock, soul, and funk lent these genres an air of "normality"; no matter how wigged-out artists like Captain Beefheart, Swamp Dogg, or Jimmy Castor were, they were still somehow organic and true to life. Disco, on the other hand, was a celebration of the fan-tastic where flash, overwhelming melodrama, sex, and fabulousness were all that mattered. Envisioning a utopia light-years away from "natural" heterosexuality, disco attempted to create a pleasure dome in which the rhythms of eroticism were inseparable from those of the machine. The roots of disco lay in the rhythmic regimentation of mid-seventies soul records like The Temptations' "Law of the Land," but the arrival of the drum machine and cheap synthesizers later in the decade inexorably changed the groove from funky to martial. As the most visible moment in a hidden history of electronic music that extends from Moog pioneer Walter/Wendy Carlos to the contemporary transgendered interventions of Terre Thaemlitz, disco used the fantastic sounds of the new machinery to imagine a brave new world of sexuality. The hypnotic, otherworldly quality of the timbres and the rigidly insistent mechanistic throbs of the Moog and ARP synthesizers used by disco producers like Giorgio Moroder, Jean-Marc Cerrone, Patrick Cowley, and Bobby

O summed up an aesthetic that sought to upset the "natural" order of things.

Giorgio Moroder was a journeyman producer from the Tyrolean ski resort of Val Gardena until he happened across the Moog synthesizer at the dawn of the seventies. The Moog's distinctly space-age timbres inspired Moroder to write "Son of My Father," which, in the hands of a group of slumming glam-rockers called Chicory Tip, became the first number-one song to feature a synthesizer. As glorious a piece of pop ephemera as "Son of My Father" was, Moroder would have to wait until he met up with a singer from Boston who was in the Munich production of *Godspell* in 1974 to define the union of flesh and machine in dance music. Little more than Donna Summer simulating an orgasm over a background of blaxploitation cymbals, wah-wah guitars, a funky-butt

clarinet riff, and some synth chimes, "Love to Love You Baby" was arranged by Moroder and produced by Englishman Pete Bellotte. It was extended into a seventeen-minute minisymphony at the behest of Casablanca Records chief Neil Bogart, who wanted a soundtrack for his sexual exploits. The song reached number two in the American charts and was largely responsible for the development of the twelve-inch single.

Even more of a landmark was 1977's "I Feel Love," which had more fake-orgasm vocals from Summer set against an entirely synthesized background. Introducing both the syn-drum and the galloping Moog bassline that would come to categorize the strain of disco called hi-NRG, "I Feel Love" was a masterpiece of mechano-eroticism. The epitome of the cocaine chill and metal gloss of the seventies, "I Feel Love" could have better encapsulated the decade's obsession with the detachment of anonymous sex only if the record had been sheathed in latex. Where synth-based records by Jean-Jacques Perrey, Kraftwerk, Tangerine Dream, and Tonto's Expanding Head Band had used Moogs to imagine the whooshing speed and gurgling weirdness of a possible

future, Moroder considered what implications the machine would have on the human body. As Summer became a bigger and bigger star, though, Moroder and Bellotte backed away from the world of artifice towards a more conventional pop soundworld that featured massed strings and guitar solos from the likes of studio hack Jeff "Skunk" Baxter. However, Moroder's proto-cybernaut findings were brought to their logical conclusion on his 1980 solo album *E=MC2*, whose cover showed the producer ripping his jacket open to show off the computer circuitry hidden in his chest.

With his soundtrack for Alan Parker's film *Midnight Express*, Moroder unintentionally came to the same sex-is-power conclusion as the Rolling Stones. "Chase" used the same materials and virtually the same sounds as "I Feel Love" to conjure up the adrenaline rush of terror

and loss of control as the film's protagonist was arrested by Turkish police for drug smuggling. Adding further to the confusion, "Chase" was a big disco hit: Was this dancing as a surrogate for sex or dancing while the bomb dropped?

At around the same time in France, another disco producer was exploring the relationship between technology and lust and trying to convince himself that he could answer "Yes" to Phillip K. Dick's eternal sci-fi question: "Have you ever made love to an android?" A former musician with Club Med (probably where he got his taste for concupiscence), Jean-Marc Cerrone was the king of disco porn. An obvious rip-off of "Love to Love You Baby," Cerrone's first hit, "Love in C Minor," featured saccharine strings, cheesy synth motifs, and choruses of g-spot vocals. His best record, "Supernature," turned the old "the freaks come out at night" tale into a bizarre parable

where laboratory mutants destroyed the humans that created them. In other words, through the transformative power of disco, the freaks shall inherit the Earth. Cruder still was "Rocket in the Pocket," which undercut its tale of masterful cocksmanship with half-man/half-machine vocals that would make Gary Numan proud.

Cerrone's countryman Didier Marouani, better known as Space, made his own contributions to this equation of machines and funkiness with 1977's "Magic Fly" and 1978's "Carry On, Turn Me On." Although "Magic Fly" was number one throughout Europe, Space was more kitsch than camp, and his impact was relatively small outside of his spaceman stage attire which has been pilfered recently by retro-ironists The Moog Cookbook. Another bizarre one-off from France was Martin Circus' epic from 1979, "Disco Circus." The epitome of disco's wretched excess, "Disco Circus" was an orgy of synth effects, hand claps, guys imitating chickens, scatting, cowbells, he-man guitars, and the kind of something-missing-in-translation lunacy that only non-Anglophiles can produce. It was all wrapped up with a sensibility that owed as much to the spatial re-orientation of Jamaican dub as it did to the gluttony of Studio 54.

Disco's aesthetic of machine sex was taken to its furthest extremes by a subgenre called hi-NRG. As its mechanical name suggested, hi-NRG was totally reliant on technology and was all about unfeasibly athletic dancing, bionic sex, and superhuman stamina. With titles like "Menergy" and "So Many Men, So Little Time," hi-NRG was, in the hands of producers like Patrick Cowley and Bobby Orlando, an aural fantasy of a futuristic club populated entirely by cybernetic Tom of Finland studs.

Patrick Cowley was best known for his collaborations with vocalist Sylvester – first as a synth player on classics like "Stars" and "Dance (Disco Heat)," and then as the producer of the definitive hi-NRG track, "Do You

Wanna Funk?" Although Cowley made two strangely effective concept albums, *Megatron Man* and *Mind Warp*, under his own name before he died of AIDS in 1982, he will always be remembered for his synth lines on the eternal "You Make Me Feel (Mighty Real)." Clearly influenced by "I Feel Love" (which Cowley would later remake), Cowley created a thoroughly inhuman bassline that, according to the disco naysayers, was proof positive of disco's destruction of the blues continuum, and thus its inherent lack of quality. But just as Jimi Hendrix remade the blues as the prismatic shards of his lysergic imagination, and Sly Stone envisioned what soul might sound like if America lived up to its civil rights promises, Sylvester (with his ultra-high falsetto) and Cowley (with his synths) interrogated the African-American musical tradition and asked what "realness" was supposed to mean to a gay, black man who, alienated from almost all of society, was forced to hide his true identity for most of his life.

The galloping synth bassline used by Moroder and Cowley became the trademark of the king of hi-NRG, Bobby Orlando (a.k.a. Bobby 'O'). Founded in 1979, Orlando's O Records was the home of impossibly camp NRG records that sang the body electric like The Flirts' "Danger," Divine's "Native Love" and "Shoot Your Shot" and Waterfront Home's "Take a Chance On Me." His most famous – and best – record, though, was the Pet Shop Boys' "West End Girls," which stripped the NRG formula of its teenage-crush, heartbeat momentum and allowed the genre to express something other than anticipation and heartbreak. With the apotheosis of the British production team Stock, Aitken and Waterman in the mid-eighties – hi-NRG once again became the soundtrack for shiny, happy people falling in and out of love on crossover hits like Dead Or Alive's "You Spin Me Round," Bananarama's "Venus," and Kylie Minogue's "I Should Be So Lucky".

The beginning of the eighties witnessed a musical and demographic meeting, particularly in New York, that will never happen again. There was little musical difference between disco, hi-NRG, hip-hop, electro, and freestyle, yet their core audiences of gay men and black and Latino teenagers couldn't have been more divergent. The only thing separating something like The Flirts' "Danger" from the synth-oriented rhythm and blues of D-Train's "You're the One" or the Latin Freestyle of Lisa Lisa & Cult Jam's "I Wonder If I Take You Home" was a bpm or two and the singer's accent. The keyboardist on the track that single-handedly created electro, Afrika Bambaataa's "Planet Rock," was also responsible for eighties disco's most crucial technological advancement. On Cuba Gooding's "Happiness is Just Around the Bend," producer John Robie concocted an entire chorus out of one syllable by using the first sampling keyboard, the Emulator. Taking this idea one step further, Robie turned signifiers of urban blight like the sound of breaking glass into percussion devices on C-Bank's "One More Shot," thus creating a sort of social realist *musique concrète*.

The use of sounds like breaking glass and toilets flushing on otherwise standard records was pioneered by Jamaican dub producers like Lee "Scratch" Perry and King Tubby (see sidebar). As Jamaicans immigrated to New York in droves during the seventies, dub techniques like instrumental dropout and echo followed them to the Big Apple's dancefloors. In the same way that synthesizers liberated the body from the supposed laws of nature, the techniques of dub provided an alternative rhythmic structure to straight 4/4 and eroticized the entire body, not just the pelvis. The Neil Armstrong of disco's spacewalk in dub's echo chamber was the legendary mixer Tom Moulton, who was the main force behind the development of the twelve-inch single. Moulton's mixing style was all about stretching the music and extending its pleasure, and his razorblade tape edits inaugurated dance music's enduring fascination with the cut-and-paste tradition that went all the way back to Pierre Schaeffer's ground-breaking experiments in the late forties.

The possibilities of dub techniques on dance music were picked up by every important DJ and remixer on the New York scene from Walter Gibbons – whose spacey remixes of Bettye LaVette's 1978 single, "Doin' the Best That I Can," and Double Exposure's 1976 track, "My Love Is Free," stretched out the grooves so much that they teetered on the edge of motionlessness – to François Kevorkian and his spatial reworkings of D-Train's "You're the One" and Jimmy Cliff's "Treat the Youth Right".

Two artists, though, took dub-disco as far as it could go: the classically trained maverick Arthur Russell and the legendary DJ at the Paradise Garage, Larry Levan. "Let's Go Swimming" and "Treehouse," both recorded by Russell with Walter Gibbons, used dub as a dislocating device, preventing disco's simple groove from developing under the dancers' feet. Russell's "Go Bang!" (released under the name Dinosaur L.), on the other hand, used dub, not to mention jazz, church organ, salsa, and calypso, to create a torrent of beats and effects that became one of the building blocks of house music.

Disco mutated into house at Larry Levan's Paradise Garage. Crafting mixes especially for his own dancefloor, Levan might be the greatest remixer of all time as his versions of Instant Funk's "I Got My Mind Made Up," Gwen Guthrie's "Ain't Nothin' Goin' On But the Rent," and Inner Life's "Ain't No Mountain High Enough" prove. It is his own production of The Peech Boys' "Don't Make Me Wait," though, that remains dub's greatest gift to disco (or vice versa). Levan kept the song sealed in an echo chamber that never let the rhythm gather momentum and forced Bernard Fowler's vocals to crumble into a disembodied, melismatic warble that undercut the lyrics' celebration of disco's potential for carefree revelry. The

plea for unfettered sexual abandon was turned into a paranoid fantasy of unrequited love and unfulfilled desire that was the disco lifestyle's inevitable curse.

Before the music to which the revelers at clubs like The Loft and the Tenth Floor danced was codified as "disco," there was no animosity, no record-burning parties at baseball games, no "Disco Sucks" t-shirts. A disco record was whatever made people dance, and this could be a funk track like Dexter Wansell's "Life on Mars" just as easily as a bit of European fluff like Barrabas' "Woman." Released on Kenny Gamble and Leon Huff's Philadelphia International, the label that would unintentionally create the disco blueprint, "Life on Mars" rode its cosmic synths and slap-bass groove into outer space, where the ghetto was a million miles away.

Just as disco was recreating the image of the human body as a cyborg pleasure machine, funk was postulating that true emancipation for African-Americans was possible only in orbit. Despite the racist chestnut that "blacks naturally have more rhythm than whites," that "blackest" of genres, funk, was largely dependent on technology to shake rumps. The very genesis of funk, James Brown's 1965 single, "Papa's Got a Brand New Bag," was the result of the engineer speeding up the tape, rather than the musicians' innate feel. Nearly a decade later, undoubtedly inspired by the galactic funk of Miles Davis and Herbie Hancock (see sidebar), Brown's backing band, The J.B.'s, linked Jesse Jackson-inspired social protest to some of the wildest Moog riffs ever recorded on their 1974 album, *Damn Right I Am Somebody*.

The message should have been obvious, but it took George Clinton's P-Funk Thang to really drive the point home. On Parliament's *Mothership Connection* album, gospel's deliverance was no longer brought forth by the white cherubs of European imagination, but by chitlin-eating, Afro-clad brothers from another planet. The "sweet chariot" of slave-era spirituals became a spaceship offering escape from the ghetto via "Supergroovalisticprosifunkstication." Clinton's sci-fi fantasy was given its musical analogue by Bernie Worrell's high-pitched synth squiggles, which sculpted the contours of Clinton's outer space in sound.

On Parliament's 1977 album, *Funkentelechy vs. the Placebo Syndrome*, Clinton used another comic-book scenario to create popular music's greatest dance-as-liberation saga. The "Bop Gun" was Clinton's metaphor for the life-affirming power of dancing in the face of the pleasure-denying, sexless Puritans who still ran America two hundred years after they founded it. With the album's closing track, "Flash Light," Clinton found a song that made his metaphor real: only a completely joyless fucker with a rump of steel could possibly deny it. "Flash Light" was not only a landmark for its implausibly kinetic groove, but for its groundbreaking use of technology as well. By taking advantage of the Moog's capacity for stacking notes on top of each other to create a gargantuan bass sound, Worrell's synth bassline on "Flash Light" remains perhaps the most important musical moment of the past twenty years: It anticipated and allowed the use of synths as rhythm machines.

In their own way, P-Funk and disco attempted to destroy the racist stereotypes that had haunted black identity for centuries. Along with Sly & the Family Stone, who used a primitive drum machine to express their post-Civil Rights cynicism on *There's a Riot Goin' On*, Stevie Wonder had pioneered this de-essentializing of black identity in the early seventies with albums like *Music of My Mind* and *Talking Book*, which were recorded with synthesists Robert Margouleff and Malcolm Cecil (later to become Tonto's Expanding Head Band). Incorporating the resolutely unearthly sounds of the Moog into an explicitly political soundworld that col-lapsed the two oppositions of the male African-American vocal tradition — the fragile, feminized falsetto and the assertive, growling tenor. Wonder not only turned soul into a genre capable of album-length statements (as everybody always notes); he also created a persona that was as complex and multilayered as anyone in pop music, black or white.

Building on Wonder's foundation, disco and P-Funk used the textures and timbres of electronic instruments as a way of rubbing against the grain of behavior and characteristics supposedly grounded in biology. By the tail end of the funk and disco era, the boundaries separating "black" and "white" music were as tenuous as they had ever been (and probably ever will be). Rock stalwarts like the Rolling Stones, the Grateful Dead, and Rod Stewart were going disco in an effort to shift product; punk and post-punk bands like The Clash, Gang of Four, Talking Heads, and Public Image Ltd. were turning on to dub-reggae, funk, and disco; New York bands like ESG, the Bush Tetras, and Liquid Liquid were taking every kind of music they could get their hands on and reducing it all to the barest essentials; Arthur Russell and Christian Marclay were bringing the avant-garde to the streets — or was it the other way around? As journalist/musician Sasha Frere-Jones has pointed out, as soon as Run DMC and Sonic Youth rose to prominence, this union was obliterated. Perhaps more than anything, this brief period when "black" and "white" music arrived at the same conclusions will be disco's lasting legacy. ❧

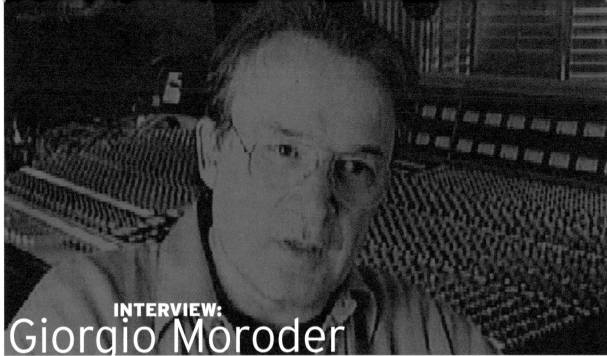

INTERVIEW:
Giorgio Moroder

I came across the Moog synthesizer towards the end of the sixties, early seventies. A friend of mine in Munich was a classical composer and he showed me this huge machine. All he was doing was sounds like [makes squelching sound], and it went on for twenty minutes. Then he showed me what else you could do with the sounds and effects. A few months later, I rented it, and I had a guy who was able to make it work and I did my first recording. The Moog was very difficult – you had to play with the patches and the tuning was always a major problem because after a few minutes, it was out of tune. I must say that at the beginning, we used the synthesizer a little bit too much as a gimmick, like making all those interesting, but I guess ultimately boring, sounds. Lately, the synthesizer has become more like an instrument than a sound effect machine. I threw away all my old synthesizers. A lot of people use them now and you can't find them, or you pay a fortune to find them. So now I feel sorry I didn't keep them. I used the Moog and then some other synthesizers for quite some time, like two or three years, and I had little success. The audience didn't really want the synthesizer, or at least that's what I thought. Then, in '76, I wanted to do a record with Donna Summer. I said: Why don't we do one with the new Moog? That song, "I Feel Love," became a big hit. Donna Summer used to live in Munich. I met her at a studio session where she was singing background. A few months later, we did a record called "The Hostage," which did very well in Europe. Then we did a few more, and then finally, in 1976, "Love to Love You Baby," which became a number-one song. I think this song "Love to Love You Baby" was all a little bit of an experiment. It was seventeen minutes long, the drum was based on the bass drum, and she sang it in a very unusual way. So I think all those things contributed to the success. "I Feel Love" broke a lot of taboos. People started to like that kind of music and then [started] doing it, not in big studios, but at home, in small recording studios. I think this whole electronic field of recording opened a lot of new ideas. People didn't need all the money to record in a big expensive studio. I think that was one of the main reasons that the synthesizer became so popular. I didn't think of the machine being erotic. I thought Donna's look and way of singing and the lyrics were erotic. *Midnight Express* was my first movie. Alan Parker heard the song "I Feel Love" and he thought I could give him that kind of sound – electronic sound. So we met, and I played him a few other ideas, and he agreed that I should do the music. It took about three weeks. We mixed it down in about a day or two days. It was my most successful movie soundtrack. I did about twelve movies in all including *American Gigolo*, *Cat People*, and *Flashdance*. I did some songs for *Top Gun*. Right now, I'm out of dance music. I have a lot of offers, but I did it for so long that I'm not interested anymore. So instead, I'm writing two musicals. I'm getting much more into computer art. I divide up my time between visual art and music. ❋

Dub

Discography:

U-ROY & FRIENDS	*With a Flick of My Musical Wrist*	Trojan, 1990
LEE PERRY	*Blackboard Jungle Dub*	Upsetter, 1973
KING TUBBY	*Dub Gone Crazy: The Evolution of Dub at King Tubby's 1975-1979*	Blood & Fire, 1994
MIKEY DREAD	*African Anthem*	Big Cat, 1997
WAYNE SMITH & PRINCE JAMMY	*Sleng Teng/Prince Jammy's Computerised Dub*	Greensleeves, 1985

It's probably safe to say that, **with the exception of punk rock, every significant development in popular music since the 1960s has in one way or another emerged from the Jamaican dancehall and its tradition of the sound system.** Originally developed after the end of World War II as a way of replacing expensive orchestras in Kingston's nightclubs, sound systems were run by an MC and a selector and consisted of a turntable, an amplifier, and enormous speakers known as "houses of joy." During the late fifties and early sixties, the two champion sound systems were those of Duke Reid and Clement Coxsone Dodd, which played the jump R&B style of Wynonie Harris, Amos Milburn, and Willis Jackson. In an effort to get the edge on the competition, both Dodd and Reid would go on record-buying trips to the U.S. to pick up obscure records whose labels were then rubbed off to prevent identification by their rivals. In the late fifties, **Dodd and Reid began to hire local musicians to record their own versions of R&B tunes on acetate discs that were played exclusively by the** sound systems. A decade later, with Jamaican rocksteady the sound of the moment, the bands associated with the main sound systems started cutting instrumental versions of popular vocal tracks on acetate. Soon enough, studio engineers began to play around with the instrumentals by reducing the tracks to their basslines and rhythms or by foregrounding certain instruments in the mix, thus laying the foundations for remix culture. The "version" opened up spaces in the song for the sound system's DJ or MC to interject and exhort the crowd to dance or to comment on the record. There had been popular DJs before the rise of the "version," like Count Machuki and King Stitt, but the DJ really came to prominence with the ascendancy of U-Roy. U-Roy made the boasting rhymes and whooping nonsense syllables of the DJ the dominant feature of the sound system, and by 1970, they became the dominant element on Jamaican records, too: He had the top three records on the Jamaican chart. All of this made an impression on the man who would emigrate from Jamaica to the Bronx, set up his own sound system and kick start Hip-Hop, Kool DJ Herc. In 1969, U-Roy was the DJ for the Home Town Hi-Fi sound system run by an engineer called Osbourne Ruddock or, more popularly, King Tubby. By 1972, Tubby had set up his own studio and was in demand as a remix engineer. Using tracks supplied to him by producers like Bunny Lee, Glen Brown, and, most famously, Lee Perry, Tubby more or less invented the techniques of "dub" by dropping parts of the rhythm in and out of the mix, using equalization effects and altering the feel of the record with echo, delay, and reverb. Tubby was a virtuoso at the mixing board, and his dubs stretched musical space into infinity. While Tubby and other influential dub engineers and producers like Errol Thompson, Keith Hudson, and Herman Chin Loy expanded and contracted music "with a flip of their musical wrists," producers like Lee Perry and Mikey Dread forsook the raw sound in favor of layer upon layer of sound and effects. Following Kool DJ Herc to New York, dub techniques would find their

way onto the dancefloors of the Big Apple's swankiest discos courtesy of remixers like Walter Gibbons and François Kevorkian. In 1974, vocalist Rupie Edwards made an entire album based on one riddim, *Yamaha Skank*, which would lay the foundation for the eighties dancehall style and for ragga. Beginning with the productions of Don Mais and Junjo Lawes in the late seventies, dancehall, like Hip-Hop, was based on DJ like Yellowman, Josey Wales, and General Echo chatting over increasingly stark reproductions of old rhythms. In the early eighties Sly & Robbie introduced synth-drums and cheap keyboards to their dancehall productions, thus creating the basis for ragga. Based on the digitized riddims of cheap Casio keyboards, ragga was inaugurated by Wayne Smith's 1985 anthem "Under Me Sleng Teng," which single-handedly shifted the focus of Jamaican music from the drums and bass to the synthesizer. As influential as any record by Kraftwerk or Giorgio Moroder, "Under Me Sleng Teng" not only inspired some 400 versions and countless imitations, but firmly established the modulating synth bassline as the sound of urban America and Britain as well as Jamaica. ❧ PETER SHAPIRO

Jazz-funk

Discography:

GEORGE RUSSELL	*Electronic Sonata for Souls Loved by Nature*	(1968) Soul Note, 1985
MILES DAVIS	*Agharta*	Sony, 1975
MILES DAVIS	*Pangaea*	Sony, 1975
HERBIE HANCOCK	*Crossings*	Warner Bros., 1972
HERBIE HANCOCK	*Sextant*	Sony, 1973
SUN RA	*My Brother the Wind, Vol. 2*	Evidence, 1969

With the exceptions of disco, heavy metal, and teeny-bop, there is no branch of music more derided than jazz-funk or fusion. Jazz purists displayed their usual condescension when jazz musicians began to experiment with the electronic instruments and gut-bucket rhythms of "vulgar" popular music, while more sensible and sensitive critics were appalled by fusion's degeneration into a cult of virtuoso technique. Fusion undeniably did become a haven for musicians who forsook jazz's fundamental tenet of swing in favor of mixolydian arpeggios. But before the woodshedders got hold of it, jazz-funk provided the space for some of music's most electroshocked explorations. Jazz-funk can trace its roots back to the 1950s when – at the same time that Ray Charles started singing about lust and money with the same intensity and style that people usually sang about God – jazz musicians like Horace Silver and Art Blakey blended elements of gospel and R&B into bebop to create a style called hard bop or soul-jazz. The effect was to bring jazz back to its roots in bordellos and nightclubs and out of the rarefied air of the concert hall. Organists like Jimmy Smith, Jack McDuff, Jimmy McGriff, and Lonnie Smith played a central role in this new, groove-based direction, and when new instruments like the Fender Rhodes, the clavinet, and the synthesizer emerged, keyboardists became the focus of the electrification of jazz. In the hands of jazz musicians, electronic instruments and effects were vehicles with which to explore both inner and outer space. Inspired by the ideas of Marshall McLuhan, composer and pianist George Russell created one of the earliest electronic events in jazz, 1968's *Electronic Sonata for Souls Loved by Nature*. A Vulcan mind-meld of treated electronic sounds and standard jazz instrumentation, *Electronic Sonata for Souls Loved by Nature* was, according to Russell's own liner notes, "meant to convey the cultural implosion occurring among the earth's population, their coming together. Also, it is meant to suggest that man, in the face of encroaching technology, must confront technology and attempt to humanize it." Russell's *Electric Sonata* contained field recordings of a Ugandan man talking to his sons as a comment on the imminent arrival of McLuhan's global village. With sitar drones, Brazilian and African rhythms, Hendrixian guitar whiteouts and a concept of music as process gleaned from Karlheinz Stockhausen, the electric recordings of Miles Davis imagined the pretechnological utopias of *Agharta* and *Pangaea* – mythical places that existed before the world was ripped asunder by continental drift and tectonic shifts. In the late sixties, Davis had turned on to the funk of James Brown and Sly Stone as an escape route from the increasing abstraction of jazz. The result was that Davis' recording sessions became open-ended jam sessions in which all of the musicians would vamp and improvise on one chord. The ensuing chaos — Reggie Lucas playing the hardest rhythm guitar imaginable, Pete Cosey producing the same sheets of aggressive psychedelia with his synth that he achieved with his guitar, Badal Roy and Mtume getting lost in a rain forest of percussion, Davis pushing

his trumpet and Yamaha organ into wah-wah oblivion — was edited into consumable shape by producer Teo Macero. Macero had been playing with jazz's conventions of "authenticity" since the late fifties and early sixties when he began splicing tape and using echo effects, but he fully brought the mechanics of the studio to bear with his loops and fade-outs for Davis' seventies records. Davis' main keyboard player from 1963 until 1970 was Herbie Hancock. When Hancock left Davis' band, he formed the Herbie Hancock Sextet, whose albums *Crossings* and *Sextant* are perhaps the definitive fusions of mind, body, and electronic circuitry. Titles like "Quasar," "Water Torture," and "Raindance" perfectly captured the sound of Hancock's phase-shifted keyboards, Bennie Maupin and Julian Priester's echo-chambered horns, and the ARP and Moog synthesizers of Dr. Patrick Gleeson. With ancestral themes coupled to spacewalking music, *Crossings* and *Sextant* were the epitome of the cosmic future-past explorations being undertaken by many African-American musicians at the time. The first musician to send back astro-blue impressions from outer space was Sun Ra. Born Herman Blount in Alabama in 1914, "Sonny" was fascinated by Egyptology and science fiction; he developed his own cosmology and became Sun Ra in the 1950s. In his "heliocentric world," the big band tradition was a conduit for a kaleidoscopic journey into the mystic. In 1956, Sun Ra's fusion of classicism and futurism really lifted off with the addition of electric keyboards, and by 1969's *My Brother the Wind* and 1970's *It's After the End of the World*, his array of organs and keyboards was augmented by the Minimoog, allowing him to truly reach "other planes of there."

PETER SHAPIRO

INTERVIEW:
Teo Macero

In a Silent Way was one of the rare times that Miles [Davis] came to the studio. I called Miles up and I said, "Look, I edited, I mixed two stacks of tapes – about fifteen or twenty reels each – I can make the cuts, I can do the edit..." [As Miles] "I'll come down. I'll be there." So he came down and we cut each side down to eight-and-a-half minutes, and I think the other side was nine-and-a-half, and he said he was leaving in four-letter words, he's going to get out of there, and that would be his album. I said, "Look you really can't do that. I mean CBS will fire you, suspend you, fire me, but give me a couple of days, I'll think about it." Then a couple of days later, I sent him up a tape and that was it. What I did, I copied a lot of it. You wouldn't know where the splices are. Joe Zawinul should give us half of his money for fixing it all up. Because at the end, I didn't know – I thought it was all Miles' music, but apparently Joe Zawinul claimed it was his. So we paid him all the royalties. When you cut and you edit, you can do it in such a way that no one will ever know. Those days we were still doing it with a razor blade. It's not like digital recording now where you got the twenty-four tracks and all kinds of equipment. You can put it on the computer. You can do all the things you want to do. If you want to move that thing over, not one beat but maybe a beat and a half or a beat and a one-sixth, you create a wash. There are a lot of things that you can do today that we didn't have the techniques to do in the late fifties and early sixties. I think *In a Silent Way* is really a remarkable record for what it is. For a little bit of music, it's turned into a classic. We did that with a lot of other records of Miles' where we would use bits and pieces of cassettes that he would send me and say, "Put this in that new album we're working on." I would really shudder. I'd say, "Look, where the hell is it going to go? I don't know." He says, "Oh, you know." So he sends me the tape. I listen to it, and I say, "Oh yeah, maybe we can stick that in here." There were a lot of times in my career with Miles that I just would do that. Put the cassette right from the stage into the master tape. We did a lot of electronic effects when we did *Sketches of Spain*. If you listen to it very carefully, you'll hear that in one spot on the record the band comes up center and splits, goes around and comes up again. We had all kinds of boxes and one engineer would be monitoring one box and I'd be monitoring the other to make this effect. I mean, not many people really have heard that record the way it should be. They've put it back out again, CBS and the Miles Davis collection, but it's not the same. There was a wealth of love to make this music boil. In Miles' music, that's the way it is anyway. To highlight it, to give it a twenty-first-century feel, is what I always wanted to do in my own music, and I still do. I wanted to do it with my artists because it made for a better record, an unusual one. That's why we got a gold and platinum record. I started at Juilliard. That was the beginning, when I was studying and working in the engineering department for fifty cents an hour to try to pay my way through Juilliard. But then I got interested in it because of Edgard Varèse. He used to be like my second father. There are some pictures here of him and the two of us and some scores I had. I was there when he was doing the *Poème Électronique* for the Le Corbusier building in Paris. He would show me all the pieces, all of the elements. He was creating sounds from other sources than electronic sounds. He was making his own, which is to me very creative. Much more so than just putting it through a filter and doing this. He created all kinds of things for that *Poème Électronique*, and I was fascinated by it. We used to see each other for lunch. We'd talk on Saturday and Sundays on the phone, and he'd come to all my concerts. He was like a second father, with a tremendous amount of knowledge. He was a sweet man and very creative. People haven't realized how great he was. It took, I think, twenty-five years before the Philharmonic played one of his pieces. He had to be seventy-five by that point. I think that's disgusting and discouraging for contemporary composers to try to write music and have to wait twenty-five years to hear it done right. Miles' stuff was mostly written down. It was worked on in the studio. I'd record everything. Then when I'd go back to the editing room, I would edit everything. I listened to everything back. Miles would say, "You remember that thing in the second take?" I said, yeah. Then I would maybe make a loop and create it. That's why those records were so good. Maybe people will say it didn't sound authentic. It is authentic because you're acting like a writer for a book. You're acting like an editor. You can't pan the book if the material is great. I'm just there to make sure that everything is in order Now, Miles, I come back to him all the time because I recorded him a lot differently than most people would think. I can't remember how far back, but I recorded him from three different sources. When the microphones first came out attached to the instruments, Miles was one of the first to use that. So I took it from the source, from the microphone on the instrument. I'd take it from the real sound into the microphone. Then I would feed another channel into the amplifier and pick it up from the amplifier. I had three different sources to work from. You could take those three sources, keep the main source, and then manipulate the other two sources and come up with *Bitches Brew*. You need that communication with the other person, [with the] engineer and research department. This is where it's coming from. All these electronics are great, but if you don't know what the hell to do with them and you're not a good composer, you might as well send it back. The funny thing is, the wah-wah pedal now is becoming more important in terms of the marketplace. The way that happened...I don't know whether I gave him the pedal, but I got him a pedal. I got him everything he needed for the wah-wah, but he couldn't manipulate it. He was just learning it. So what I did, I told him "Don't worry about it. We'll fix it." When I got the tapes out of the studio into the editing room, I got a wah-wah pedal, and I wah-wah'ed those things to death. I don't think anyone could duplicate those records today. I think he made two records like that. I think the wah-wah pedal and all the sort of electronic effects that you have with the guitars is really marvelous. Miles was very careful; he liked to try new things. ♣

Afro-Futurism

Afro-Futurism has more than one beginning. *Planet Rock* is certainly one of them. You could also say George Clinton's *Mothership* collection in 1974 was one of them. You could even push it further back to Sun Ra in the 1950s, and the compositions that he worked out with his Arkestra. One of Sun Ra's many innovations was to transform jazz into an electronic music. He wasn't in the least bit funky. He was extremely atonal – a difficult, serious composer. And he wasn't really jazz, either. He was somewhere between jazz and electronic, somewhere between electronics and music, that doesn't even have a name yet. In this sense we still haven't really caught up with Sun Ra. Although he made music from the fifties to the nineties, in some sense he still comes from the future. Like Varèse or Miles Davis. Their music, even though it was made twenty years ago, arrives from the future and kind of impacts on the present. It abducts us into a new sonic universe. Sun Ra made over two hundred records. And there's a point where he's saying to you, "Give up your life. Listen to my

SUN RA

records. Listen to me. Enter my universe. Enter my mythology." He created a series of different, overlapping universes. He created overlapping mythologies. Overlapping cosmologies. He created what he called "the Omniverse," which is a series of sonic universes in sound. And the idea was that you would literally give up your life and become an acolyte, make listening your full-time vocation. Sun Ra is a challenge. He's the James Joyce of organized sound. You can only really know a little aspect of his music because it encompasses such a huge area. ⚘ KODWO ESHUN

4

We must break out of this limited circle of sounds and conquer the infinite variety of noise sounds. **LUIGI RUSSOLO,** *The Art of Noises,* 1913 Life and being alive and excitement and sex is full of noise. Death is quiet. **ALEC EMPIRE** I think making melodies is important, but people have a cliched idea of what a melody is. A melody, I think, could be constructed of noise or different sound. **BILL LASWELL** "Noise is politics." If you have noise, that reflects chaos, and people don't really want to see that because mentally it blows things a little bit out of focus. People want clarity – even if it's an artificial clarity. **DJ SPOOKY**

POST-PUNK

SNARL: A POST-INDUSTRIAL AUTOMATON

BY PETER SHAPIRO

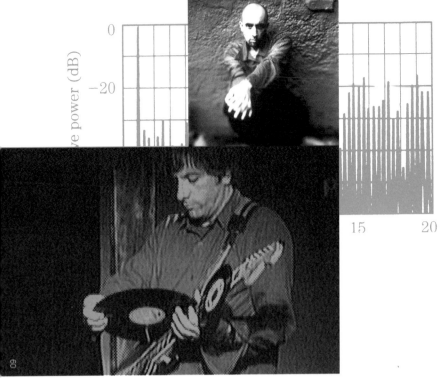

0

−20

ve power (dB)

15   20

Discography:

CABARET VOLTAIRE	*Red Mecca*	Rough Trade, 1981
CHROME	*Alien Soundtracks*	Siren, 1978
COIL	*Time Machines*	Eskaton, 1996
DAF	*Für Immer*	Virgin, 1982
FRONT 242	*Front By Front*	Epic, 1988
THE RESIDENTS	*Meet the Residents*	Ralph, 1974
SUICIDE	*Suicide*	Red Star, 1977
THROBBING GRISTLE	*20 Jazz Funk Greats*	Mute, 1979

LEE RANALDO / SONIC YOUTH   MEAT BEAT MANIFESTO   TRANS AM

Before we became accustomed to associating the synthesizer with gloss, sophistication, and "the new," musicians on the fringes of the punk and post-punk scenes were using the new technology to expose the alienated underbelly of society. Combining the Farfisa organ peals of ? & the Mysterians' garage classic "96 Tears," the metronomic pulse of the Velvet Underground and the lo-fi electronica of sixties experimentalists like the Silver Apples and Walter/Wendy Carlos, these musicians realized that punk's snarl would be even scarier on the face of a post-industrial automaton.

Originally a performance-art troupe called COUM Transmissions, Throbbing Gristle was a group of art-punks inspired by the literary cut-ups of William Burroughs and Brion Gysin, who were hell-bent on shocking Britain's tabloid press. Wallowing in the abject, Throbbing Gristle surrounded their grating electronic noise with Nazi imagery, quotes from serial murderers, and anonymous death threats, and called the bricolage Industrial Music. Although they occasionally ventured into disco grotesques and ironic exotica, TG was all about creating ugly music for an ugly world. TG split in 1981 and ringleader Genesis P-Orridge and Peter "Sleazy" Christopherson formed Psychic TV. Initially a TG rehash with a larger tonal palette, Psychic TV progressed from an obsession with cults, through an obsession with the sixties to an embrace of the drug-shamanism P-Orridge found in club culture. Christopherson was the electronic mastermind behind TG and Psychic TV, and his own project, Coil, has produced some of the most disturbing electronic soundscapes imaginable.

Less gruesome, but just as shocking to the rock

brigade was Sheffield's Cabaret Voltaire. While their punk contemporaries had appropriated the in-your-face attitude of sixties garage rock, Stephen Mallinder, Richard H. Kirk, and Chris Watson merely appropriated the organ stabs. On early records like the *Extended Play* EP and "Nag Nag Nag," Cabaret Voltaire made synth riffs and tape loops sound as aggressive as anything by the Sex Pistols. By the time of 1980's *Voice of America* and 1981's *Red Mecca*, the found-sound collages of their Dadaist namesakes had worked their way into the band's ominous electronic noisescapes to create dark portraits of Thatcher's Britain.

Although they were similarly influenced by the organ drones of sixties garage rock, New York's Suicide seemed to embrace rock 'n' roll rather than seeing it as the enemy. Vocalist Alan Vega and synthesist Martin Rev were Lower East Side bohemians in love with rockabilly, American sentimentality, the Velvet Underground, church hymns and cheap drum machines who got together in the early seventies to form a performance-based art project. With almost rhythmless drum machine programming, two-note bass drones, Vega stalking the stage in Western shirts and leather tassels, and the band mimicking the famous Sun studio sound by surrounding Vega's hiccuping, yelping vocals with echo and reverb, Suicide reimagined rockabilly as the sound that an army of Andy Warhol's Elvis reproductions would make. While Suicide's sound has been enormously influential, no one with the possible exception of Soft Cell's Marc Almond (who has attempted to ally the melodrama of Northern Soul and Jacques Brel with the detachment of electronics) has picked up on their blend of alienation and kitsch, stylization and authenticity.

Meanwhile, in San Francisco, the fallout from Haight-Ashbury had left a bitter and twisted fringe scene that dabbled in electronics as a vehicle for communicat-

SENSORBAND

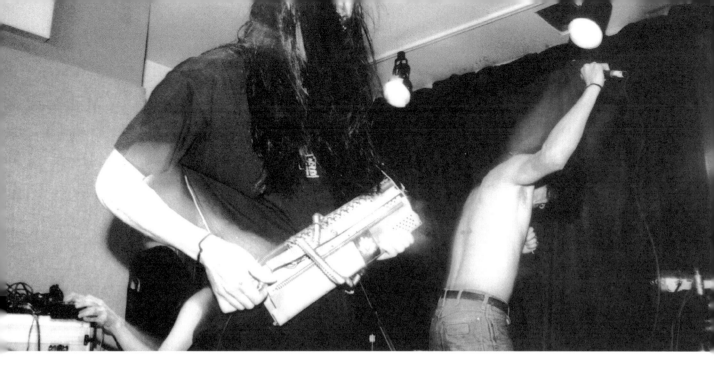

ing their bizarre visions. Comprised of Damon Edge, Helios Creed, Gary Spain, and John Lambdin (a.k.a John L. Cyborg), Chrome initially attempted to bridge The Stooges, Can, and Jefferson Airplane, but by 1978's *Alien Soundtracks* album, they had started creating music for android strip shows, and their music became more electronic. Although they never fully gave up guitars, Chrome has often been called "the American Throbbing Gristle," and they certainly shared a sense of postindustrial alienation.

Down the road apiece in San Mateo, The Residents used cheesy synths and tape manipulations to desecrate pop music's sacred cows, creating deliberately awful covers of Nancy Sinatra's "These Boots Were Made for Walking" and James Brown's "This is a Man's World," brutal parodies of George Gershwin, and a cover of "The Twist" in which Chubby Checker morphs into Adolf Hitler.

At the other end of the spectrum, shrouded in a dour Teutonic image, DAF (Deutsch Amerikanische Freundschaft) were the early-eighties champions of electronic minimalism. Robert Görl and Gabi Delgado-Lopez attempted to mix Kraftwerk with Wire and, on 1982's *Für Immer*, they succeeded with dainty love songs that nuzzled up to ascetic social-realism. In the hands of Front 242, such synth-pop turned into Belgian New Beat. Making digital technology the sonic analogue of the repressive practices of the state, Front 242 made aggressive, sloganeering music about control and the new world order that, at least on 1988's "Headhunter," you could dance to.

MERZBOW

INTERVIEW:
Genesis P-Orridge

I've always seen music basically just as a tool, a platform to access people – preferably reasonable numbers of people, not huge numbers, but enough. I have no love affair with music in and of itself. I have never called myself a musician. In fact, I'm always incredibly offended if I see someone refer to me as a musician in an article or a book. I refer to myself as a cultural engineer: That's more accurate. Music is there and people already like music. People are already listening to music. It is in the cultural pot of society, as is television. Anything that's there that people are working with, affected by, or conditioned by, is my territory, too. In Throbbing Gristle, in the early 1970s, my first, absolute, adamant request to everybody involved was there should be no drummer, no lead guitarist, and no rhythm guitarist. I thought, rightly or wrongly, all Western popular music was derived from feudal slave music, and I had no great urge to declare myself a bastardized former slave. I'm a white middle-class boy. I had many arguments with punk bands, who would say "Learn three chords and form a band." I thought, "Why on earth learn three chords?" Therein lies the problem of punk to me – they wanted to learn to play music. To learn to play music based on rhythm and blues is to become a slave of the system once more, so if you're going to play slave music, let it be about post-industrial slave society, where people worked in factories and mills. No one had really done that. No one had actually decided to make a music rooted in the experience of western European and industrial society, so that's what we did. We took the conveyor belt, the factory, the power station, and mass-produced luxury goods as the stepping-stone for the form of the music and experimented with that rather than guitars. This meant we had to look beyond traditional instruments – Roland was making equipment that we were very excited about and that didn't require normal musical knowledge, only logic and inspiration. But their use seemed preordained, specific, and very limited, like all tools and all toys. If you give a baby a guitar, he'll jump on it, smash it, hit it. The baby won't play chords or a beautiful piece of classical music. He will see what the entire thing does. Everything is about learning to think. A friend of mine,

Dr. Timothy Poston, who is a chaos mathematician, once told me (way back in the early days in 1969/'71 when it was still called catastrophe theory and fuzzy geometry) that what's exciting about science since the atom was split is you go to the bottom of the castle of science and you tear up the final stones in the bottom of the castle and you look through and it's an empty space. It's the stars. It's the universe. There's nothing there. The world is not meant to be good/bad, black/white, one/zero. It's not binary. It's chaos. Chaos is not a digital system, and if there is a programmer, something is wrong, because you should be the programmer. It should always be your program, not someone else's program, not somebody else's software, not their boundaries, and not their limitations. Why would I enter their world? I don't want to be them. I have to be honest and confess that I have a great hatred for digital culture. I think that it's passive. I think popular culture should be trying to generate opportunities for a truly psychedelic and hyperdelic expansion of consciousness towards the creation of an experience that could not be recorded in any possible way. That's been lost. All the excitement that I felt in the mid-eighties, when I came across white labels in Chicago, and all the excitement I felt when people began doing drug-riddled events in Britain, which were later called "raves," but at that time were just drug-riddled events, you know, is gone. I feel there's just formalization, commodification, assimilation — all the things that were the enemy in the seventies are back with a vengeance and it doesn't excite me. I was excited by music in the sixties because it was sexy, rebellious, and everyone hated it. It confused even me. I'd never come across it before, and I didn't know what the next sound was going to be. Adding to this appeal was the fact that often I couldn't go out and buy it anywhere. I couldn't see it on television and it wasn't in magazines, except scare stories saying it was destroying civilization. I liked that, you see. I think that's what we're supposed to be doing. We're supposed to scare everyone. We're supposed to try and find things that are sexy. We're supposed to feel confused and exhilarated and to have experiences we never had before. We're not meant to get jaded. We're not meant to know the ruling peer group's approved mode of dress or how to dance to it in advance. The expected is the enemy. When I woke up one morning and realized I knew what the flyers for the raves would look like and what software was used to do the graphics and that there would be Hindu deities on the back, even the choice of typefaces and how long it was going to last. When I even knew all the DJs and what they were going to play, and I knew the people who did the light shows, and I knew exactly what videos they were going to use I thought, "Why do I go? Why on earth would I go to this?" "So it's on a beach...big deal. You know, I can go to a beach and take drugs anyway. I don't need to go and deal with 10,000 people who do not think, you know?" The joy of true creativity is the exploration of the unpredictable. At the point that creative energy becomes fully predictable and formularized, the flickering spirit of the divine is extinguished and camouflaged conservatism takes over, fed by the desire of many to be safe within the familiar. We should imagine what will surprise us next. I'm not in the game of the expected. I like the idea of the dematerialization of identity, and I think it's inevitable now. As people communicate more and more frequently and globally, they can invent new personas and identities — probably the first impulse is to imagine celebrity as being one of the great big deities of our time. But if celebrity is about mass media and mass contact, then at some point an anti-celebrity status and a way of behaving that destroys the celebrity, destroys the ego and the personality and identity until we do not exist, becomes revolutionary. Self-immolation. Self-immolation is actually going to be one of the contemporary ways of behaving, and you can see it already in some performance art — with Orlan, who does plastic surgery, and Stelarc (www.stelarc.va.com.au/), both people that I know and respect a great deal. I think they're both leading the way to a much more intriguing and dangerous vision of what technology might do, and also addressing the body as a malleable physical container, which, interestingly, relates to the Heaven's Gate people. Part of the spillage we've had from technology is that the body is seen as a container now. The Heaven's Gate suicide was a fantastically modern event. Their refusal of sexuality with its replication of a flawed species, the negation of individual identity, the utilization of the world wide web to maintain an immortal presence beyond biological death is probably the most modern action we've seen. Far more modern and intriguing than just making audio recordings. So I think that we've got to look to the extreme. All culture is fed by the extreme. **Throbbing Gristle, in 1975, printed a newsletter that we gave away free, and it said all you need is a cassette recorder with a condenser microphone and you can make an album. We made our first album that way. We put the tape on the table and we played live and released it as an album, which has never been deleted since.** We set up really deep frequencies with custom-made speakers and reflex bins in a concrete basement of a factory. We found that the frequencies got so intense that our clothing started moving, even though there was no draft. Just the actual sound made everything move. Our clothes, the fluorescent lights hanging on chains, objects on tables, all moved. Finally, after about an hour, we got tunnel vision and went blind. **Throbbing Gristle only ever played for one hour at a time. We had a big digital clock that ran from zero to sixty minutes. As soon as it hit sixty, we all stopped, irrelevant of where we were. But we all had our own smaller clocks, too. During the last five minutes we did what we called the "Whorl Of Sound," boosting everything to maximum, taking all the middle out with maximum treble, maximum bass. Then we basically just hit everything that made a noise and put it through every possible processor we could until it was just beyond white noise, beyond** *Metal Machine Music,* **just something that the brain could not comprehend. It became almost the same as a silence, it was so overwhelming. There had to be something to put after that because it stopped so abruptly, and people were so disorientated at that point, physically and mentally. So we chose two things. One of them was Martin Denny. If you hear the live recordings of Throbbing Gristle, you'll always hear a little touch of Martin Denny at the end.** The brain loves the easy ways to work. Give it a rhythm and it won't work hard for you. It won't look for surreal and unexpected options. It will just lock down and sleep, dancing and moving to a rhythm. It's not clever or innately radical. You know, moving two or three discs of plastic so that they go at the same speed is not really that clever. It's artisan work. Being a DJ is a matter of getting the speed of plastic the same. That's it. And, I'm not impressed, you know? I'm sure it's like chimpanzees at the zoo. If you gave them three record decks long enough, they'd get the same speed and then they'd be DJs. People should think a lot harder. Push their own limits of what is possible and impossible on behalf of their chosen tribe. **William Burroughs and many other thinkers would agree that the ultimate challenge is to see if we can access our own DNA and adjust the program. Sexuality is definitely one of the keys. All paths lead to a focused sexuality. Clarity of intent is definitely a method of deprogramming and reprogramming ourselves. Refuse all previous programs, refuse all socialization, all imprints, all authority and control, all inherited values, all inherited modes of behaviour in order to prepare ourselves as an emptied, positive vehicle and container to fill with what we choose, in order to go where we wish.** I met William Burroughs in 1970 in London and sat for many, many hours with him talking about tape recorders and magic and experiments with cognition designed to change expectations, how to destroy things, how to create things. It was a long time ago, and apart from recommending the tape recorder, he also showed me techniques, with photographs, where you cut the photographs up, remove what we don't want and reassemble the photograph to remove from your life things that you don't like. He also said that in his mind, the most important project for anyone to work on was how to take your individual consciousness and somehow find a vehicle or a technique for it to continue on, without the body and outside time. I thought that was a remarkable concept. I was twenty years old and I was thinking, "Hmmm?" Then Burroughs said to go and think about it and I have. I've thought about it ever since, so there were two jobs. One was to short-circuit control, and the other was to take your brain – your neurological sense of being – and separate it from the body, so that it could continue without the body. Spiritual transcendence and sexuality are exactly the same thing. When I used to do performance art, way back in the early seventies, I would do different actions related to my body and sexuality that, surprisingly, also had neurological effects. I would speak in tongues, I would have visions, I would leave my body and, actually, once was declared dead in a hospital, but I was still conscious, thinking, why are they saying that? I'm fine. I just can't move. But the doctors could find no heartbeat, no pulse. I didn't know why it happened, but I was very interested, so I began to investigate. I wanted to know if I could repeat those experiences. With Psychic TV, we used to use very, very, very high intensity strobes that would activate the left brain more. We worked with brain theories and discovered that you could actually use red strobes, and they would be more left brain. We'd have different strobes at the sides of the stage, large mirrors behind or in front of us and we'd use frequencies that were very sensual. We were very happy one day, in about 1986, to have several people say they had spontaneous orgasms whilst they were dancing and watching what we were doing. We were like a research lab, and we would throw up lots of ideas, too many for us to follow through on all of them. Other people would expand on them, amplify them, and do incredible things with them that we would never have thought of. Life is fun. Isn't it? I like it. I'm having a good time. ꙮ

Synthpop

Discography:			
	HUMAN LEAGUE	*Dare*	A&M, 1981
	HEAVEN 17	*Penthouse & Pavement*	Virgin, 1981
	DEPÈCHE MODE	*Catching Up With Depèche Mode*	Sire, 1985
	NEW ORDER	*Substance*	Qwest, 1987
	DEVO	*Greatest Hits*	Warner Bros., 1987

Given its emergence from the scattered rubble of the artier end of the punk scene, synth-pop's combination of pizzazz and alienation may very well have started with Kraftwerk or David Bowie's ARP-fuelled mega-downer from 1977, *Low*. In its golden age, though, synth-pop had far more to do with the Eurodisco of Giorgio Moroder and Cerrone (which expressed much more emotional and physical dislocation than critics will ever give it credit for) than with anything by Kraftwerk or Suicide, despite the authentic post-punk credentials. Synth-pop qua synth-pop can be most usefully dated from 1979, when automatons like Gary Numan's Tubeway Army and Visage crawled out from the remains of a cosmetics factory explosion and dressed up in a detached Warholian glamor (via David Bowie and Brian Eno) in metallic blue and shocking-orange make-up. Where Bowie was a glammed-out pseudo-aesthete who cocooned himself in conceptual grandeur, Numan and Visage weren't pretentious enough to really believe that they were artistes: Compare Numan's matter-of-fact line

DEVO

GARY NUMAN

"Here in my car, I feel safest of all/I can lock all my doors" with any of the Thin White Duke's ridiculously oblique lyrics. While Numan and Visage were musing about electric friends and trading tips on foundation and mascara, M and Telex imagined that the synthesizer would take the world in a love embrace on their global-village anthems "Pop Muzik" and "Moskow Diskow". Despite the chart successes of M and Telex, synth-pop continued to be the preserve of angry young men with a tenuous grasp of Marxism. At the start of their career, the Human League was, just like their neighbors Cabaret Voltaire, achingly earnest post-industrial doomsayers who released records called *Being Boiled* and *Dignity of Labour*. Out of nowhere, though, the League discovered that the humans they supposedly represented responded better to pop hooks than being hectored about historical materialism, and they released New Wave's magnum opus, *Dare*, in 1981. A landmark of plasticity, garish artifice, and shimmering surfaces, *Dare* made synth-pop's sangfroid the soundtrack to the look-but-don't-touch eighties. As Heaven 17, ex-Human Leaguers Ian Craig Marsh and Martyn Ware also embraced the logic of capital, but songs like "We Don't Need This Fascist Groove Thing" and "Penthouse and Pavement" proved that you didn't have to give up politics to be catchy. As definitive as *Dare* was, though, the real pied piper of synth-pop, and the one who truly made the synthesizer the instrument of beach holidays and summer romances, was Vince Clarke. Starting his career with Depèche Mode and the *sui generis* single "Just Can't Get Enough," Clarke went on to recreate synth-pop in the image of Eurodisco — the sound of heroic heartbreak — with Yaz(oo), The Assembly, and Erasure. Plastic soul boys like Martin Fry of ABC and Nick Rhodes of Duran Duran took Clarke's idea one step further by trying to make synth-pop more hedonsitic by merging Chic with Roxy Music. The flip side to this sybaratism was New Order, who took good old-fashioned British miserablism into New York's Fun House to create "Blue Monday," the biggest-selling twelve-inch single of all time. Synth-pop was almost exclusively a European phenomenon: Even the few American bands, like Berlin, who ventured into this territory had to cloak themselves in the mantle of European grandeur. Akron, Ohio's Devo, on the other hand, was synth-pop's evil twin. A bunch of smart-ass miscreants, Devo turned rock classics like the Rolling Stones' "(I Can't Get No) Satisfaction" and Johnny Rivers' "Secret Agent Man" into the robotic parodies that guitar fascists always feared, proving that androids were capable of satire as well as imperturbability. 🔹

You don't have to have had any piano lessons, drum lessons, any kind of musical lessons to make this kind of music. Any guy can go and spend $2000 or $3000, sit in his bedroom, and he can make music. What you like is what you sample and what you use. **LTJ BUKEM** Everybody now works with screens if they work in digital technology. It used to be that one person worked with a pencil and another person worked with a violin – totally different forms of technology – but now there is a convergence on the screen. There is something I call a screen ceremony, where the work is created on the screen. **DAVID TOOP** I just like the idea of getting out of bed and getting your breakfast, coming back and you're in the studio. You don't have to go down the road, you don't have to get on a bus to get to the studio. You are just there, it's hands-on straight away, you wake up in the middle of the night and do a track – that's what's revolutionized it for me. **SQUAREPUSHER** Our Japanese bamboo flute called shakuhachi is a very difficult instrument to learn. People would say that it takes eight years just to master one note. It might be interesting to sit for eight years trying to make a sound. Maybe in another lifetime I would do that. **RYUICHI SAKAMOTO** I think technology, in the sense of new kinds of rhythm machines, new kinds of sound machines, certainly allows new mutations of music. But what really defines western culture are the specific thresholds that get crossed at any one point. It's the specific new limits of rhythms, the new limits of tones, the new rhythms of melodies that a machine allows. Sound machines allow new kinds of tones that don't belong to the old system of notated music. You get things that are in-between texture and rhythm: texture-rhythms. You get things that are in-between rhythm and melody: rhythm-melodies. You get a whole series of new kinds of musical forms that have nothing to do with that traditional way of making music. In this way, I'd say technology allows a new kind of music that doesn't really have much to do with the West anymore. It's more to do with particular kinds of personal music systems. Almost like machine mythologies. **KODWO ESHUN**

5

Dance music, as I define it, is rhythm-machine music. The machines augment bodily

thought. They allow the drummer to become a superhuman percussionist. They allow

you to play lots of different tones and lots of different rhythms that you wouldn't be

able to play normally. It's about opening out a new kind of physical interface. And in

fact, machines de-physicalize music. In other words, if you can just push a button for

percussion, then you don't need to practice lots of hours on the drums. So in that sense,

you have to think more about the music you're playing, or you have to think more about

the organization of rhythm and the organization of sound. **KODWO ESHUN**

HOUSE

THE REINVENTION OF HOUSE

KODWO ESHUN

DJ PIERRE

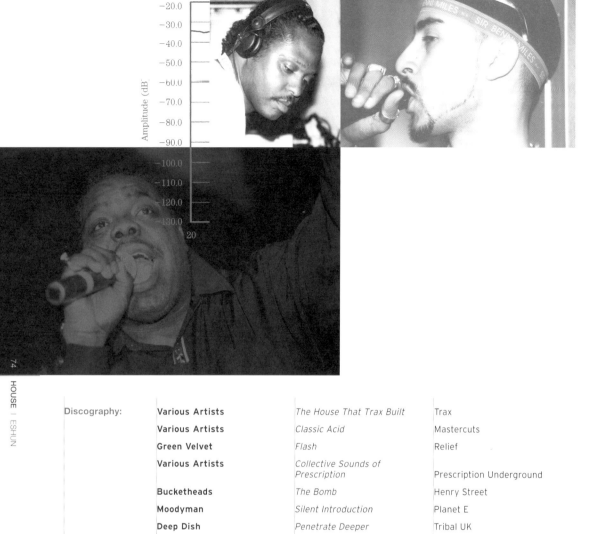

Discography:			
	Various Artists	*The House That Trax Built*	Trax
	Various Artists	*Classic Acid*	Mastercuts
	Green Velvet	*Flash*	Relief
	Various Artists	*Collective Sounds of Prescription*	Prescription Underground
	Bucketheads	*The Bomb*	Henry Street
	Moodyman	*Silent Introduction*	Planet E
	Deep Dish	*Penetrate Deeper*	Tribal UK
	Daft Punk	*Homework*	Virgin
	Tori Amos	*Professional Widow*	Armand Van Helden Mix, Atlantic
	St. Germain	*Alabama Blues Revisited*	Todd Edwards Vocal Mix, F Communications
	187 Lockdown	*Gunman*	East West Dance
	Dem 2	*Destiny*	New Vocal Mix, Locked On
	EZ	*Presents Underground Garage Flava's*	Breakdown Records
	Basic Channel	*Phylyps Track 1/11*	Basic Channel
	Jephte Guillame	*The Prayer*	Spiritual Life

DARRYL PANDY   JESSE SAUNDERS   ARMAND VAN HELDEN

At the same time as Giorgio Moroder was unleashing his synthesized sex fantasies with Donna Summer on the world, an aspiring disco DJ from New York was recruited to play at Chicago's new pleasure dome, The Warehouse. During his residence at the club, DJ Frankie Knuckles discovered that his crowd of two thousand gay, black revelers enthusiastically responded to the electronic feel of tracks like Summer's "I Feel Love." As a result, he began to augment his Salsoul and Philadelphia International records with the more rigid beats of a cheap drum machine; the dancers responded with remarkable intensity. Legend has it that this combination of disco with drum machines and reel-to-reel tape edits became known as house music after people kept asking record stores for "the records they played at the Warehouse."

When Knuckles left the Warehouse in 1983 to form his own club, The Power Plant, the owners of his old club opened the Music Box, which was presided over by a young Californian named Ron Hardy who had a harder, more percussive style than Knuckles. The fierce competition between the two DJs led to gimmicks like introducing sound effects and mixing trickery into their sets. With this quest for novelty, local musicians began making "tracks" (so named because they were little more than a drum track) for the DJs, to play and house's low-end minimalism was born.

Most people agree that the first house record was Jesse Saunders' version of "On and On" in 1983. The following year, a local entrepreneur named Larry Sherman started the Trax label to cater to the growing demand for these tracks. Its first release was another Jesse Saunders

record called *Wanna Dance*. Another local label, DJ International, started releasing house records and scored the first real house hit with yet another Jesse Saunders record, his collaboration with Farley Jackmaster Funk on a version of Isaac Hayes' "Love Can't Turn Around," which had hit the British Top 10 in 1986.

The dance to house music was called "the jack," and it was as jerky and twitchy as its name implies. "Jack tracks" were hard and minimal records whose only human touch would be a voice exhorting you to "jack your body," but these were nothing compared to 1987's fad for "acid tracks," which were even more fiercely minimal. The hallmark of the "acid track" was its bizarre, squelching bassline that was created by the Roland TB-303 bassline machine. Originally designed to provide bassline accompaniment for solo instrumentalists, the

303 was an abysmal failure at its assigned task, but in the hands of the Chicago house producers, it became capable of generating tense, frightening, and orgiastic music. The first "acid track" was, naturally enough, Phuture's "Acid Tracks" which was created by DJ Pierre, Spanky, and Herb Jackson and produced by Marshall Jefferson. Little more than a typical four-to-the-floor Chicago house-drum pattern and various permutations of this twitchy, droning bassline, "Acid Tracks" created such mayhem when it was first played at the Music Box that everyone thought the club's water supply had been spiked with LSD, a rumor that allegedly gave the record its name.

The Moroder-on-steroids feel of the acid tracks was predated by a few months by Mr. Fingers' "Washing Machine." Produced by a jazz-fusion afficionado called

FRANKIE BONES W/ TECHNO ARTISTS HEATHER HEART AND ADAM X

Larry Heard, "Washing Machine" was a gurgling, spinning, tumbling instrumental record that didn't feature a 303 but was just as inhuman. It was an anomaly, though, as most of Heard's records, like *Mysteries of Love* and *Distant Planet* pioneered the warmer, more "musical" sound known as deep house. Heard's deep house sound seemed to move house away from its post-human tendencies and back towards the lush disco of old Philly International and Salsoul records, and connected with the discofied garage sound of New York.

It's widely agreed that the first acid-era wave of house from 1986 to 1989 reached a creative peak at the point where dancefloor appeal and extreme experimentation converged. But the upheavals of mid- to late-nineties house have gone unnoticed, overshadowed by the breakthroughs of jungle and drum and bass on one side and by techno/electronica's self-image of conceptual breakthrough on the other. Listening back to the house music of 1994-1999, it's immediately audible how much house has reinvented itself.

Back in 1989, acid producer Bam Bam's "Where's Your Child?" played on parental fears (about music, drugs, raves) with the insidious expertise of an Aum Shinrikyo cult leader. "Where's Your Child?" the chorus demanded, gloating, "Don't you know they don't know right from wrong?" Fast-forward six years: Producer Curtis Jones, a.k.a. Green Velvet, answered acid's taunt with "Flash," his 1995 track that epitomized the second wave of Chicago house.

"Flash"'s narrator gleefully leads parents on a tour through a rave where they "See a bad little kiddy doing bad little things/Sucking on a balloon filled with nitrous oxide/Laughing gas hee hee hee ha ha/But this is no laughing matter." As he gives the order, "Cameras ready, prepare to flash," the parents fire off their Kodak in a hair raising fusillade of double-time military snares.

With singles like "Flash," "The Stalker (I'm Losing my Mind)," "I Want to Leave My Body," and "Answer Machine," Green Velvet and other producers such as Tim Harper, Boo Williams, Nate Williams, and Gemini used the Relief label to release "tracks," updating acid's tradition by jettisoning the 303 but intensifying its brutal funk-tionalism. Rejecting melodies in favor of stark synthetic patterns, the Relief producers tuned their Roland drum machines into concussive kick drums, punishing snares, and hooks of harsh noise. Tracks like Tim Harper's "Enter the Dragon" effectively abolished the distance between house and techno, inducing a mood of psychopathic aggression in Velvet's fictional scenarios.

New York's Armand Van Helden released Relief-inspired house throughout 1995. Tracks like "Witchdoktor," with its blaring klaxon, harsh drum tattoo, and bellowing vocals, spoke volumes about house music's new aggres-sion. "Musically, I get a lot of tips from the techno scene," Van Helden said to i-D magazine in February 1995. This mid-nineties minimalist militancy followed the path opened by DJ Rush, the Chicago producer whose 1993 Knee Deep EP had single-handedly reprogrammed house rhythms. Instead of an inexorable galloping momentum, Rush retriggered the drum-machine tones at intervals so that rhythms backed up, rolled out, and stepped to the side, hooking you in before falling back into sequence. Triple- and double-timing step patterns generated tum-bling hooks, as did extreme filtering that sounded as if a jet fighter was landing on a record.

U.S. house followed two tendencies: the metal machine music of the "track" and the gospel humanism of the "song." Relief's brutalism/brutality was paralleled by the beseeching succor of anthems like vocalist Dajae's "Brighter Days," produced by Green Velvet's other per-sona, Cajmere, on Relief's sister label, Cajual. Simultaneously, Chicago labels like Prescription Underground, its sister label Balance Recordings, and Circulation pioneered an introspective take on spiritual-ity. Instead of uplift, melancholy; instead of piano refrains, minor-key synthesizer soloing; instead of kick drum, drum machines tuned to congas. Founded by producers Ron

Trent and Chez Damier in 1994 to "provide a certain level of healing for people," as Trent explained to i-D magazine in November 1995, Prescription Underground EPs like vocalist-producer Romanthony's Prince-like The Wanderer and Abacus' Relics spatialized house by sculpting space into elegiac intimacy. Instead of dry, machine tones or the sweeping, phasing variations, these producers opened a depth of field that allowed wind currents and heavy weather to charge through the horizon of the mix. 1996's Romanworld was a concept album, an audiodrama where Romanthony took an elevator "deeper underground to Romanworld – an imperial Roman Empire, where you can feel free to indulge your every whim."

Abacus' Relics EP was house at its most sumptu-ously interiorized. Credited to Timeless Children, the sleeve read, "We caught up with the man who made up all the rules, and he said that it's OK to make new rules." On "Relics 1 Mix 2," bell-like bass tones and hi-hats simmered through a lachrymose synth refrain of the actor Ossie Davies delivering a peroration at Malcolm X's funeral.

Fusing spirituality with space, the Chicago producer Derrick Carter, a.k.a. Sound Patrol, whose eighteen-minute track "Tripping Among the Stars (A Necessary Journey)" took up the first side of his 1994 debut album, Sweetened No Lemon. A three-note gospel piano refrain loops into a fugue swelling with expectation and driven by a stately, even regal, synthesized bass pattern, while an extended sample of Timothy Leary rhapsodizing about the sacrament of LSD steered the track through wistful synth soloing. When the sample – "Now energy comes/Float beyond the fear/Float beyond desire/Into this mystery of mystery" – comes in, ominous horns sound on the horizon of the mix, and the mood turns baleful. At eight minutes, everything drops away for Carter to duet the chorus with himself in an exalted tone: "Walking in the stars/I see somewhere far away."

DERRICK CARTER & DJ SNEAK

In New York, producers Kenny Dope Gonzalez and Little Louie Vega, better known as Masters at Work, became The Bucketheads for their disco cut-up smash, "The Bomb," released on the Henry Street label. Like Todd Terry's "Jumpin," DJ Sneak's 1997 single "You Can't Hide From Your Bud" and Armand Van Helden's "You Don't Know Me," a U.K. Number 1 in February, 1999, "The Bomb" surgically extracted peak moments in disco classics and reconstructed them as a beat suite. Neither a song nor a track, the cut-up is a loop-da-loop groove. Here, the irrepressible horn fanfare, as gladiatorial as a disco in Nero's amphitheater, propels the self-reflexive sample: "These sounds, these sounds, these sounds fall into my mi-i-i-nd." DJ Sneak's "You Can't Hide From Your Bud" similarly looped string swirl and rubberhead bass with two meaningless, and therefore purely sonic, vowel snatches from Teddy Pendergrass' "You Can't Hide From Yourself."

From Washington D.C., the vocalist De Lacy's stentorian declaration "I don't need no man to take care of me" declaimed itself across England's dancefloors throughout 1995. Originally written by Blaze, the veteran production duo of Kevin Hodge and Josh Milan, the Deep Dish remix of "Hideaway" became *the* anthem of the year. The Iranian-American duo of Ali and Dubfire set De Lacy's commanding voice at the bottom of a cavern with waves of white noise pounding against the walls. "Hideaway" announced Deep Dish's signature syncussion sound (only paralleled by Mark Bell's production for Björk's *Homogenic*), which crashed like boulders scraping the seabed, while their mix cd, Penetrate Deeper, confirmed them as house music's most innovative producers.

Josh Wink's "Higher State of Consciousness" resuscitated acid house's Roland TB-303 in 1995. Over rudimentary, deliberately primitive, proto-hardcore, troglodyte-style breakbeats, acid tones writhed and roiled, their screeching mid-frequencies firing the plea-sure centers like a Dinosaur Jr. guitar solo. The snare roll in "Higher State" caught the ear of both junglist producers Aphrodite and Big Beat producer Fatboy Slim, influencing the future singles, "Bad Ass" and "Rockafeller Skank."

By 1995, the deep house tradition inspired by Mr. Fingers/Larry Heard's 1987 single, "Can You Feel It," had reached a dead end; producers listed back to Heard's moods of exalted expectancy and hushed warmth as a blueprint to be refined – not innovated, but rarefied. Under the name Nuyorican Soul, Masters at Work had reinvented deep house with "The Nervous Track" back in 1993 and with "Mindfluid" in 1995. With its conga-tuned drum machines programmed for Latin rhythms and its lead bass tone that surged ahead with an inexorable curved tone like a hovercraft, "The Nervous Track" exerted a major impact on later producers like 16B and his fretless, synthesized bassline debut album, *Sounds From Another Room*.

In Paris, St. Germain, a.k.a. producer Ludovic Navarre, released the three-part *Boulevard* series of EPs for Laurent Garnier's FNAC label. "Alabama Blues", a somber, down-home blues sample with a vibrant hook of gospel chorale, was the standout. Todd Edwards' remix was U.K. underground garage before it had a name, extracting vowel sounds that were stretched enough to register but so transient that they teased and tugged, then crosshatching them with curlicues of guitar that licked your ear.

In the U.K., house DJ-producers like DJ Harvey and labels like Paper, Other Music and 20/20 Vision yearned for the early-eighties era of experimental house epitomized by producers, mixers, and groups such as François Kervorkian, Walter Gibbons, Liquid Liquid, ESG, and Arthur Russell. London's Junior Boys own axis of producers – Ballistic Brothers and Black Science Orchestra –

released *Walter's Room* as an homage to Walter
Gibbons, while Faze Action released the album *Plans and
Designs* on Nuphonic. In East London, Harvey played six-
hour sets full of looped Salsoul, Prelude, and 99 Records
classics, while his Black Cock label applied the cut-up not
to disco classics but to Dick Hyman's Moogie
Wonderland version of James Brown's "Give it Up or
Turn it Lose," splicing and incising until it sounded like a
proto-Coldcut track. The best U.K. producers at updating
the approach, if not the sound of Arthur Russell's tradition, were Dan Tyler and Conrad McDonnell, the Idjut
Boys, whose U-Star and Disfunction labels hosted
Santana-influenced guitar and keyboard solos.

In New York, Daniel Wang's Balihu label harked forward to the same point when house sprawled and
swaggered across funk, psychedelia, rock, and boogie —
when it was expansive rather than coercive. "Tracks like
DJ Pierre's "Masterblaster" are all in one measure
instead of classic two-measure disco basslines and
grooves," Wang complained to *Muzik* magazine in
August 1996. "Tracks end up sounding mechanical and
repetitive," he insisted, pinpointing the tyranny of the
4/4 beat that was so enjoyable in the Relief sound. "A cut
like Dinosaur L's "Go Bang" is fantastic because you
don't know when the breaks are going to come in.
Instead of everything happening on the four, the track
shoots off in twos, threes, fives and sevens."

Loose joints for a loose music. Of all the U.K. house
duos, only the South London duo Basement Jaxx broke
decisively with the well-meaning dead end of homage.
Even while sampling Flora Purim for their track "Samba
Magic," producers Felix Buxtona and Simon Ratcliffe
arranged a track whose soaring synth lines and ecstatic
yelps of carnival built and built into a sustained symphonic sunburst of a track. DJing at their monthly
parties, the two moved restlessly, never repeating them-

DANNY TENAGLIA

selves. In 1996, the syntharmonic arrangement of "Be Free" gave an irresistible sensation of courage, of swimming through the air, of looking down through the clouds, being pulled inexorably forward by the momentum of the music, which was punctuated by exhortations sampled from *Blade Runner*. On "Fly Life," blaring klaxons met the rasping ragga of Glamma Kid and the commanding voice of collaborator Corinna Joseph, while the remix filtered the slashing string loop until it swooped and phased across the soundfield.

In 1995, Motorbass – French producers Etienne de Crecy and Philip Zdar – revealed a sampladelic, heavily spatialized house with extreme depths of field on their brilliant album *Pansoul*. The heavy bass drop was rounded and warm, adapting reggae's implied rhythm –an approach also used in Etienne de Crecy's 1996 collaborative album, *Super Discount*. Fellow French producer I-Cube's "Disco Cubism" reveled in mutant jazz loops, Moog synth patterns, and a signature, tight, coercive syncopation that people heard as clicking. In September of that year, Armand Van Helden released his remix of Tori Amos' "Professional Widow," in which Amos' vocal was sliced into a three-word lyric that demanded to be misheard. Van Helden designed a deliberate, maddening, mondegreen loop (misunderstood lyric) that eventually resolved itself into the hook, "Gotta be big." More significant still was his "Dark Garage" mix of Sneaker Pimp's "Spin Spin Sugar." Adapting the baleful, but buoyant bassline from the 1994 junglist anthem "Dred Bass" by Dead Dred, the "Dark Garage" mix dramatically energized a moribund U.K. garage scene with its brooding but spirited low end.

If Van Helden supplied a new approach to bass, then it was Todd Edwards, along with Masters at Work, who led the way in the reinvention of rhythm. MAW ranged across the rhythmic spectrum from the thuggish stomp of "Everybody Needs Somebody" to the astral-fusion of "Our Mute Horns," pioneering an organic, woodblock percussion sound. Characterizing his sound as "that real good swing, the hard clicking sound," Edwards cut up the vowels, alternately stretching and compressing the center into bubbles, multiplying them into a honeycomb – a tugging mathematics of super-sexy syncopation. In a brilliant series of mixes – his own "Save My Life," Tuff Jam's "Just Got Better," and the Songstress' "See Line Woman" – Edwards honed his signature sound, weaving a web of vo-o-u-wels that teased and tickled the ear. By 1997, these three American inputs (Van Helden, MAW, and Edwards) had converged with London producers eager to adapt junglist techniques into house, giving the U.K. a sonic and emotional attitude it had never had before.

Pirate radio stations like Freek FM, Addiction FM, Rush FM, and Deja FM emerged in what journalist Simon Reynolds called "a new clandestine cartography." Four key tracks – Kelly G's mix of Tina Moore's "Never Gonna Let You Go," Double 99's "Rip Groove," Scott Garcia's "It's a London Thing," and 187 Lockdown's "Gunman" – all crashed the British Top 30. Peaking at Number 16 in the national charts on the strength of Morricone guitar licks, a gun being cocked and fired that acted as a hook, and a cue for woodblock programming that locked into a swaggering Dred Bass bassline that gallops straight at you, "Gunman" was a total ride: a track that seated you in the saddle of snappiness.

Later the same year, U.K. garage DJ-producers adopted Chicago producer Roy Davis Jr.'s "Gabriel" and broke the track across London's pirates. "It was one of the first two-step tracks with two beats to the bar instead of four," U.K. producer MJ Cole explained. Shedding the sensation of speed and roughness, the effect was to slow garage right down, introducing an edgy, on-the-verge, bristling feel, which matured into full-fledged musicality.

Two-step garage was further intensified by the production duo Dem 2 and KMA. Their 1997 release "Destiny" and 1998's "New Vocal Mix" revealed them at their most brilliant with android vocals whimpering for mercy and breaks interlocking with a micro-intricacy. As their mixes of Tina Moore's "Nobody Better," SJ's "I Feel Divine," Doolally's ska-step "Straight From the Heart" (which featured a chorus of kids chanting "The whole world's going doolally,") and Richie Boy and Klass E's "Madness on tha Street," with its *Love Story* refrain, showed, two-step allowed room for songs and samples to roam with an attitude that updated hardcore's exuberant, cheeky bravado.

On tracks like "Lovebug" and "Style" on their own Bug label, Ramsey and Fen exchanged the bad boy b-line for synthesized bass curvature, combining patterns with stab chords to give a push-pull notion. The chord stabs alone created a snare pattern that traded places with off-key stabs for an intricate crosshatching of beats.

If one garage tendency reinvented the song through beats, another integrated voices into musical arrangements. On their mixes of N Tyce's "Telefunkin'," Johnny Gill's "Angelbody," Conner Reeves' "Read My Mind," and Madie Myles' "I've Been Waiting," producers Groove Chronicles pioneered a lush lovers' garage style, as did the producer MJ Cole with his 1998 song, "Sincere," which showcased an expansive, wide-screen dynamic for vocalists Caspar Nova and Jay Dee Coler.

In March 1997, Thomas Bangalter and Guy-Manuel de Homem Christo, a.k.a. Daft Punk, released their debut album, *Homework*, introducing a radical, simple efficiency to the new jack sound. Early singles like "Da Funk" and "Musique" brutally intensified this approach with loops that locked into interminably filtered grooves so that the slightest modulation in frequencies triggered a jolting sense of relief. Later hits like the vocoderized electro of "Around the World" and "Burnin'" added a driving dis-comotion to the Relief style that had sent the duo onto the U.K. charts. Recorded as Stardust and released on his Roulé label, Thomas Bangalter's "Music Sounds Better with You" became 1998's most inescapable record. A disco guitar loop full of solar feeling from Chaka Khan's late 1970s track "Fate" drives itself through your body while the "Ooh baby, feel like the music sounds better with you" vocal stretched and yawned, creating a sound that was sated and urgent all at once.

Like "Music Sounds Better with You," UltraNaté's "Found a Cure" left you feeling brave and elated at once. Sung with an irresistible force, "Found a Cure" was an empowerment anthem – the follow-up to 1997's "Free," with its chorus of "You've got to live your life and do what you want to do" – riding in on a guitar hook created by Mood II Swing, the production team of John Ciafone and Lem Springsteen. Like Deep Dish, Mood II Swing moved from collaborations to eerie, mesmerizing dubs. On labels like Nitegrooves and Music For Your Ears, tracks like the amazing *Hoop Dreams*, sampling epic "Move Me," were drastically subtracted gossamer dubs where beats traded places with synth stabs – a music implied as much as stated.

Along with Deep Dish and U.K. producer Matthew Herbert, Mood II Swing productions like "Do It Your Way," "Driving Me Crazy," and "Call Me" all revealed the impact of Berlin producers and label runners Basic Channel. "I love Basic Channel's sound," Ciafone said in 1995. By lightening the weight of the kick drum and emphasizing the alteration of timbre, Basic Channel singles like the influential "Phylyps Track 1" and "11," "Radiance," and "Octaedre" generated chiming, metallic tunnels that "rolled without end" – timbral travelator tones adapted from DJ Pierre's track, "Inside Out."

In these tracks, the fiercely held distinctions between house, dub, and techno dissolved. History volatized itself into mirage moods. In 1997, Basic Channel's Moritz Von Oswald and Mark Ernestus started a new label called Main Street for house music, collaborating with reggae vocalist Tikiman as Round Two to release "New Day" and "Acting Crazy" as Round Three. "New Day" in particular reinvented the song as a slow-burning and sepulchral lullaby, excising the sustained strings to reveal a spooked, revenant exaltation.

By 1998, Prescription Underground-style electronic introspection had given way to an organic sound where congas replaced rhythmatics and flutes supplanted the sustained tones of synths. Joe Claussel's Spiritual Life and Ibadan became the key labels for house's new Afrocentricity, and New York's Body and Soul was the major club. Spiritual Life released Jephte Guillame's invocational "The Prayer," while veteran New Jersey producer Kerri Chandler released the yearning, Nina Simone-sampling "See Line Woman" on Ibadan. Recording as Urban Sound Gallery and New African Orchestra, Ron Trent released records like the rootsical "Village Dance" on Nite Grooves.

"You go to a club now and you just get real hard music," house veterans Blaze complained to *Muzik* in August 1996. "It's like being on speed, it's not a spiritual experience." Blaze's second album, *Basic Blaze*, released in August 1997, continued the super-syncopated space funk of 1995's *Moonwalk* EP, the wide-eyed child's perspective of 1997's "Lovelee Dae" twelve-inch and 1998's Dexter Wansell update, "New Directions Part 1." Throughout 1998, producers paid homage to the musical – if not the libidinal-political – approach of the Nigerian bandleader-arranger Fela Kuti, who died of AIDS-related illness in 1998. Kuti's songs were long-form chants with pliable, undulating conga and electric piano grooves.

JOSH WINK
CARL COX

Masters at Work released a respectful version of his "Expensive Shit," while Black Science Orchestra became Black Jazz Chronicles to release the album *Future JuJu*.

Against the prayerful tone of house's spiritual turn, Detroit's Moodymann, a.k.a. Kenny Dixon Jr., adopted a militant nationalism previously encrypted in the techno of Jay Denham and Underground Resistance to create a sound some called "beat-down house." With loops of guitar and piano obscured by a deliberately scuzzy sound, the extreme filtering on his 1997 EP, *U Can Dance If You Want To*, created a sleazy ambience that invited you in while keeping you out at the same time. On 1997's *Silent Introduction* on Carl Craig's Planet E label, Dixon mumbled about "Niggaz who are deep," allowing an intimidating edginess to seep into feel-good tracks like "I Can't Kick This Feeling When It Hits," which sampled its chorus from Chic's "I Want Your Love."

Two albums epitomized house innovation in 1998. Deep Dish's debut album, *Junk Science*, featured "Stranded," in which forlorn but bright-eyed Cocteau Twins-style melancholy converged with a surging synthetic groove to generate compellingly mixed feelings. "Muhammed Is Jesus Is Buddha Is Love," sang by their engineer Richard Morel, was even more unique: an expansive, soothing call driven by heartwarming keyboards and a twinkling guitar refrain. August saw Herbert and chanteuse Dani Siciliano refracting "the song" through dry, intricate, tap-dancing rhythms, crystalline synths, and domestic *concrète* to generate the bewitching sound whorls and fragile sanctuaries of the exquisite *Around the House* album. By renovating the three main traditions of house – the song, the dub, the track – from inside those legacies, late-nineties house music invigorates rather than rejects the dancefloor. In the world of house music, the future soothes as much as it shocks: Catchiness converges with confusion, immediacy feeds into extremism, and pop coincides with futurism in Möbius loops that obsolesce the inherited distinctions between over and under.

6

What we hear on released records of the sixties is the product of a great deal of analog tape editing, which is no different now with computer manipulation of sound. The edits determine the piece of music that you bought in a store in the seventies even. I think we didn't know that then; we thought this was the way people played music. No more than when we hear a record now based on techno or hip-hop, we think that this is how it happened, but it's all manipulation. **BILL LASWELL** I made the turntable an instrument. If you want to just play a record, just play a record. But if you want to play the turntable, you have to learn how to do it. You have to train, just like any other instrument. **DXT**

HIPHOP

IRON NEEDLES OF DEATH AND A PIECE OF WAX

BY DAVID TOOP

KID KOALA

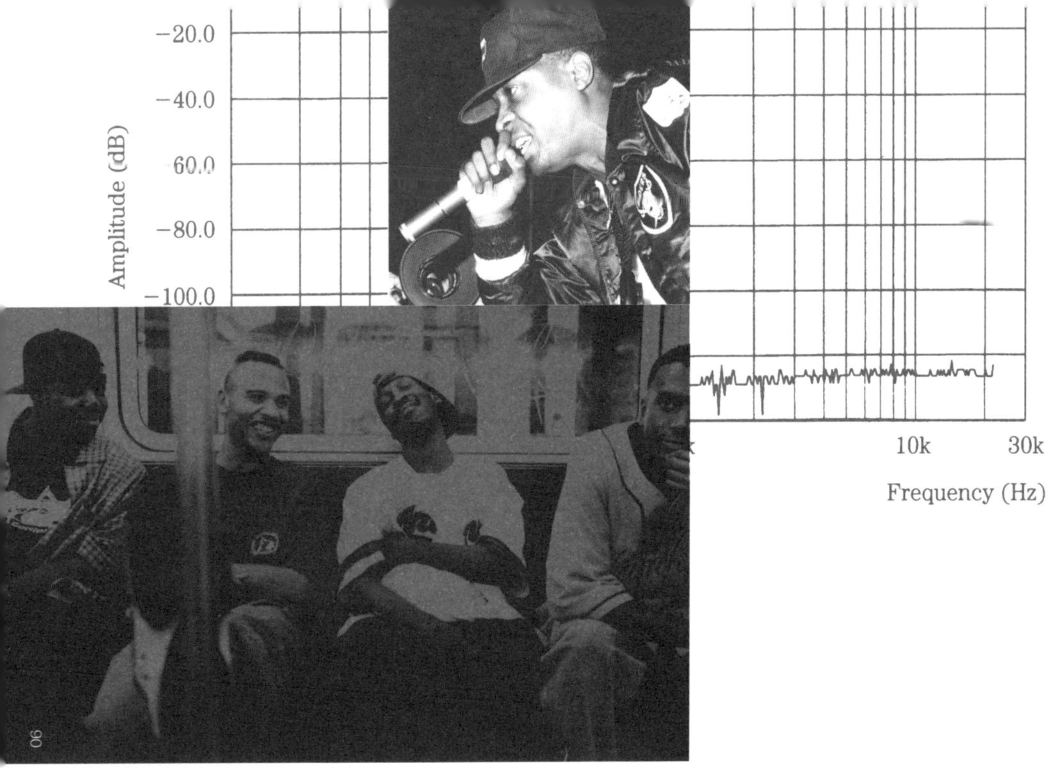

Amplitude (dB)

−20.0
−40.0
60.0
−80.0
−100.0

10k   30k

Frequency (Hz)

Discography:			
AFRIKA BAMBAATAA			
& SOUL SONIC FORCE		"Planet Rock"	Tommy Boy
GRANDMASTER FLASH		"Adventures of Grandmaster Flash on the Wheels of Steel"	Sugarhill
RAMMELZEE VS. K-ROB		"Beat Bop"	Profile
DE LA SOUL		"Plug Tunin'"	Tommy Boy
THE FEARLESS FOUR		"Rockin' It"	Enjoy
ERIC B & RAKIM		"Follow the Leader"	MCA
PUBLIC ENEMY		*It Takes a Nation of Millions To Hold Us Back*	Def Jam
WU-TANG CLAN		*Enter the Wu-Tang*	36 Chambers, RCA/BMG
PHONOSYCOGRAPHDISK		*Ancient Termites*	Bomb Hip-Hop
OUTKAST		*Aquemini*	LaFace

X-ECUTIONERS   CHUCK D

In the 3rd of January, 1984, in midtown Manhattan: Lil' Rodney Cee of the Funky Four Plus One More and Double Trouble says, "OK, at that time, I'm going back to the competition. It was so strict that, to play with Flash, we had to bring as many people as he'd bring to a party. So when he gon' play, he got a thousand followers. Wherever he play at, he got a thousand people come to see him. So in order for us to play with him, we had to bring a thousand people. And that's the only way we played with each other. So other than that, if you couldn't bring as many people, you just wasn't as good. Who you could say is better between Flash and the Funky and the Soul Sonic is up to the individual, 'cause they all are out there, and we all are doing the same thing, but then, you didn't play with nobody they couldn't do as well as you did, and that's how it was."

His compadre with the quieter voice, K.K. Rockwell, sniffs out some amusement, then cuts in with, "That's like inna real business, heh."

Before myth there was reality, and before reality there was myth. Hip-hop's origins are wrapped in mystery. We know that in the mid-seventies a Jamaican-born DJ, Kool Herc, began playing reggae records at parties in the Bronx. Meeting a hostile reaction to Jamaican music, he switched to funk records and at that time, as Lil' Rodney Cee has explained, MCs were being engaged to chant praise to the DJ. With "to the Eastside, to the Westside, make money, make money," the MCs celebrated territorial rivalry, a benign shadow of urban turf wars and gang-banging.

Hip-hop is low-tech and local, hot-wired to an electrical source, the DJ's at the service of the crowd and the

MC's at the service of the DJs. Yet a strange chemical reaction took place that has remained the central mystery of the music. The holy trinity of hip-hop innovators – Kool Herc, Grandmaster Flash, and Afrika Bambaataa – created a new music with music that (within the reference frame of the music industry, copyright law, and received morality) did not belong to them. This appropriated music was then edited on record turntables in real time, in order to eliminate the verse, chorus, verse, bridge structure of popular song, leaving only repetitions of an internally complex percussive cell, a fragment and memory trace of the history of a track known as the break.

The break took it to the bridge, to paraphrase James Brown, and held that bridge in a looping mechanical stasis, thereby aligning hip-hop with other musical developments of the seventies including disco, minimalism, heavy metal, James Brown's funk, Fela Anikulapo-Kuti's Afrobeat, Jamaican dub, and Miles Davis's electric music – all of them exploring entrancing elaborations and variations on repetition. The bridge became a bridge to another world, revisiting the past, suspending time, and transforming the familiar into something unrecognizable.

Thrust center stage in a dangerously competitive atmosphere that fomented rivalry, MCs were forced to elaborate on their early praise songs to the "pulsating, inflating, disco-shaking, heartbreaking man on the turntables." Their subject matter in the majority of cases was themselves, transposed into a myth universe of champagne, fur coats, fast cars, easy women, and death-dealing oral fluency (or "fluence", a hypnotic power). The message had been summarized in the early 1960s in one notorious sentence by the young Cassius Clay: "I am the greatest."

Lil' Rodney Cee maintains that the late Cowboy, a founding member of Grandmaster Flash and The Furious Five, was the first hip-hop MC to do this. Although contemporaneous with Rodney Cee's Funky Four, the Furious Five pioneered and perfected the art of intricate group rapping. According to Danny Glover (known in the Five as Kid Creole), Funky Four rapper Raheim transferred to the Furious Five because of the Funky Four's inability to provide a soloist with support on stage. In its own eyes, and in the eyes of his audience, each moment of hip-hop demanded displays of absolute, annihilating greatness, an impossible pressure that accelerated technical and technological innovation.

"It's always been a struggle, even before recording," said Grandmaster Flash, speaking on the 29th of December, 1984, in London, "because it's a highly competitive form of entertainment. We couldn't just go out there and just cool out. I couldn't just go out and think, This blend will make it to the next. They [the Furious Five] couldn't just go out there and just talk on the microphone. We were forced to add gimmicks. Like the beatbox. I had to scratch; they had to start dancing. This shit all had to be necessary in order for this shit to really work."

Hip-hop's history (circa 1975 or 1976 until the present) can be read as a series of mutations of its origins in a simplicity of means: the art of creating entertainment (as Flash describes it) using pyrotechnic techniques of verbalization, turntable manipulation, spray-paint art and body movement. As Flash suggests, the unadorned art of freestyle rapping over a DJ cutting breaks was not spectacular enough to hold the attention of volatile crowds, nor sufficiently distinctive to crush equally gifted competitors. Although a number of solo rappers (DJ Hollywood, Kurtis Blow, Eddie Cheeba, King Tim III, Lovebug Starsky, Busy Bee Starsky, Spoonie Gee, Tanya Winley, etc.) recorded tracks of either artistic or historic significance in the earliest days of hip-hop, few of these soloists survived. Until second-generation soloists such as LL Cool J began to incorporate stage sets, lighting effects, and on-stage drama into their shows, hip-hop was dominated by groups whose inter-play offered some security against the potential humiliation risked by any rapper or DJ who dared to step up to the mic.

Once hip-hop had found its initial shape, the gim-micks of professional stage presentation, whether dance moves inspired by The Temptations or innovations like scratching, were the first mutation. Far more damaging in its impact was the second mutation: the translation of hip-hop's turntable futurism (the assault on conventional music practice, copyright law, and musical form) into a retrogressively musical version of itself. Among the first musicians to enable hip-hop's inevitable transition from underground to overground were Positive Force at Sylvia and Joe Robinson's Sugarhill Records in Englewood, New Jersey, and the late Pumpkin at Bobby Robinson's Enjoy Records in Harlem. At Sugarhill, the drums, bass, and guitar trio of Keith LeBlanc, Doug Wimbish, and Skip McDonald took over from Positive Force and label arranger Jiggs Chase almost immediately, establishing themselves as the undisputed house band for the label and consolidating the sound of old-school hip-hop.

"It's not easy going in the studio," said Doug Wimbish in 1985, recalling the translation process. "You go in there blindfold' and you've got a rapper who can't really give you the proper directions: 'OK, the song goes like this' [hums tunelessly]. We said, 'huhhh?' We devel-oped a whole new talent – 'I can translate rappers.' We

did one tune that's a classic example 'That's the Joint.' There was another song that we had cut before that, but the way Rodney Cee put it, that was for an 'older crowd.'"

"Funky Four, the first tune we cut for them, Jiggs [Chase] had done an arrangement that was pretty slick but it wasn't the raw stuff they wanted," added Keith LeBlanc. "One of them was almost in tears, 'cause they thought they were going to have to do it. And then Rodney was just, 'Man, this sounds like it's for an older crowd. What is this shit?' So then we cut 'That's the Joint' and they liked that much better. You couldn't do those boring disco tracks – everything was four-on-the-floor all the way through. The rappers, they wouldn't have that shit. They were into old James Brown. They were trying to force us to keep it straight at Sugarhill but then I'd have a rapper in my ear telling me, 'I don't want that, I can't rap on that.' So basically, once we went with a rapper's idea of how it should be, it clicked."

At a crucial show at New Rochelle High School north of New York, Grandmaster Flash and The Furious Five appeared as a support act to The Sugarhill Gang, three lucky pretenders with no apprenticeship in hip-hop who were nevertheless enjoying the hit sensation of the era with their first single release, "Rapper's Delight." "We had to actually prove ourselves," said Flash. With little exposure to the killing floor of hip-hop, most participants in the show were amazed to discover that by using only their voices and two turntables, Flash and the Five could electrify a huge audience. Yet this unstable, difficult technology presented unique problems, requiring responses that were both conscientiously prepared in advance and mutually supportive spontaneous reflexes in moments of crisis.

"Doing our show, we used turntables," recalled Danny Glover, "so if somebody jumped across to the turntables [and made the needle skip] or if the record's

scratched, it'd go to a whole other part. You have to almost have it memorized, so when the music's doing this, the words is saying that. I listened to the song a lot in order to do that. We used to just be out there and something would happen, like the turntables, somebody'd just pull out the plugs for the turntables, like sabotage us, and then somebody'd say, 'Flash, turn the music down,' and the music is already down! And then we would go into something where we didn't even need music. We'd just do something with the crowd."

Understandably, years of honing these skills in front of audiences that might riot or even shoot firearms if things went badly wrong nurtured conservative attitudes, contradicting the radicalism of this approach. As trumpeter Jon Hassell has said, "It's a problem to know what to do with [instrumental virtuosity] in the age of

sampling and audio sleight of hand because the audience is looking for the final result, basically. They don't care if it took you twenty years to arrive at it or whether somebody just sampled it off of a record and used it."

Turntable scratching is a means of gouging quick, semi-identifiable traces of music from the grooves of a record and transmuting these electronically transmitted traces into furred and splintered drum noise. Due to their source in complex waveforms, each individual scratch has the quality of tropical birdsong, a richness of tone spiked with percussive impact. Each scratch was what we would call, in the digital age, a sample. The irony was that analog scratching − a performance medium demanding high levels of coordination and musical intelligence refined through the traditional "woodshedding" approach of dedicated, regular, and repetitive practice

– evolved only a short time before the invention of digital sampling, thus raising the crisis of performance integrity pinpointed by Hassell.

For a virtuoso of scratching and break montage, the use of fake scratches, produced by digital samples, was a betrayal of hip-hop principles. "What I feel bad about," said Grandmaster Flash, " is that, here it is, it was considered an underground form of entertainment, right? Scratching, I'll speak on the scratching. Now, scratching is considered a noise. Scratching is done with a piece of wax, whether it's an old record, a new record, your mother's record, your father's record, and you put it on a turntable, and you go back and forth. Now, it's considered a noise, and it's up to the particular DJ to make it sound as less noisy as possible.

"To bring in instruments like the Fairlight [an early sampling keyboard], you're talking about putting out a product internationally and calling it scratching when it's not scratching. That I take as a personal insult. If there's a DJ in a group of rappers, if he can't scratch well, let him just do what he do best and make it fit on that record. Why come in with a Fairlight and program one zhuuup into this machine and then play it? Ridiculous. I mean, it's

a great machine, I hear this machine is like wondrous, but at the same time, in that respect, zilch.

"The human factor to scratching is like, the quicker you move the disc the more of a risk factor of it jumping out of the grooves, OK? Now, here it is, you can scratch fourth notes, eighth notes, you can go as far as sixteenth, chhh-chhh-chhh-chhh-chh-chh-chh-chh. But when you're talking about going into thirty-twos and sixty-fours, it's humanly impossible to do. Let's not be ridiculous now. Brrrrr-duh, brrrda-da-da-da. And behind that, it's like there's a edit, right? They have fake scratching, like brrrrr, and then, a second later, a whole 'nother scratch. I mean goddamn, you need to bend over and do what you gotta do."

Flash, who had written the bible of scratching with his 1981 Sugarhill release, *Adventures of Grandmaster*

Flash on the Wheels of Steel, clearly regarded the technique's expression of physicality – the virtuosity of the body – as a major element of its meaning. His scorn for "impossible" machine sequences of digitally sampled scratch simulacra rang the same bells as drummers like Keith LeBlanc, who before his conversion to the beatbox, admitted to pouring cans of Coca Cola into any drum machine he encountered in a recording studio.

The drum machine, pioneered by Flash in live performance, was destined to take over from the turntable. In the heat of technological development, turntable cutting seemed to be the equivalent of early rhythm boxes installed in electric organs. Both played loops that could only be chained in sequence or overlaid with other elements. The possibility of programming each element of a rhythm – kick, snare, hi-hat, ride, toms, cowbell – seemed to be a vast leap forward.

The breakthrough was "Planet Rock" by Afrika Bambaataa and Soul Sonic Force. Released by Tommy Boy in 1982, the track was assembled by a team that exemplified hip-hop's journey downtown into clubs where Soft Cell meant more than Dyke and The Blazers. Again, the record was a translation of live DJ performances. Afrika Bambaataa's DJ style was based on wild eclecticism rather than turntable trickery. His reputation for collecting obscure records was notorious. Spies would wait for him outside record stores, then follow him in and automatically buy two copies of whatever he had bought (even when Bambaataa bought a Hare Krishna album simply for home-listening).

In 1981, Tommy Boy founder Tom Silverman had already made one attempt to record instrumental breakbeats with Bambaataa. The tape was lost, but with the collaboration of producer Arthur Baker and electronic keyboardist John Robie, "Planet Rock" successfully translated Bambaataa's enthusiasm for Kraftwerk, Yellow

AFRIKA BAMBAATAA

Magic Orchestra, and Gary Numan into a b-boy anthem. Working with limited, though very new, electronic instruments — notably a Roland TR-808 drum machine — they created one of the most startlingly tangential records in popular music history. For Baker, the limitations of the available technology had been rationalized into a positive. "You have to use the equipment you have," he said in 1984. "The reason the Motown sound was the way it was, was because they had shitty equipment."

The record was made quickly and cheaply. Mistakes were left in. At one point during the session, Tom Silverman asked if it would be possible to play a polyphonic orchestral hit on the studio's Fairlight keyboard. Robie obliged, and the resulting noise, a tearing jolt of electricity, rocketed hip-hop into a new dimension. The effect combined the qualities of a Grandmaster Flash scratch, amplified to monstrous bandwidth, with the science-fiction suggestion of ten orchestras, all playing a single chord in perfect synchronization. The sound became a trademark of many subsequent records, so leading to Flash's condemnation of the technological annexation of scratching as a bodily function.

Yet scratching also represents a virtuosity of the imagination, a device for simultaneously disrupting and maintaining hip-hop's peculiarly retro vision of a now constructed from slivers of the past. Underground hip-hop sought to maintain a sacrosanct "book" of source breaks — most of them originating in a period that predated the emergence of hip-hop itself — yet these breaks were transformed over and over as hip-hop producers and DJs rocketed the music into the future. As hip-hop's first generation faded in the mid-eighties, some artists began to confront the compromised condition of recorded rap and its studio technology. In a world of monstrous, arthritic 808, DMX, and Linn drum-machine beats exploding in slow motion, the twelve-inch single

release of Eric B & Rakim's "Eric B for President," (produced by Eric B and mixed by Marley Marl and MC Shan) recovered b-boy breaks — The Mohawk's "Champ," Otis Redding, and Carla Thomas's "Tramp" — from their legendary status, slicing them in and out of the mix like sword cuts in order to recreate the dislocated structure of breakbeat montage as pioneered in the Bronx. And as overheard, for those who were not there, on unauthorized releases such as Afrika Bambaataa's "Death Mix" and "Live Convention '82, volumes 1 & 2".

The primacy of the turntable and its revolving vinyl software stayed alive, despite changing fashions and more than one revolution in music technology. Calling himself The 45 King, New Jersey DJ Mark James synchronized the new digital samplers with b-boy tradition by looping sampled breakbeats into seamless new versions of the 45 rpm vinyl singles from which they were born. As minimalist as Steve Reich's phase-shift tape loop exercise, "It's Gonna Rain," The 45 King's "songs" released by Tuff City Records in New York — "The 900 Number," "Mr. Smith & Mr. Wesson," "Forty Dog," and "Roach Clip" — distilled the chaotic mania of live cutting into an insistent purity, a simple perfection.

At the beginning of his career, Mark James had served time as a record boy (an apprenticeship towards the hallowed magus title of Master of Records given to Afrika Bambaataa) for The Funky Four's DJ Breakout. He had also been given access to the extensive collection of R&B and soul 45s owned by ex-music-business journalist Aaron Fuchs, founder of the Tuff City label. So the furtive researches of the collector and the ceaseless hoarding of the archivist, were rejuvenated through the active legacy of the turntable.

Although the technology through which hip-hop tracks are created has played a critical role in the mutations of the music, different schools of rapping techniques have also catalyzed significant changes in the music. The differences can be illustrated by Kurtis Blow's attempts to explain the mid-eighties schism between street rap and commercial rap. "You had the two different markets," said Blow, speaking in his dressing room at Madison Square Garden in New York City on December 27th, 1985. "Where I came in, I was the disco guy, majored in communications at college, announcer of WCCR radio, City College radio. I used to imitate Hank Spann on WWRL. He was always my idol, 'This is Hank Spann on WWRL super sixteen.' That sounds just like him. I used to imitate him and that's where you get that whole sucker MC disco thing.

"Also, I was a street DJ. There are a couple of us like that. For instance, Lovebug Starski. He's versatile. He could go into the disco and rock the disco people – have that kind of class for them and not seem like an idiot or a bum or something. A nigger – you know what I'm saying? There were two different markets. The street hip-hoppers came out of disco. This is what I was trying to tell Flash. Flash says, 'Yo, Kurtis Blow, you're disco. You were never street'. I tell him, 'Flash, I played with you! And Melle Mel, at the Webster PAL Center up on 183rd and Webster Avenue in the Bronx.' I used to go to the Kool Herc parties and dance against the Nigger Twins, the best b-boys in the Bronx."

In retrospect, it is possible to trace a strong line connecting radio jocks and soul rappers such as Barry White and Isaac Hayes or the radio raps of George Clinton on "Mr. Wiggles" and "Chocolate City" through to the early solo rappers such as Kurtis Blow, King Tim III, Lovebug Starski, and Spoonie Gee. This line continues onto the gangsta soloists: Ice-T (also influenced by his literary heroes Iceberg Slim and Donald Goines), Snoop Dogg, Tupac Shakur, and The Notorious B.I.G. In a sense, this style of rapping is closely related to the recital of poetry over jazz, its musical underpinning (gravitating towards the bass-heavy grooves of Funkadelic and Zapp) a less disruptive force, its rapping a story text that values the flow and intimacy of the storyteller over the hyperkinetic, disrupted, oblique anti-narrative of a Public Enemy, the Ultramagnetic MC's, or the Jungle Brothers.

The paradox of hip-hop's dedication to constant change is its unchanging allegiance to the past: looking back at "the good old days" of its own history; paying homage to the archive of musical history through sample loop montage (the majority of samples now declared, cleared, and paid for in obeisance to copyright law), turntable cutting, and scratching. But, to quote the Wu-Tang Clan's sample of Gladys Knight & the Pips, "Can it be that it was all so simple then?"

As K.K. Rockwell of The Funky Four surmised, hip-hop's competitive core was immediately comprehensible within the dog-eat-dog context of business. Hip-hop's entry into the record business in 1979 made a shocking impact upon a culture that had developed in a state of relative innocence. The first manifestation of that impact was technological: the switch from turntables and breakbeats to studio musicians. In the ensuing twenty years, rap's ascendancy to a prime position in music markets has proved that the record business showed remarkable foresight by insisting upon the changes that have become second nature to rap artists. Yet the artistic state of the music in the late nineties – either formulaic and cynical or nostalgic and retrogressive – suggests that a heavy price has been paid in return for financial gain.

Only in the underground are there signs that hip-hop's musical innovations are being developed in stimulating new directions. Growing numbers of turntable artists such as the Invisbl Skratch Piklz, DJ Disk, the X-ecutioners, Kid Koala, DJ Faust, and Peanut Butter Wolf are confronting hip-hop's mutated, now-depleted condition with a new slant on turntable funda-mentalism. The turntablists return to hip-hop's source, the unstable, real-time, improvisatory performance medium that can transform recorded history into a lurch-ing octopus creature with scratch elaborations waving like tentacles in every direction.

In the first half of the century, the virtuosity of jazz musicians such as Louis Armstrong and Charlie Parker swept aside received notions of the possible. Similarly, the dexterity and speed of the new turntablists such as DJ Disk contradicts Grandmaster Flash's claims that the body sets final limits on scratching's musical possibilities. Hip-hop's active use of the record turntable (perhaps the most influential item of music technology of the twenti-eth century) as a recycling agent and transforming tool has been one of the most innovative abuses of electronic technology in music history. Steeped in old-school history, the turntablist rewrites the bible of breaks, drops the nee-dle to the wax, and launches yet another phase.

QUEEN LATIFAH

Scratching and cutting were a whole new technique, new operations applied to sound. They activated vinyl – switched it on. Before that, all people did was put the vinyl on the record player and listen to it. Suddenly, the turntable became a musical instrument in its own right. Vinyl became a kind of useful archive, not just the commodity that you bought and listened to and then put back. It became something that you could use to build a new sonic composition of your own. Everybody knows that these things have been tried out before by people like John Cage and people like Pierre Schaeffer. However, by definition, these were avant-garde ideas that were restricted to a tiny amount of people. The difference between John Cage and Grandmaster Flash is like before and after electricity. What Grandmaster Flash did went around the whole world. What John Cage did was restricted to a few people in New York, a few people in London, a few people in Berlin, etc. But people like Grandmaster Flash and Grand Wizard Theodore invented not just a new operation of sound, but a whole new conceptual attitude toward sound: The idea that every record is open to misuse and can be combined with a second record. **KODWO ESHUN**

INTERVIEW:
Arthur Baker

In 1981, when we [Afrika Bambaataa] started what we originally thought was just hip-hop – the "electro" tag I think came from England. We were all turned on by Kraftwerk. I was turned on by "Autobahn" when I was working in a record store in high school. When I moved to New York, you would continually hear "Trans-Europe Express" and "Numbers." With *Planet Rock*, we married that sound with the Bronx and with the hip-hop culture that was developing there. We created something great by combining two really different elements, two diverse cultural things that were clashing, and made a really cool record. I knew that it would work because when I was hanging out and going to the park I would hear people rap over "Trans-Europe Express." It was as simple as that. It was just being aware of what was going on and picking up on what was happening in the street. We took that, my partner John Robie, Bambaataa, and I, and made *Planet Rock*. When we started, Bambaataa and Soul Sonic Force had never been in a studio before. So it was sort of an educational process. The rappers were really impatient. Bambaataa was this great idea man. He'd get an idea and then before we could implement it, he'd come up with another idea. He was doing wild tracks where he would just get on the mike and sing and do all these crazy things. He'd never do the same thing twice. After doing it once, he'd get bored with it. It was a bit frustrating. We had fights with the rappers. The process wasn't easy. The music for *Planet Rock* was all done in one night. It took about eight hours. I took the tape home. My wife at the time was there, so I popped the tape in and said, "We've made musical history tonight." She remembers I just said it. Before the rap was done, I already knew that we had done something great.

Freestyle

Discography:			
SHANNON	Let the Music Play	Mirage 1983
LISA LISA & CULT JAM	I Wonder If I Take You Home	Personal 1984
SA-FIRE	Let Me Be the One	Cutting 1986
TKA	Is It Love	Tommy Boy 1986
LISETTE MELENDEZ	A Day in My Life	Fever 1991
JOCELYN ENRIQUEZ	I've Been Thinking About You	Classified 1994
VARIOUS ARTISTS	Freestyle's Greatest Beats	Tommy Boy/Timber199

Sure, Bronx kids thinking Kraftwerk were the funkiest thing since James Brown was pretty bizarre. Even stranger was that New York Latinos heard ancestral echoes of salsa piano lines and *montuno* rhythms in Afrika Bambaataa & the Soul Sonic Force's rewrite of the Kraftwerk blueprint. In the hands of producers like the Latin Rascals, Chris Barbosa, Carlos Berrios, and Andy "Panda" Tripoli, the video-game bleeps, synth stabs, and Roland TR-808 clavés became an android *descarga* called Freestyle that was emblematic of New York culture clash. With its vaguely Latinate vocals and subdued clavé, Special Request's "Salsa Smurph" (1983) was probably the bridge between Electro and Freestyle, while John Robie's contemporaneous productions for C-Bank defined the sound and tempo of freestyle without the explicitly Latin feel. Freestyle's ground zero, though, was Shannon's "Let the Music Play" (1983). Although it didn't have the hi-hat sound that would come to characterize freestyle percussion, the electro-woodblock-and-cow-bell percussion and kick drum/snare

drum interaction "Let the Music Play" sounded like a cross between Gary Numan and Tito Puente and provided the blueprint for freestyle's street-smart tales of innocence and experience. Former Fun House dancer Lisa Velez was discovered by production team Full Force and, as Lisa Lisa, became freestyle's biggest early star. With a dub-like synth effect stolen from John Robie's Emulator keyboard and a Roland woodblock pattern, Lisa Lisa & Cult Jam's debut record, I Wonder If I Take You Home (1984), was an anthemic update of the eternal question first posed by The Shirelles: "Will You Still Love Me Tomorrow?" Their follow-up, "Can You Feel the Beat" (1985), merged soaring salsa-tinged keyboard lines with the rhythm from Billy Squier's "Big Beat," while a more straight-forward R&B sound predominated on their two U.S. number ones, "Head to Toe" and "Lost in Emotion." For all of Lisa Lisa's success, freestyle was dominated by one production team, the Latin Rascals. The duo of Tony Moran and Albert Cabrera first made a name for themselves on New York radio station WKTU, where their edits and mixes were the only challengers to KISS' François Kevorkian and Shep Pettibone. Their own "Arabian Nights" (1984) was an early freestyle classic, but it was their hip-hop-influenced productions of the Cover Girls' "Show Me" (1986) and Sa-Fire's "Let Me Be the One" (1986) that showed that, at its best, freestyle was a potent mix of the best of disco and hip-hop. Moran's own project, Concept of One, continued their hit parade with "Dance With Me" and "Saving all My Love." The duo continued to produce freestyle's biggest names like TKA, Noel, George Lamond, and Lisette Melendez until the early nineties when Moran went on to produce AOR ballads for the likes of Gloria Estefan and Cyndi Lauper. ✑
PETER SHAPIRO

Miami Bass

Discography:			
MC ADE	"Bass Rock Express"	4 Sight Records 1985
2 LIVE CREW	"Throw the D"	Luke Skyywalker 1986
MC SHY D	*Got to Be Tough*	Luke Skyywalker 1987
DYNAMIX II	*Just Give the DJ a Break*	Joey Boy 1987
DJ MAGIC MIKE	*Drop the Base*	Cheetah 1989
LUKE	*I Wanna Rock*	Luke 1992
TAG TEAM	*Whoomp! There It Is*	Life 1993
QUAD CITY DJS	*C'mon N' Ride It (The Train)*	Atlantic 1996
BASS MEKANIK	*Sonic Overload*	Pandisc 1998
VARIOUS ARTISTS	*Biggest Bass Hits from the Bottom*	Pandisc 1996
VARIOUS ARTISTS	*Ghetto Style DJs Bass Volume I*	L'il Joe 1996

That gut-churning rumble you feel coming from those neon-lit IROCs and Cherokees that crawl the malls in the southern US is Miami Bass. The guiltiest of guilty pleasures, Miami Bass is about one thing and one thing only — booty. With more unrepentant ribaldry than Rudy Ray Moore, Redd Foxx, and Blowfly put together, the collected works of Miami Bass serve as a Satyricon for the late-twentieth century. What's interesting about booty music, though, is not so much that it's lasted for some fifteen years with its only subject matter being a fascination with the female posterior, but that its earthiness is expressed exclusively through the most purely electronic sound this side of Iannis Xenakis. The preponderance of thongs in south Florida made booty inevitable, but the obsession with the bottom end didn't start until the electro-bass cruised down the I-95 autobahn from New York in the early eighties. Exploiting the surreal popularity of Düsseldorf's showroom dummies in New York discos and block parties, Afrika Bambaataa, keyboardist John Robie, and producer Arthur

Baker welded the melody of Kraftwerk's "Trans-Europe Express" to the synth-bass of "Numbers" and the percussion from Captain Sky's "Super Sperm" to create "Planet Rock" (1982), the song that taught the world that machines were just as funky as James Brown. While "Planet Rock" introduced the Roland TR-808 drum machine, Juan Atkins, the kingpin of Detroit techno, and Richard Davis, a.k.a. 3070, moved with a machine glide and truly dropped the BOOM with Cybotron's "Clear" (1983). As if kids from the Bronx and Detroit grooving to Teutonic man-machine music wasn't bizarre enough, MC ADE (Adrian Hines) imagined what Kraftwerk's Ralf and Florian would sound like cruising south Florida's strip malls in their bass-booming rides. Basically a cover of "Trans-Europe Express" — with additional 808 clavés, archaic scratching, a vocoded voice listing the equipment used to make the record, a snippet of the Green Acres theme, and an overmodulated synth bassline — "Bass Rock Express" made booty bounce all over the South in 1985 and became one of the founding records of Miami Bass, even though it came from Fort Lauderdale. From even further afield, Riverside, California's 2 Live Crew relocated to Miami and defined the sound and subject matter of Bass with "Throw the D" (1986). With primitive scratching and megaton bass, "Throw the D" was probably the Crew's best record, but it was 1989's "Me So Horny" that brought the group, and Miami Bass, to public attention. Based around samples of Mass Production's "Firecracker" and *Full Metal Jacket*, "Me So Horny" got exposure on MTV and embroiled the group in a whirlwind of controversy. As a solo artist, 2 Live Crew's Luke (originally Luke Skyywalker) released the all-time classic, "I Wanna Rock" in 1992. "I Wanna Rock" set Luke's scurrilousness to a beat with so much relentless forward momentum that you'd forgive him for spending the rest of the record talking about his favorite position from the Kama Sutra (which, in fact, he does). Afro-Rican's "Just Let It Go" (1989) and DJ Magic Mike's *Drop the Base* (1989) followed "Me So Horny" as commercial successes for Miami

Bass, but it would require a journey up north to Atlanta and Jacksonville for its biggest hits. With less of an emphasis on the 808 sound, tracks like Tag Team's "Whoomp! There It Is" (1993) and Quad City DJs' "C'mon N' Ride It (the Train)" (1996) had more fluid basslines and cleaner catchphrases than their Miami rivals and became two of the best-selling records of the nineties. While it might have had its commercial apotheosis elsewhere, Miami is still the undisputed center of a subgenre called boom 'n bass. The overlord of this bizarre subculture is The Dominator, who is responsible for arming a militia of Camaros, Jeeps, vans, and drop-top Cadillacs with bowel-damaging infrasound riffs. Played almost exclusively at competitions that serve to test the lower limits of automotive bass bins, boom 'n bass is the ultimate example of music as a toy for boys. ✈
PETER SHAPIRO

7

It's all called techno or dance music now, 'cause it's all electronic music created with technological equipment. Maybe that should be the only name, "dance music", because everybody has a different vision of what techno is now. **KEVIN SAUNDERSON** Detroit's an industrial city. It's a wasteland of ideas. Detroit is the type of place where you can only dream of what the rest of the world is like. **DERRICK MAY** Techno is totally futuristic . . . and for kids it's brilliant 'cause all you're thinking is sci-fi, space, future, what's this, excellent, computers, wicked, music made on electronic gear, I can do that. **SEAN BOOTH (AUTECHRE)**

TECHNO

DAYS OF FUTURE PAST

BY MIKE RUBIN

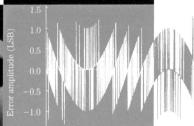

Error amplitude (LSB)

1.5
1.0
0.5
0.0
−0.5
−1.0
−1.5

Discography:			
	MODEL 500	*Classics*	R&S
	MODEL 500	*Deep Space*	R&S
	CYBOTRON	*Clear*	Fantasy
	DERRICK MAY	*Innovator*	Transmat/Never
	KEVIN SAUNDERSON	*Faces & Phases*	Planet E
	E-DANCER	*Heavenly*	Planet E
	PAPERCLIP PEOPLE	*The Secret Tapes of Dr. Eich*	Planet E
	69	*The Sound of Music*	R&S
	PSYCHE/BFC	*Elements 1989-1990*	Planet E
	VARIOUS ARTISTS	*Intergalactic Beats*	Planet E
	PLASTIKMAN	*Consumed*	M_nus/Novamute
	UNDERGROUND RESISTANCE	*Revolution Through Change*	Network
	UNDERGROUND RESISTANCE	*Interstellar Fugitives*	Submerge
	MOODYMANN	*Silent Introduction*	Planet E
	THEO PARRISH	*First Floor*	Sound Signature/Peace Frog
	DREXCIYA	*The Journey Home*	Warp
	DREXCIYA	*The Quest*	Submerge
	VARIOUS ARTISTS	*From Beyond*	Interdimensional Transmissions
	VARIOUS ARTISTS	*Techno Bass: The Mission*	Direct Beat
	VARIOUS ARTISTS	*Detroit: Beyond the Third Wave*	Astralwerks
	DJ ASSAULT	*Belle Isle Tech*	Assault Rifle/Electrofunk

CARL CRAIG

Long before the Prodigy ever learned to count to 303, Detroit-area teenager Juan Atkins and his high school buddies Derrick May and Kevin Saunderson were wired-up wunderkinds, mixing up the elements of techno in their bedroom labs and setting the periodic table for groups like the Chemical Brothers. Back in the mid-eighties, the so-called "Belleville Three" (named after the small town outside Detroit they hailed from) took the post-disco house music that had been nurtured in Chicago and refined it, upping the electronic content and adding a forward-thinking, defiantly cosmic worldview cobbled together from the writings of *Future Shock* author Alvin Toffler and Atkins' own ruminations.

In the city where the assembly line became a staple of modern life, techno's Henry Ford and his accomplices welded Motor City funk, European avant-garde composition, and Japanese gadgetry together to form a whole new chassis, but found their invention unappreciated in the American marketplace. Like jazz musicians from Ben Webster to Dexter Gordon in the postwar years, Atkins, May, Saunderson, and the ensuing generation of Detroit musicians they inspired – including the so-called "second wave" of producers like Carl Craig, Stacey Pullen, and

Kenny Larkin – went to Europe in the late 1980s to seek their fame and fortune. Thanks to a variety of factors – including a more enlightened European attitude toward dance music culture and a smaller, densely populated landmass that allowed for faster dissemination of data – they found it. By the early nineties, the English music press, like-minded musicians in Berlin, and ecstatic crowds from Amsterdam to Zurich had all embraced the Detroit pioneers as dancefloor deities.

Derrick May once described techno's man-machine fusion as "George Clinton and Kraftwerk caught in an elevator with only a sequencer to keep them company," but at some point during techno's global proliferation – maybe while Ralf and Florian were pushing the buttons for all the floors – Dr. Funkenstein got off the lift and left the building. While the homogenized byproduct of their

creation now provides the soundtrack for countless cola and car commercials, the Detroiters have been all but ignored here in the States, receiving virtually no publicity and even less airplay.

More disturbing to the Motor City posse is that techno has been portrayed as a "white" music. As techno's digitized signals crisscrossed Planet Rock, most of the producers and consumers who tuned in were white, and the identity of the music's funky forefathers often got lost in the transmission. Meanwhile, black audiences and musicians ceased to see techno as their own art form, leaving the electronic pioneers of Detroit not only feeling spurned by indifferent white-owned record companies, but estranged from their own community as well.

The tug-of-war for spin control at the heart of techno merely mirrors the tortured record of race rela-

tions of the city it hails from. Detroit is still recoiling from the repercussions of July 23, 1967, when a police raid on a black after-hours drinking spot touched off six days of violence, the worst U.S. civil disorder of the twentieth century until L.A. in 1992. "White flight" to the suburbs was already well under way, but the riot put some serious horsepower behind the city's abandonment. In the first twenty years after the riot, Detroit lost one-third of its population; a city built for two million people has today dwindled to half that. In one generation, Detroit went from 70% white to almost 80% black. The area's de facto balkanization led the local NAACP chapter president to declare in 1987 that "Detroit is the most racially polarized city in the nation."

Though blacks rose to political power with the election of Mayor Coleman Young in 1973, whites continued

JUAN ATKINS

to control the economic clout. Those that fled took the money and ran, building not just their homes but their factories, businesses, and stores in suburbia, too. Some suburbanites have gone years without once actually venturing into the city that gives their metropolitan area its name. Not that there's much reason to go: Detroit in the seventies and eighties was devastated by a decline in the auto industry, skyrocketing unemployment, and cuts in urban assistance programs. Between 1967 and 1982, Detroit lost about 45% of all jobs in the city, and by 1987, more than half of the city's manufacturing, retail, and wholesale base had disappeared. Ironically, it was automation, computerization, robotics, and technological advances in manufacturing that fueled the city's precipitous loss of blue-collar jobs – the same developments that would pave the way for techno.

The fancy term for this process is "deindustrialization," but sometimes the oldies are best: "ghost town." Far from the chaotic lawlessness that the national media has envisioned in Detroit, the prevailing feeling is actually an eerie emptiness. Prewar skyscrapers in the heart of downtown stand forlorn and abandoned. Streets dotted with ramshackle shanties amidst untended grass and scrub look more like backcountry roads in the Mississippi Delta than arteries in an urban core.

Detroit's post-apocalyptic mystique is crucial to the mythology of Detroit techno. It's from this blighted backdrop that techno comes forth, like the city motto, *"Resurget Cineribus"* – "It will rise from the ashes." The contradictions in imagining a future while both the past and present sit in shambles all around you are rich indeed, as are those of having a high-tech movement hail

from a burnt-out urban shell or a sophisticated art music flourishing amidst such a stubbornly close-minded, culturally intolerant, blue-collar town like Detroit.

Techno's roots in Detroit date back to an FM DJ named Charles Johnson − better known by his on-air alter ego, the Electrifying Mojo. From 1977 to 1982 on WGPR, followed by three years at WJLB, Mojo practiced a philosophy he calls "counterclockwiseology": ignoring the strict formatting that afflicted the local airwaves. A typical evening's session of Mojo's "Midnight Funk Association" (which each night featured an audio simulation of the landing of Mojo's own interstellar craft, "the Mothership") might include Parliament's "Flash Light," the J. Geils Band's "Flamethrower," the B-52s' "Mesopotamia," Visage's "Frequency 7," Yellow Magic Orchestra's "Firecracker," and anything and everything

by Prince and the Time. Most importantly, the DJ had fished Kraftwerk's *Autobahn* out of the discard bin at a previous station, where it had been used as backing music to cut commercials over, and soon after acquired a copy of *Trans-Europe Express.* "It was the most hypnotic, funkiest, electronic fusion energy I'd ever heard," Mojo gushes. "I couldn't imagine what the mindset was of a band who could be that funky on purpose."

When Kraftwerk's *Computer World* came out in 1981, Mojo played virtually the entire album every night, making a lasting effect on impressionable young listeners like Atkins. Growing up in northwest Detroit, Atkins had known he'd be a musician from age six or seven. When Atkins was in high school, his family almost moved to California, but instead ended up in Belleville, a fishing town of roughly 3000 about thirty miles southwest of

PLASTIKMAN (RICHIE HAWTIN)

RYUICHI SAKAMOTO

Detroit. Belleville in the early eighties was perhaps the only place more unlikely than Detroit for a high-tech movement to begin: a rhubarb (a rural town taking on the trappings of a suburb thanks to metropolitan sprawl) only eight blocks long at the time, where a general store/bait and tackle shop was the town's biggest business. Because there were so few black families in Belleville, Atkins struck up friendships with two pals of his younger brother Aaron: Derrick May and Kevin Saunderson. Atkins turned his pals on to Mojo's radio show, and the trio began doing pause-button mixes and trading tapes while Atkins, May, and May's friend Eddie "Flashin'" Fowlkes began spinning and mixing at parties under the name Deep Space Sound.

At Washtenaw Community College after graduation, Atkins met Rick Davis, a Vietnam vet twelve years his senior whose own noodling with synthesizers was more advanced than Atkins embryonic experiments. The duo soon formed Cybotron, Davis rechristening himself "3070" (his dog tag number, according to legend), and in 1981, they released the heavily Ultravox-influenced "Alleys of Your Mind" as a seven-inch single on their own Deep Space Records. Although they weren't the first local crew to put out their own electronic record – that title goes to "Sharevari" by A Number of Names – Atkins and Davis were blessed with plenty of airplay on Mojo's show, and "Alleys," and its 1982 follow-up, "Cosmic Cars," sold ten to fifteen thousand copies in Detroit alone. A contract with Berkeley, California-based Fantasy Records for *Enter* soon followed, and while the album was as much spaced-out new-wave funk-rock as it was ur-techno, a remix of the instrumental "Clear" became a top-twenty hit nationally

STACEY PULLEN

on *Billboard's* black singles chart. However, when Davis decided the follow-up single would be "Techno City" (despite its title, the song is heavily guitar-based), Atkins decided to strike out on his own.

Frustrated by his less-than-fantastic first taste of the record business, and fed up with his demos getting rejected by other labels, Atkins decided to press a twelve-inch record himself with the goal of simply attracting a larger label's attention. In 1985, he started Metroplex, taking the name from Cybotron's "techno-speak" glossary of Toffleresque terms. Atkins chose the name Model 500 for the project as a way of "repudiating ethnic designations" and cloaking his persona behind a machine-like veil; May, Saunderson, and many others would later follow suit. It would be this elimination of any telltale emblems of African American identity that would eventually come back to haunt the Detroiters in their search for a black audience.

For his debut release as Model 500, Atkins unleashed "No UFO's," his attempt at working out George Clinton and Mojo's Mothership issues. Eight years before the *X-Files*, Atkins sang of now-familiar themes of extraterrestial encounters and official conspiracy, but with an urban twist: "They say 'There is no hope'/They say 'No UFOs'/Why is no head held high?/Maybe you'll see them fly." "The government always tries to cover up the fact that there could be other life in the galaxy," explains Atkins. "To me, the system is bent on keeping people in despair, hopeless, not wanting to achieve anything, so if you keep your head up high maybe you'll start realizing things that you never thought possible, and seeing a UFO is probably the ultimate impossibility."

Beneath the sci-fi scenario was an implicit subtext of self-empowerment, both in the lyrics and in the fact that Atkins was taking the modes of record production into his own hands. Like a black version of punk rock,

techno musicians around Detroit suddenly started their own labels — most notably, Saunderson's KMS and May's Transmat — and began releasing their own records, a case of brothers doing it for themselves. The aesthetic of anonymity that would become techno's trademark arose initially due to "straight economics," explains Atkins: blank record sleeves were a financial necessity because "we didn't have enough money to print full-color jackets and stuff. We were so used to doing it that way that we never even thought about it after that." Besides the blank packaging, the musicians camouflaged themselves behind a dizzying variety of alter egos, particularly Saunderson, who holds the unofficial record for aliases. Since releasing "Triangle of Love" as Kreem in 1986, he's recorded as Reese, Reese and Santonio, Reese Project, Keynotes, Tronik House, Inner City, Inter City, and E Dancer. The multiple monikers were "to help Detroit seem bigger," reveals Saunderson, to make it appear "that there was more going on."

The Detroiters' creative fires were fueled by some good-natured competition with Chicago's house DJs. May had moved to Chicago for a few months after high school to soak up the vibe of house DJs Ron Hardy and Frankie Knuckles; now May and Atkins traveled to the Windy City, hoping to have their new records played by Knuckles. It was May — desperately needing rent money — who sold the 909 drum machine to Knuckles that allowed the Chicagoans to become a record producing force in their own right. The Detroiters' initial records were also heavily indebted to the progress made in Chi-town - "If Chicago had not done what they did," says May, "we would not have had anywhere to take our music" — but where Chicago's sound was heavily reliant on disco, the Motor City remained steeped in funk, albeit accelerated to heretofore unexplored beats per minute.

But Detroit didn't really distinguish itself as distinct

from house until the name "techno" itself was first popularized with the 1988 British compilation *Techno!: The New Dance Sound of Detroit* on Virgin's 10 Records subsidiary. The huge success of that compilation helped propel the term that Atkins lifted from the chapter "The Techno Rebels" in Toffler's *Third Wave* into the English vernacular. Following the compilation, the poppier, house/techno blend of "Good Life" and "Big Fun" by Inner City (Saunderson and female vocalist Paris Grey) became enormous hits across Europe and the locus of Detroit techno began to shift across the pond.

Crowds of thousands of ecstatic carousers greeted the Detroiters when they went to England in 1988 and 1989, and the continent soon became Motown's home away from home. Back in Detroit, May had become the house DJ and for eventual co-owner of the Music Institute, the most legendary local venue since the Grande Ballroom played launching pad in the late sixties to the MC5 and the Stooges gettin' Iggy wit' it. The after-hours downtown club was open for a year and a half, from May 1988 to late 1989, drawing a predominantly black clientele. Crowds of six to seven hundred people packed the Institute each weekend despite no liquor license, pulled in simply by the attraction of get-down-to-basics dancing from midnight till six or eight in the morning.

But the Institute closed in 1989, a victim of the Detroiters' success abroad. "We all got too preoccupied with our own lives," says May. "The world started calling and we started answering." In the kitchen of May's stylish pad above the offices of his record label Transmat, four clocks tell the time in London, Tokyo, New York, and Detroit, a constant reminder of where his bread is buttered. During the height of Detroit's foreign success, May moved from Detroit for stints in Amsterdam, Paris, and London, but each time he's returned to the place he calls "an ugly beautiful city." "There's not too much more to

do here," says May, "except either be very creative or be very negative."

The English press often refers to May as "the Miles Davis of techno," but the My Bloody Valentine or Guns N' Roses of techno might be a more appropriate description of his musical disappearing act. Recording under the pseudonyms X-Ray, Mayday, and Rythim is Rythim (May's accidental misspelling, which he ultimately kept because "my rhythm *is* my rhythm"), May raised Detroit techno to its most majestic, elegant heights and transformed the music into epic, complicated compositions. From 1986 to 1992, May rapidly turned out some of the best singles that Detroit ever produced – "Nude Photo," "Strings of Life," "It Is What It Is" – then abruptly stopped making music in favor of travelling the world performing DJ gigs, enjoying wine (just a little), women (a lot), and song (just not his own).

But while May may be a superstar in techno circles, in Detroit he's almost invisible. "Nobody knows who Derrick May is in the black community like they knew who Derrick May was back in 1990 and 1991," says May's good friend Carl Craig. "Derrick is like Sam Malone, a serious legend, but more people who are involved in this whole electronic music rave thing know who Derrick is, and all those people are white kids."

"We may have left here too soon," admits May. While the Detroiters were building bridges in Europe, they were allowing the foundation of their home to crumble. No one was left minding the store in Motown, and the momentum that had built up over the four years since Atkins launched Metroplex began to dissipate in 1989. "Once the guys got the notoriety and acceptance in Europe," says Stacey Pullen, "they couldn't be found in Detroit at all. So it just left us, like, 'Where are we going to go next?'"

The answer was Canada. Windsor, Ontario, may be

the only place from which Detroit looks like a bustling metropolis. From a vantage point across the Detroit River, all the Motor City's racial and social problems disappear, and only the recent gleaming real-estate developments on the riverfront are visible. "This is one of the best locations to get that overall picture of Detroit," says Richie Hawtin, a.k.a. Plastikman, as he sits on a couch in the living room of his home in a former firehouse nicknamed The Building. "It gives me an interesting perspective. My music from the beginning is definitely based in Detroit techno, basically influenced by people like Derrick May and Kevin Saunderson, but it hasn't progressed or come out in the traditional Detroit techno way. It's partly due to my background, but also partly my location."

Since he launched Plus 8 (a reference to the fastest pitch adjustment on a turntable) with partner John

Acquaviva in 1990, Hawtin has become the most controversial character in the evolution of Detroit techno, so much so that there are plenty of people who feel that he shouldn't be considered part of Detroit techno at all – whether it's that his home base is across the river in Windsor, or that, as James S. of the electro group Drexciya once commented to an interviewer, he's of the "Caucasian persuasion."

Hawtin earned his white devil status by almost single-handedly bringing rave culture to Detroit. Since 1992, he's thrown what are widely acknowledged to be the city's best parties in some of Detroit's worst neighborhoods, taking advantage of Detroit's surplus of vacant warehouse and factory space to stage huge, conceptual affairs, like the one that helped give him his Plastikman persona, where he completely covered a building in black plastic.

When Detroit's techno movement had disappeared across the ocean, Hawtin reenergized the Detroit scene with a new infusion of creativity. Releasing records as States of Mind, Cybersonik (with Acquaviva and Dan Bell), Fuse, and finally Plastikman, Hawtin built an intense following in Detroit as well as across the Midwest, and in the

process totally reshaped the racial makeup of the local techno audience. After Hawtin stepped in to fill the vacuum created by the originators' European vacation, scores of young Caucasian fans followed him into the inner city in a startling reversal of white flight.

While Hawtin was shifting the constituency of Detroit techno to the vanilla suburbs, Mad Mike Banks and his Underground Resistance label tried to steal the course of the scene's original black identity. Banks is the conscience of Detroit techno, a combination of Chuck D and Ian MacKaye running a fiercely do-it-yourself operation where keeping it real means keeping it independent. Forming the group Underground Resistance with Jeff Mills (and later Robert Hood) in 1991, Banks brought a new aggression to Detroit techno, with UR song titles like "Riot," "The Punisher," "Elimination," "Predator," and

"Sonic Destroyer," and the motto "Hard Music from a Hard City." The stylistic approach of UR's tracks has ranged from pummeling hardcore to jazz-inflected melodicism, but the ideological content has never wavered, delivering puritanical anti-major label broadsides on songs like "Message to the Majors" and "The Theory," where a voice repeatedly chants "Remain underground!" In an era when most black pop stars boast far and wide about living large and getting paid mad money, Banks' anticommercial *modus operandi* is a radical concept.

A formative influence on Alec Empire (of Berlin's Digital Hardcore label), Banks manages to pull off the difficult task of imbuing his instrumental tracks with a political subtext. One single, for example, is inscribed, "Message to all murderers in the Detroit Police Force –

We'll see you in hell!" and is dedicated to Malice Green, a black motorist beaten to death in 1992 by two white Detroit cops. As part of his self-reliant approach, Banks also helps run the distribution and mail-order companies Submerge and Somewhere In Detroit, "the world's most exclusive record store," which is open by appointment only – you can't get much more underground than that. Banks is the inspirational force behind Detroit's unique strain of black nationalist techno, which ranges from Drexciya – the mysterious collective who propose a scenario in which pregnant African women thrown overboard during the Middle Passage might not have drowned but instead gave birth to a race of water-breathing Afronauts who, any day now, are coming back up to the surface to deliver whitey a beatdown – to the crypto-fascist themes of Dopplereffekt, whose Gerald

Donald even posed for the matrix photo of the "Racial Hygiene and Selective Breeding" EP wearing a brown-shirt uniform and SS bars (which ended up being magic-markered out on the actual record).

The twenty-nine-year-old honcho behind Planet E, arguably Detroit's most innovative and important label these days, Carl Craig is the bridge between the original era of the Belleville Three and the various "waves" that followed, developing from the "boy genius" of techno, who made his first recording in 1989 under the tutelage of Derrick May, into the most consistently inventive Detroit artist of the last decade. Since launching the company in 1991, Craig hasn't just concentrated on the work of him and his friends, but also new local talent like the enigmatic Moody Mann, who had issued a stream of house-inflected twelve-inches on his own KDJ label

before Planet E released his outstanding debut album *Silent Introduction*, as well as non-Detroiters like Berlin's Quadrant and Britain's Mark Bell (who provided the beats on Björk's *Homogenic*). Recently, Craig has taken the next step and begun releasing full-length albums on compact disc, both of which had been heretofore untapped formats among Detroit labels. He's also initiated the practice of compiling retrospectives of out-of-print material, including the *Faces and Phases* collection of Kevin Saunderson's essential late-eighties underground singles and Craig's own early work as Psyche and BFC.

It's often said among electronic circles that there's a maximum of ten people with innovative ideas in techno at any one time, with everyone else who's making records simply ripping them off. If so, Craig is a constant among that talented ten, consistently heading off into new directions that alternately delight and confound techno's tastemakers. His Paperclip People and 69 projects, for example, are some of the most irresistibly funky grooves to come from Detroit since George Clinton received his discharge from Uncle Jam's Army, while the two albums recorded under Craig's own name are more mellow, almost ambient affairs. Just to further derail the trainspotters, his Innerzone Orchestra album, *Programmed*, makes the oft-suggested jazz/techno analogy explicit — it has far more in common with a Herbie Hancock record than a 4/4 beatdown.

Craig is as close as techno comes to having a prodigy. He started listening to Mojo in first grade, and though he was a fan of Prince, Led Zeppelin, and the Smiths in high school, it was just after graduation that he discovered the scene developing at the Music Institute. "It blew my mind," remembers Craig, leaning back on a couch at Planet E's headquarters in a downtown high-rise office building. "The Music Institute was my coming out of my shell, freedom kind of thing. I finally found where I wanted to be, what I wanted to do, who I wanted to become. It was like for gay people, coming out of the closet. It was finding my musical identity, my lifestyle."

But young black audiences today aren't having experiences like Craig's electronic epiphany. Craig traces techno's divorce from its original black following to the point it began to veer from the street-oriented grooves of Italian disco and early hip-hop and began to get more spiritual and soundscapey. "Rap stayed street, rap stayed urban, it stayed within the community," observes Craig. "Techno went somewhere else." While hip-hop became the (purportedly) *verité* narrative chronicling the inequities of America's inner cities, techno's sci-fi soundscapes became the soundtrack to a cerebral ticket out, not so much escapist as transcendent; it wasn't a report of what was going on around them, but rather an open-ended prophecy of what might yet be. "Techno is no words, no lyrical content," Craig continues. "We were like, 'Here it is, like it or not, let your body move to it, it's African rhythms mixed with European melodies, let's see what you can do with it,' and they were like, 'Fuck you.' So we went to Europe."

While many of his colleagues are still focusing their energies on the continent, Craig is taking active steps to make sure techno becomes the soundtrack to all tomorrow's parties. Toward that end, Craig has hatched a plan to invest a few thousand dollars in distributing free techno tapes to kids, hoping to get them hooked early enough so they grow up thinking that techno is normal. "Nobody knows our music because they can't hear it," says Craig. "Radio is not playing it. We need to take the initiative and promote ourselves in formats that people can actually listen to." Craig pauses to look out the window at the city below. "It just comes down to what we can do to make it happen," he says. "This is our hometown, and for us to be alienated like this isn't right."

But is it too late for techno to reclaim the streets?

Booty music is the newest "new dance sound of Detroit," as well as the oldest – it's been around in one form or another since the early eighties. It's sometimes called "Detroit bass," "ghetto bass," "techno bass," or "ghetto tech," or often just lumped in as "electro," from which it's derived. The terms are more or less interchangeable – sort of. "Electro is the meeting point between techno and hip-hop and funk," says Brendan M. Gillen, who runs the Ann Arbor, Michigan-based experimental electro label Interdimensional Transmissions. "It has inherently science fiction elements because you're using machines to talk for you rather than instruments, and it comes from a time when the future seemed so bizarre and exciting."

Booty, on the other hand, is electro's illegitimate love child, with most of its practitioners obsessed with recapturing the early eighties sound of Cybotron and Model 500. Harder and faster than the similarly salty bass music of Miami or Atlanta, booty takes the Detroit tradition of speeding up the music to the extreme, with high-velocity beats, call-and-response chants, and potty-mouthed lyrics in obnoxious high-pitched voices that put the "scat" back into "scatological" – like Alvin and the Chipmunks if they hung with the Long Beach Crips. Booty is street level, working class, and incredibly reactionary in its homophobia and misogyny, with all the coochie-popping and bitch-slapping anyone could possibly hope for (or stand); call it "cum and bass."

Regardless of its exact handle, booty/bass/electro has won not only the hearts and minds but the asses of Detroit's black community. Techno has never been considered ghetto music, but now it's lost the battle for the streets to not just hip-hop but its own perverted cousin. Booty is the soundtrack of choice booming out of car speakers on weekend nights at Belle Isle, Detroit's popular island park, and cars cruising down Jefferson Avenue with trunks full of woofers. Booty/bass is getting the local radio airplay that techno could never achieve, especially on weekend mix shows on WJLB and WCHB that are broadcast live from clubs. Local sales are booming, with entrepreneurs selling records out of the back of their cars and testing their records at strip clubs to see if the tracks have shake appeal.

Booty's reigning titan is DJ Assault, a.k.a. Craig Adams, whose *Belle Isle Tech* CD carries the front-cover message, "Warning: This product has no social [sic] redeeming value whatsoever." Inside, there's enough unbridled testosterone to give C. Delores Tucker a field day, with such tunes as "Asses Jiglin" (sic), "Drop Dem Panties," "Bitch I Aint Yo Man," "Big Booty Hoes and Sluts Too," and three versions of "Ass N Titties." Unlike techno, where the subject matter is inscrutable and open to interpretation, booty's topical preoccupations are easy to divine: in the words of the chorus to "Ass N Titties," "ass/titties/ass n titties/ass ass titties titties/ass n titties." With one tawdry tale after another about the world's oldest business, the only thing remotely "futuristic" or "sci-fi" about it is the sonic similarity to Luke Skyywalker (a.k.a. Luther Campbell).

Like just about every black musical genre before it, white musicians have now moved into the neighborhood. Assault's main challenger for bass supremacy is DJ Godfather (Brian Jeffries), whose "Player Haters In Dis House" and "Pump" have become local standards. Brian Gillespie, who describes himself as "a white kid with a black soul," runs two electro labels (Twilight 76 and Throw) and a bass imprint (Databass) and is trying to challenge Assault's Electrofunk and Assault Rifle record companies for the title of the Berry Gordy of booty.

Perhaps not surprisingly, there's considerable disdain from techno's artistic forces towards the booty men. Even Atkins, to whom booty claims paternity by dint of his Cybotron and Model 500 pedigree, is skeptical. "It's too silly," he says. "All that hoopin' and hollerin' and whoopin' 'It's your birthday!' - it's too corny."

It may be that booty is corny (as well as horny), but it certainly resonates in Detroit in a way that techno hasn't since its earliest days. "Detroit techno for the most part doesn't really exist here," says Lawrence Burden, co-owner of the electro/techno bass label Direct Beat, "and it really hasn't for quite some time." Booty's bottom-line-driven hustlers have been willing to make the compromises that Detroit's proud techno artists refuse to consider. Crass as they are, booty's sex-obsessed lyrics make the tunes more accessible than techno's purely instrumental song structures, which lack a human voice to relate to. White kids were drawn to gangsta rap by exaggerated stereotypes of what black behavior was supposed to be, and booty samples that formula; where techno rejected racial sterotypes, booty plays into them.

But the issue of Detroit techno's low U.S. profile is bigger than just the Motor City and booty. Like soccer, Detroit techno has yet to fire the passions of most Americans. In their quest for domestic acceptance, the Detroiters have been stymied by a variety of factors outside of their control, including racism, conservatism in radio programming, the immensity of the U.S. marketplace, lack of record company support, and commercial and critical indifference to their brand of instrumental music — if not instrumental music in general — all compounded by the city's isolation from the industry, especially after Motown Records left for Los Angeles in 1972.

Some culpability can also be laid square at the feet of the creators themselves for issuing limited-edition singles under a sometimes staggering number of aliases on poorly distributed, vinyl-only independent labels, most with blank sleeves that carried little or no information except on the matrix label (and even that space was oftentimes left blank to create the much-sought-after "white label" release). It's an approach almost hell-bent on obscurity. "People in Detroit say, 'Oh, we didn't get the dues that we deserve and we didn't get this and that,'" observes Hawtin. "And then there are people like ostriches, they stick their heads in the ground, they want to be so underground that you've got to feel sorry for them. If you go out and work for it, you have to make some concessions to get what you believe in to a bigger stage. Some people don't understand that." Ten years after their singles first lit the fires of a youth culture revolution, the question about Detroit techno still remains: do Motown's electronic pioneers want to be art music snobs or urban dancefloor guerilas? The forefathers of techno still don't see why they can't have it both ways.

With Detroit techno, Derrick May, Kevin Saunderson, Juan Atkins – they were looked up to as the successors of Kraftwerk, the guys who took techno to the dancefloor. **STACEY PULLEN** Some of my best stuff has come from mistakes. You'd be surprised with what I come up with. **JUAN ATKINS** Robot music . . . I don't know, that's just what it seemed like. It just seemed like robot music. Not just dead robots. Really kind of alive. **SQUAREPUSHER** We do not represent the future. We represent the eternal now. **FUTURE SOUND OF LONDON** I see boundaries between musical styles as being very arbitrary: It all goes onto a CD and it all comes out of the speakers. **MOBY** What grabbed me when I first heard Kraftwerk and Derrick May was the futuristic qualities of this music. Every time you heard a special record, not only did it have a special feeling and a special sound, it was unlike any feeling you'd had before, it was unlike anything you'd heard before. **RICHIE HAWTIN a.k.a PLASTIKMAN** We're not going to arrive at a brand-new sound or a note or anything. It has to be a combination of elements that create another, two together create a third, and all these different things go into creating something new: The only way, I think, to arrive at something a little different is by combining things now. **BILL LASWELL** The actual beat for a dancefloor, to keep a dancefloor dancing all night, is 133 beats per minute. I play faster than that, but that's the speed for a normal crowd. You have people on drugs, people drinking, but an average person on the dancefloor wants to dance to music at 133 beats per minute. That's what I've learned after ten years of doing this every week. You keep it at that tempo, and you keep the floor going until early morning. You start playing jungle, happy hardcore, gabba, whatever, you get a little testosterone jumping, they're like this for half an hour and you lose it. **FRANKIE BONES** Before I was experimenting with music, I was probably experimenting with something else. Making different kinds of drinks, with sugar and lemonade and . . . cornflakes, milk. **RONI SIZE** Life is hard. You gotta go bust your ass at a job eight hours a day, making shit money, barely able to pay your bills. You need a good six hours where you don't have to worry about shit. Even if it's raining outside, you got two dollars, your girlfriend left you, and on the way here you locked your keys in the car...You need to be able to have a chunk of time to go somewhere, no matter what. **DERRICK CARTER**

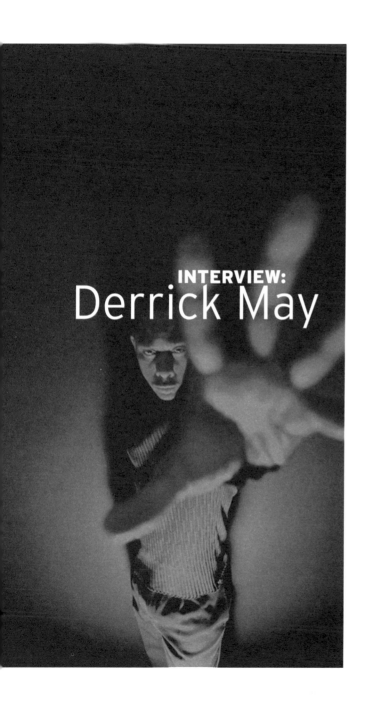

Derrick May

Detroit's an industrial city. It's a wasteland of ideas. Detroit is the type of place where you can only dream of what the rest of the world is like. You find yourself trying to get out of there, wanting to put yourself in a position where whatever you think about, whatever you feel, you believe that it's going to help you get out of that city. I don't mean that in a negative way; Detroit is a cool town for some people, but in many ways you come up with this perception of the world by not having anything. By not having the same opportunities as some people have in other places. And that tends to put you in a position where your imagination begins to play a really strong role in everything you do. That is one reason why so many artists have come from Detroit or places like Detroit. Cities or places that don't have so much tend to create opportunities. People tend to use their imaginations to compensate. People tend to dream of what others have or dream of what it's like to be in other places. That's when the imagination gets hungry and when opportunities come around; you more or less push yourself to the next level. Not to have is to want. To have is to not want. Black science fiction and Alvin Toffler's, *The Third Wave*, have very much happened already. *The Third Wave* is here. The technological revolution is here. We're speaking now with a video camera that is not a video camera. It's a digital camera. I'm speaking to you, in the future, right now. We are here. The technological revolution, which is a phase after the industrial revolution, has already happened. Once again, we're in the future. Every second, we're in the future. The music [techno] started off being made by young black men from Detroit. It branched off to Europe and became bigger. Over there, it was mainly white kids doing it. When it came back to America, it was mainly white kids doing it. The music doesn't have the same feel, nor does it have the soul or love that it had when it first started. People know what's good. In their hearts, people can feel what's right. The individual is far more intelligent than the masses. The right people will find the music, cherish it, and help it move to the next level, the so-called "futuristic level." "Strings of Life" was a mistake. A friend of mine came over to my home to make a ballad. He had put down a basic piano riff, and maybe one year went by between the time he did this five-minute piano sequence and the time that I listened to it. I was looking for something else on my sequencer, going through all my disks, and I found this little piece of music. It didn't mean anything to me at the time because it was, like I said, a five-minute-long ballad. But the tempo that I had had on the sequencer at the time, compared to the tempo that he recorded it in, freaked me out. I did a digital edit on it. I chopped it down and did a basic loop. I didn't sample anything, but I looped the main part of the piano, and I created a song around it. One guy said to me, "Man, how is it possible that that song is a song without a bassline?" I never thought about it having a bassline. It never dawned on me that it didn't have a bassline. Not once. I didn't think about it. The DX 100 was not the machine of Detroit. It was my machine. What happened was, a few guys in Detroit decided to use it. It never was the machine of Detroit, because I wouldn't let anybody know what I was using. I was really secretive about all that. I was very secretive with all of my gear for a long time. Because I knew that in this business, once you release a record, it's public domain. Once people know what you do and how you do it, they try to do it like you. The music business is a vicious business. It's all about other people making money. It's nice to be an artist, but it's also very much a money-making business. I'm in it to make money too. I love to be an artist. I love to create, but I also enjoy making money. Most of hip-hop is made by black artists. Most black artists are not imitating, they're reliving their most gratifying moments, the most interesting times of their life. That's why they sample and loop these classic old tracks from years and years ago – and also, they're funky loops. I think more than anything, that's what they get the loops from. I think to put anything more into that is really being far-fetched. I think about modern music today – for instance, techno music from Detroit – I don't think it was a mimic of anything. Motown was Motown. Detroit techno was Detroit techno. Chicago house is Chicago house. It is inspired subconsciously by something. Everything is subconsciously inspired by something. Nothing just...comes from nothing. Everything comes from something.

INTERVIEW:
Mixmaster Morris

I'm not interested in categorization. See, I thought we had a revolution. But you know, the revolution seems to be well and truly lost. You sometimes wonder whether it's worth fighting for that revolution anymore, seeing as how its initial aims have been so perverted. I guess I have the same sort of feeling that the Bolsheviks would have had – by the time they got to Stalin they're thinking, "Do I support this anymore?" By which time you're in the gulag, it's too late. The techno revolution was very necessary, but it certainly allows the music industry to do a lot of scummy things. The music that's played in the clubs in London at the moment, I don't think I've ever heard music so bad. Really, I think it's the lowest standard. Even the worst disco, before the whole empire collapsed. I just don't see how it could continue. I mean, it will continue because millions, untold millions will be spent on hyping that music till kingdom come. But I can't see how anyone can put up with it. I went last Saturday to about six or seven London clubs and I was in tears by the end of it because I didn't hear any music that wasn't disgusting. Nowadays you can go to a party in England and hear twelve major label A&R men play all their new releases and call themselves underground DJs. People are having to fight harder to create an alternative. I've always been part of an alternative culture. I don't expect to like what every sixteen year old in the country likes. I didn't when I was sixteen and I don't now, when I'm thirty-five. I like the people who go the extra mile to find something more individual with more integrity than what you get in the charts. When you're a kid, you're brainwashed because all you ever hear is chart music, especially on daytime radio. It's only when I was like a teenager that I started to realize that there were albums and people making songs longer than three minutes. A vast wealth of music from all around the world, none of which ever gets heard on the radio. I have twenty or thirty thousand records in the house and none of it is chart music. It's all obscure and brilliant music from around the world. I make no apologies for that. It's not my fault it's obscure. But it's all music that maybe takes more than one listen. It's music that's worth persevering with. It actually gives you something back in the end, instead of just a cheesy feeling of having been ripped off. It's like the difference between organic food and junk food. I think that the majors are turning the club scene into a junk food franchise, like "Kentucky Fried Beats" or something. Greasy, tasteless, disposable food that doesn't even satisfy your hunger and gives you cancer in the long term. Everything is up for grabs. PMT: Pre-Millennial Tension. The end of the millennium is a good time to reassess what's happened in the century and to save the careers of people that have been forgotten for the last twenty or thirty years. I think now is the time to do it because people look with a longer lens. This time of the century, people look with a long lens at the whole century and try and put it in perspective. I think a lot of rewriting of music's history is going to be done before this century is over, because most of the greats never figure on the commercial rosters. I mean, if you compare techno to jazz, say, Miles Davis never had a hit record. Ornette Coleman never had a hit record. Thelonious Monk never had a hit record. But Kenny G. has sold twenty million albums. That doesn't make him the best, it just makes him the blandest. I think the same is true with techno. None of the greats of techno ever figured on the pop charts because they don't work for the major labels. That doesn't mean we can write them out of the history books any more than you can write Miles Davis out of the history of jazz. It seems that every form of music that's of black origin suffers — each one suffers even more than the previous ones because people don't get any respect for what they've done. And to me that's really disgusting. ❧

8

Jungle is definitively recombinant music – it takes aspects from all kinds of music and combines them. So in that sense, it represents an alienation from an older form of making music. The point is not to pledge allegiance to one particular form of music, but to surf between all kinds of music. What it looks for is a certain kind of amplification. **KODWO ESHUN** Jungle has the potential of creating two times at the same time, so you can have a half-time and a double-time. You could play a dub- or reggae-sounding line along with things that accelerated and doubled. You can have two things happening at once. **BILL LASWELL**

JUNGLE

MODERN STATES OF MIND

BY CHRIS SHARP

RONI SIZE

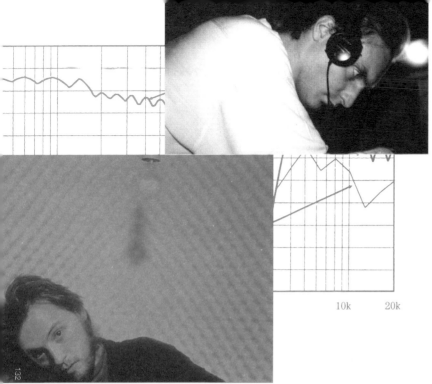

10k   20k

Discography:			
METALHEADZ	"Terminator"	(Synthetic Hardcore Phonography) proper dark hardcore
HYPER ON EXPERIENCE	"Lords of the Null Lines"	(Moving Shadow) cut-and-paste breakbeat mayhem
DROPPIN' SCIENCE	*Droppin' Science Volume 1*	(Droppin' Science) drum and bass breakthrough
SHY FX AND UK APACHE	"Original Nuttah"	(S.O.U.R) ragga jungle
LTJ BUKEM	"Music"	(Good Looking) ambient /"intelligent" drum and bass
OMNI TRIO	*Volume Four*	(Moving Shadow) symphonic breakbeat science
GANJA CRU	*Super Sharp Shooter* E.P	(Parousia) jump up anthem
ED RUSH	*Skylab*	(Metalheadz) twisted techstep
APHEX TWIN	*Boy/Girl* EP	(Warp) arty precocity
PHOTEK	*Ni Ten Ichi Ryu*	(Science) minimal oriental neurofunk

SQUAREPUSHER   APHRODITE

Looking back, the rave phenomenon is difficult to explain to anyone who wasn't there: You could call it an unruly union of disparate influences that proved temporarily explosive. Drugs, dance music, the libertarian spirit of the eighties, collective nostalgia for the counter-cultural engagement of the sixties, and the casual hedonism of British kids looking for a buzz – rave was an unpredictable day-glo cocktail of all this, and it transformed thousands of lives. Between 1988 – the second summer of love, as it was dubbed by smiley-sporting acid house hipsters – and 1991, dance music became more than just something to dance to. It was the gateway to collective euphoria, a huge shared secret and a massive in-joke incomprehensible to the mainstream. A whole generation was in on it, meeting at motorway service stations in the dead of night to follow coded directions to illicit parties and dance until dawn.

In keeping with the fine tradition inaugurated by the Beatles, British musicians and producers were captivated by American imports, but didn't merely try to copy them. Instead, homegrown house music (as it continued to be called, no matter how far it deviated from the original blueprints generated by Farley "Jackmaster" Funk, DJ Pierre, Frankie Knuckles, and Larry Heard) was driven by a magpie spirit and an instinctive understanding of the way that certain samples and sounds pushed drug buttons and unleashed dancefloor mayhem. By the time bands like The Prodigy made their appearance in 1991, rave music was a finely honed set of signals with a plethora of comedy accessories – a full-fledged culture, brandishing glowsticks and smeared in Vick's Vapo-Rub.

But the comedown was swift and crushing. The out-

break of outlaw spirit that spurred hundreds of thousands of people to break into warehouses and set up sound systems in remote fields was hunted down by the police and local government officials with decibel counters, bled dry by quick-buck promoters with a closer eye on their profits than on their promises, and laid open to ridicule by a string of infantile pop-rave hits like The Smart E's "Sesame's Treet" and Urban Hype's "A Trip To Trumpton." Dance music retreated back into the clubs, opting for constraint and control, and in the process created its first generation gap. Older fans, graduates of acid house clubs like Shoom in London and the Hacienda in Manchester, were happy to abandon rave's Balearic inclusiveness, to regroup in small cliques of like-minded afficionados and make their choice from the classical four-to-the-floor poise of Chicago house or the

processed neo-disco of New York garage. But this movement left ravers in suburban outposts and pirate radio DJs in London's unfashionable enclaves with a thirst for speed and rhythm that the new dance establishment could not satisfy. Out of this thirst, hardcore was born.

During hardcore's dark ages, which lasted from the collapse of the rave adventure until jungle's charge overground in the summer of 1994, the British media had a simple, serene policy towards the music. They ignored it. Those august publications reverentially referred to as "taste-makers" by marketing types saw hardcore as a scrofulous parasite clinging to the margins of acceptability, a moody, psychotic blare consumed by zitty suburban adolescents and Ecstasy casualties with ill-mannered car stereos. They trained their spotlights instead on the tasteful, manicured pulse of "progressive house" and the

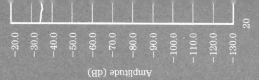

smooth, metallic sheen of "intelligent techno," implying by omission that hardcore – or "'ardkore," as it was pronounced by matey initiates – was neither progressive nor intelligent.

As hindsight has triumphantly shown, this was as much a blessing as it was a mistake. Unencumbered by the demands of the critics, fuelled by the siege mentality of the true believer, and propelled into complexity by the constantly increasing power of their equipment, the 'ardkore pariahs turned their spurned and derided music into the most electrifying sound to emerge from the U.K. in thirty years. The most expressive, too. Despite its emphasis on sheer speed, hardcore came to articulate misty nostalgia, momentary rapture, urban dread, criminal moodiness, and sci-fi futurism.

Hardcore's breakneck momentum was generated by a quest for intensity – partly an attempt to recapture rave's lost Eden of MDMA bliss, partly a reflection of the flicker-frame stimulus offered by urban experience. Producers and DJs were driven by an urge to make the drums more percussive and the bass more physical than they had ever been before. Even though some desperados went to the extreme lengths of forcing open their Technics 1210 turntables and butchering the variable resistor that regulates the pitch control, Roland TR-909-generated house music running in 4/4 time at a stately 126 bpm was never going to deliver a heavy enough sound. There was only one alternative: The renegade hardcore pioneers began to experiment with the possibilities inherent in the breakbeat.

As early as 1990, proto-jungle pioneers Shut Up And Dance (a.k.a. PJ and Smiley) were using breakbeats to

inject a bit of urgency into dance music. Coming out of northeast London, SUAD saw themselves as making twenty-first century hip-hop rather than house music – working with the same armory of breaks and samples, but speeding up the beats from hip-hop's standard 80–90 bpm to 126 or 130 bpm. SUAD's sound was a kind of slow-motion jungle before the fact – a celebration of urban piracy and rhythmic manipulation that existed uneasily alongside the stilted Brit-house sound of their contemporaries, but that managed to attract a huge following. Instinctively, PJ and Smiley had grasped the many advantages that breakbeats lent to dance music. Although they were limited by the equipment of the time and could only explore them in a rudimentary way, another two or three years would see their vision explode into life.

Breakbeats have an aura of villainy. Plundered from aging slices of funk and rare groove, lifted and looped from quasi-legal *Breaks and Beats* compilations, they are of uncertain ownership, a delicious grey area. Breakbeats evoke hip-hop, plugging hardcore directly into urban experience, nodding backwards towards DJ Kool Herc and Grandmaster Flash, giving the music an unshakable, grainy immediacy. Breakbeats mean syncopation – chinks of fraught silence that keep space and tension in the rhythms, even at high speeds.

Between 1992 and 1994, breakbeats were outcasts – they had carried The Prodigy, SL2, Altern 8, and Shades of Rhythm onto the charts on the back of the huge rave fan base, and the new "progressive" dance music shrank from them in visceral disgust. Clinging to breakbeats through that time was a gesture of defiance, a statement of intent and an invigorating and obnoxious "fuck you" to the mainstream house crowd to boot. In that spirit, one of the very first full-fledged hardcore records – "Some Justice" by Urban Shakedown, featuring Mickey Finn –

RONI SIZE

gleefully defiled Ce Ce Rogers' unimpeachable house classic "Some Day" with accelerated old-school hip-hop rhythms, a rolling bassline, and the kind of videogame-style samples that were guaranteed to get right up the nose of house purists. Pitching up the vocal sample also had the half-irreverent, half-unsettling effect of transforming Rogers' silky, masculine tenor into the helium soprano peal of a technologically violated diva.

But hardcore progressed with dizzying rapidity. 1993 was the crucial year, as the music's hyperactive, cartoony garishness was focused down into a succession of precision-tooled explorations. During that time, the music held the DNA for practically every future variation in fertile suspension – five or six years later, the lines of inquiry that started then are still being worked out in drum and bass' multiple, schismatic fragmentations.

At the time, the dominant force was the dark sound typified by Dollis Hill's Reinforced label. The music mirrored the degeneration of the rave dream, celebratory ecstasy rushes rendered queasy and menacing by overload and adulteration. The late-eighties/early-nineties Belgian sound of Joey Beltram, T99, and CJ Bolland was revisited at delirious, choppy hyperspeed. 4 Hero documented this shift in their epochal "Journey from the Light," which took the moody sparseness of their earlier 'ardkore smash "Mr Kirk's Nightmare" into ramshackle hyperspace, subjecting lush string sounds to distorting G-forces and stabbing, bleak, nameless squirms and squiggles into the heart of the mix. Nebula II's "X-Plore H-Core" went further into de-tuned psychosis, writhing ectoplasmically around a bastardized snatch of the Wizard Of Oz, and arriving at a Teutonic climax that hammered mercilessly away at a clammy synthesized orchestral stab. Doc Scott reveled in this murky playground. Recording as Nasty Habits (a celebration of pariahdom if ever there was one), his "Dark Angel" and "Here Comes the Drumz" were the apotheosis of the dark sound – bone-chilling funk shot through with viral smears of noise.

All of which might sound pretty unappealing to the uninitiated – but the hardcore-as-horror-movie vibe managed to articulate moods and sensations that had remained voiceless. At the very least, it was a way of working the poison of the rave comedown out of the music-generating system – and at best it was an utterly compelling affirmation of hardcore's identification with the new urban underclass of post-Thatcherite Britain. Like hip-hop in the States, dark hardcore reveled in its status as a product of its environment: The joyless inner cities of the late-twentieth century: have a physical presence in the sound.

Using noises from video games and video nasties was a way of celebrating the cheap, unreflective, pirated pleasures of suburban life while simultaneously evoking the sheer moodiness of the decaying, crime-ridden inner cities in the rolling bass and hypertense, metallic percussion. The sheer delight with which the dark sound plundered these defiantly lowbrow sources deepened the scorn of the house and garage hegemony. This despite the fact that these sounds are exactly what enabled it to evoke the ultimate suburban, late-capitalist paradox of transient thrills and casual misery. Hyper-On Experience's "Lords of the Null Lines" took its "fucking voodoo magic" sample from the sub-Schwarzenegger gore-fest *Predator 2*, but added a knowing glance at the essential hollowness of this kind of low-rent pleasure: Halfway through its relentlessly choppy, channel-surfing undulation, a disembodied female vocal croons the single line "There's a void where there should be ecstasy," before being sucked into the music's percussive vortex. This isn't simply a drug-reference, a gripe about defective pills, or a glum admission of inviolable tolerance levels. It's a vibrant snap critique of late-twentieth century consumer life – a pointer to the redemptive creativity that animated even the darkest sounds and lead to less oppressively monumental achievements.

In fact, despite its dominance within hardcore's inner circle, the dark sound was only one of the mutations adopted by hardcore as it evolved. The total flexibility of the music left vital sonic space for the kind of unrestrained playfulness that would have been condemned as "self-indulgence" or "experimentation" in more sober, traditional music forms. And as sound-manipulation equipment became more powerful, the essential jouissance that flickered constantly through the music flowered into different forms. Other labels emerged purveying variations on the sound, among them Suburban Base and Moving Shadow.

Suburban Base developed out of the Boogie Times record shop in Romford on the border between London and dour suburban Essex. Moving Shadow was based even further out of town, among the concrete grids of Stevenage, a new town in the depths of Hertfordshire. During 1992 and 1993, the two labels were closely allied, developing a punchy breed of breakneck hardcore that swung energetically through pools of moodiness but whose essential appeal lay in its flicker-frame, plunderphonic approach. Hyper On Experience's triumphant "Lords of the Null Lines" has already been mentioned; in similar restless and hyperkinetic vein were "Mixrace Outta Hand" by Mixrace, "The Slammer" by 'ardkore stalwarts DJ Krome & Mr Time, and "Breaks The Unbreakable" by Sonz of a Loop Da Loop Era, whose name managed to boast affiliation to old-school of rhythm manipulation even as it heralded the arrival of a new generation.

Danny Breaks was the man behind Sonz of a Loop Da Loop Era, and when he joined up with that new generation, he took his knack for nomenclature with him. His next project was one of several that helped to define the shift from hardcore to full-fledged drum and bass. The name he chose came as close as anything else to describing the creative nature of that shift – no longer simply a Son of a Loop Da Loop Era, Danny Breaks (together with other producers around the country) began Droppin' Science...

The Akai S1000 sampler was first produced in 1989 but took a few years to become a standard item in the budget producer's armory. The S1000 was also impressively futureproof; Akai produced regular upgrades in the early nineties, and each one made cheap and powerful sound manipulation more of a reality. A chunky gray box with a small LCD screen, a fully-upgraded S1000 offered trimming, looping, crossfading and splicing facilities, all in 16-bit, cd-quality sound. It also incorporated a new device called time-stretching, which allowed the tempo of a sample to be increased without the pitch going up as well. It's not too much of an exaggeration to assert that drum and bass could not have come into being without this box and its successors.

Hardcore's graininess and garishness were largely forced on it by the limitations of the equipment with which it was made. The expense of memory and slow processors meant that sampling time was scarce, sound quality was low, and complex blending an impossibility. The advent of the S1000 changed the rules, and as producers got to grips with what it could do, it changed the music, too. If hardcore was a collage – a roughneck ride through a succession of intense experiential instants – drum and bass synthesized those experiences into a swathe of new texture. Armed with the S1000, drum and bass producers could suddenly become high-tech ver-

sions of the decadent hero Des Esseintes (from J.K. Huysmans' *A Rebours*), who spent hundreds of hours constructing elaborate perfumes from an enormous array of scents. Goldie and 4 Hero have spoken of a three-day session in the Reinforced studio during which they sampled, manipulated, and resampled, filling DAT (digital audio tape) after DAT with hours of mutant sound and creating a priceless storehouse of raw material. Results like "Terminator", the rampaging, cyborg apogee of dark, and "Angel," which matched jazzy female vocals with loungey piano, twisted strings, slurps, shudders, and viscerally crunchy beats – and which marked the beginning of the journey back towards the light – spoke volumes about the increased power of sound manipulation technology.

Goldie clearly understood the opportunities opening out for the music. The sleeve notes on "Angel" are a manifesto for the progressive wing of the hardcore movement: "Dedicated to those who have strived to keep the underground alive and develop this once raw sound into a music all of our own design. A new dimension in music is upon us, a time when the cutting-edge of hardcore must be pushed to survive. Ever forward is how it was always supposed to be..."

Moving Shadow's releases began to reflect a similar tendency. Label owner Rob Playford was a gifted producer (as one-third of 2 Bad Mice, he was responsible for a string of future hardcore classics like "Waremouse," "Hold It Down," and "Bombscare," and he would later collaborate on Goldie's first album *Timeless*). He was swift to recognize that the music was now equipped to strain against its own boundaries. In the second half of 1993, he began to release groundbreaking sounds from the likes of Omni Trio and Foul Play.

Foul Play's remix of "Lords of the Null-Lines," released several months after the original, pinpoints the shift in the music's sensibility perfectly. While it respects the bpm count of the original, it seems to run in slow motion, shot through with quizzical shivers and nameless moans. The frenetic rush is halted, ionized, held in suspension. The effect is curiously ambivalent, and introspective, somehow suspended between emotional states. If hardcore was a constant oscillation, a rollercoaster through e-rush and comedown, euphoria and regret, the friendship and the villainy of the rave experience, then drum and bass, as produced by Foul Play, compounded those feelings into strange new textures, holding them all in exquisite stasis even as the articulated beats rolled through the mix, "Open Your Mind" and "Being With You" are similarly evocative, tinged with regret, and morphing through complex, modern states of mind.

Rob Haigh's Omni Trio project was even more fluidly emotional. His first release for Moving Shadow, "Mystic Stepper," threaded a plangent four-note quaver through lush clouds of strings and placed a lugubrious Morricone bell chime at the heart of flurried, back-masked beats. A series of EPs through 1993 and 1994 explored similarly lush, beguiling territory. What really set Omni Trio apart was not Haigh's command of minimalist melody or his ability to arrange swathes of orchestral sound, but the way that he intensified the rhythmic complexity of the music.

Although a string of hardcore releases sought to do more than simply loop and accelerate breakbeats – often running two patterns simultaneously, animating the tune with the tension and release generated by the clashing breaks – Omni Trio pioneered the technique of constructing his rhythms from discrete percussive samples. Even as early as "Mystic Stepper," his beats have a glittering, exoskeletal quality of technology, and they flicker and shift with alien, cybernetic dexterity. By the time he released "Soul Promenade" eighteen months later, he was a master of this particular art (an art brought into being by the capabilities of the Akai sampler), and he had helped bring into being a whole new field of enquiry – breakbeat science.

Other producers, including Danny Breaks, were soon mainlining on this quest for rhythmic complexity, forcing their percussion through breathtaking plastic pirouettes whose combination of grace, complexity, and sheer speed was even more remarkable given the hours of painstaking studio labor required to generate them. The drum patterns on a track like the ectoplasmically sensual "Droppin' Science Volume One" are incredibly articulate and genuinely musical. In Bristol, Roni Size was sticking to sampled breakbeats but pursuing similar lines of enquiry, meshing three, four, or even five separate loops together and fully demonstrating in tracks like "Music Box" and "11.55" that, in the right hands, time-stretching could give birth to mind-mangling rhythmic complexity.

If Goldie, Foul Play, and Omni Trio were among those who were trying to bring musicality back into drum and bass, they were trying to do it without abandoning the locomotive force of the hardcore mentality. Others, however, had more deep-rooted reservations about hardcore's almost paranoid hyperkinesis. As early as 1991, LTJ Bukem had mapped out an alternative future for breakbeat house with an EP whose title made his view of things abundantly clear – "Logical Progression."

Unlike, say, Goldie, who came to hardcore from a solid hip-hop background, Bukem was a veteran of the London's eighties rare-groove and acid jazz scenes. His music amply reflected that grounding. The three tracks on "Logical Progression" come swathed in breathy, soft-focus keyboard chords, and the slow-motion breaks patter rather than tear at the listener. The warm, jazzy piano stabs, and live vocals (which gently inquire "Do you wanna have a good time tonight?") blend good old-fashioned soul stylings with the kind of dewy-eyed romanticism that made Liquid's "Sweet Harmony" a dawn-chorus rave anthem.

By the time that Bukem made "Music" in 1993, he had his own label, Good Looking, and his own vision firmly in place. More jacuzzi than Uzi, Bukem's beats were an intricate, fibrillating flow of soft-edged pressures billowing like tiny bubbles through the mix, buoyed up by waves of strings and accompanied as often as not by sampled whale song and the oceanic ebb and flow of tidal water. The darkness that was coursing through the bloodstream of hardcore had been utterly drained off, and in its place was a blissful rapture not a million miles from that purveyed by horizontal mixologists in the ambient house scene like The Irresistible Force and The Orb.

During 1994, Bukem gradually gathered like-minded souls around him – PFM, Sounds of Life, Studio Pressure (a.k.a. Photek), Peshay, Wax Doctor – releasing their music, playing their dub-plates, and in the process guiding his musical, uplifting approach away from the margins – the 4 a.m. "wind-down" sets and the sparsely populated back rooms – and right into the heart of the drum and bass movement. Eventually, he started a club night in the West End of London called Speed, a night that was to be devoted entirely to what had come to be known as "intelligent drum and bass". This tag – implying, of course, that any music with a trace of hardcore's streetwise energy was somehow unintelligent – did no end of casual violence to the considerable programming skills and talents of those who chose not to make their music in this way. It did, however, go some way to guaranteeing a hipster audience when events at the other end of hardcore's sound spectrum suddenly brought the music to the attention of the world at large.

The Speed sound had plenty of coffee-table appeal,

but no mass following. In fact, the club was practically deserted during its first few months. The events with an enthusiastically burgeoning audience at that time took their musical cues from somewhere else entirely – ragga. Reggae had been pumping its DNA into hardcore rave since the early nineties. Tracks like Prodigy's "Out Of Space", which sampled "Chase The Devil" by Max Romeo, and SL2's "On A Ragga Tip," which looted Wayne Smith's dancehall classic "Under Mi Sleng Teng" were chartbusting hands-in-the-air anthems. And despite the advances being made in studios around the country, producers who stuck to the simple and exhilarating amalgamation of high-velocity breakbeats and strident ragga vocals knew that they had an increasingly dancefloor friendly formula. While rave had been a predominantly white movement, events in suburbs

with high black populations started to attract more and more black punters into the music. Temples of low-end sound like the Lazerdrome in Peckham and Roller Express in Edmonton offered ragga-style MCs and pumping basslines to a multiracial audience. By the time that sound came exploding out of the bass bins at the 1994 Notting Hill Carnival the fusion universally known as jungle was well on its way overground.

The new breed of jungle fans had no interest in the producers who had kept the faith with hardcore, laboring through the dark ages to perfect their programming skills. They just loved the tracks that gave them the best buzz, and the one track that they loved above all the others that summer was "Incredible", a collaboration between Ragga MC General Levy and the youthful producer M Beat. "Incredible," was a top ten UK hit – a feat

PHOTEK

achieved by no other jungle or drum and bass release before or since. "Original Nuttah" by Shy FX and UK Apache followed it into the charts a few months later. These records, booming belligerently out of the sound systems at Notting Hill and riding roughshod over mainstream chart pop, announced to the world that jungle was massive. And when the media smells a mass movement – and a potential new audience of consumers – it leaps on board. Within a few months, hardcore dance music was thoroughly rehabilitated, the subject of broadsheet profiles and style press guides, a fully accredited cultural phenomenon. Not long after that, jungle was advertising breakfast cereal.

This turn of affairs provoked consternation within the scene, especially as it looked unnervingly as if the main movers behind the sound's genesis weren't going to be the ones who got paid. A committee was briefly formed to protect what the participants saw as the integrity of the music. Edicts were issued that prohibited certain records from being played, and some events and promoters were boycotted. It's difficult to know whether these extreme and faintly paranoid measures had any real effect. It's certainly the case that the really overt ragga elements in jungle began to be toned down, reduced in later jungle anthems like "The Burial" by Leviticus and "Callin' All the People" by A-Zone to brief snatches set against moody swathes of ambience. It's also the case that 4 Hero, Roni Size, LTJ Bukem, and Goldie all ended up with major-label record deals, while General Levy and M Beat haven't been heard of since.

It's not hard to see why. "Intelligent" drum and bass may not have had the street following that jungle enjoyed, but its unthreatening textural carnival had an obvious appeal for music critics as well as the potential to appeal to a "home-listening" audience in the same way that "intelligent" techno had a few years before.

Most major label A&R men would have been hopelessly adrift in sweaty cauldrons of bass like AWOL and Thunder and Joy. The music that was purveyed at Speed and heralded by Goldie's "Angel" manifesto was, whether by design or not, far more approachable for people who didn't have a background in hardcore. Deals were concluded, money was invested, and a definitive caste of media-friendly "big names" began to emerge. The old informal network – club flyers, specialist record shops, pirate radio transmissions – lost its territory as mainstream sources of information and influence began to shoulder aside the underground. 1995 saw the U.K.'s major radio station, BBC Radio One, initiate a series called "One in the Jungle" and a slew of compilations called things like "Artcore" appeared in the racks of chainstores like HMV and Our Price that had previously been oblivious to the music's existence.

All this activity took place at a great pace. No one saw fit to hear the warning inherent in the first real full-length drum and bass album, 4 Hero's 1994 collection "Parallel Universe." The record is sporadically amazing. "Wrinkles in Time" shudders and shivers through spangling frequency ranges and microscopic bpm shifts – but it's also an illustration of what could happen if drum and bass' rhythm-driven aesthetic was to be compromised by attempts to prove its musical "legitimacy". There's an unwelcome emphasis on sax doodlings and chilly vocal gymnastics that gives the record a disconcerting middle-of-the-road flavor, and demonstrates that "mature" and "intelligent" jungle wasn't a foolproof way forward.

Nevertheless, the stage was set for drum and bass to move away from the dancefloor and venture into the world of the album. Goldie's 1995 Timeless was impossible to ignore, partly because of the sheer scale of its ambition – the title track was a twenty-minute orchestral epic – and partly because of the enormous marketing

campaign that accompanied its appearance. It sold over 100,000 copies, although whether the income generated by those sales actually offset the amount that had been spent on advertising it is debatable. Musically, it was another partial success, by turns astonishing and emptily grandiose. At around the same time, S.O.U.R.'s T Power released *The Self-Evident Truth of an Intuitive Mind*, which revealed in its painful title as much as in its distinctly floppy music that "intelligent" drum and bass – like progressive rock and jazz fusion before it – could so easily embark on a voyage up its own backside.

By 1995, the secret was out. Drum and bass was public knowledge, a fully mediated musical genre. Naturally, outsiders began to make it. Musicians who had previously been drawn to the arty end of alternative rock like Graham Sutton from Bark Psychosis and Kevin

Shields from My Bloody Valentine were enticed by this new area of avant-gardist sound manipulation. Techno auteurs like Aphex Twin, Luke Vibert, and Mike Paradinas were fascinated by the new rhythmic space that the music offered. The wayward talents of these people often imbued the music with amazing new textures – Aphex Twin's "Boy/Girl," for example, is plangently emotive and rhythmically ferocious in equal measure – but some newcomers seem to have been attracted to the music for dubious reasons. Tom Jenkinson (a.k.a. Squarepusher) is a case in point . At the forefront of the arty drill and bass micromovement, he seems concerned less with drum and bass' exhilarating sense of community than with the opportunities for virtuoso programming flashiness that it provides. The simple fact of drum and bass' velocity was appeal enough for others.

GROOVERIDER

It provided industrial electronica merchants in the U.K. and Northern Europe – Techno Animal, Alec Empire, Frankfurt's Position Chrome roster – with another framework for their queasy monochrome extremism, bringing into being what is described helpfully by Panacea as "industrial hatecore terrorstep."

Others saw drum and bass as a way to revitalize their careers. The miserable folk-pop duo Everything But the Girl enjoyed a massive freak hit in 1995 with the Todd Terry remix of a song called "Missing." Suddenly alerted to the regenerative powers of dance culture, they retreated into the studio with symphonic neo-junglists Spring Heel Jack to make an exquisitely mournful and immaculately tasteful collection of drum and bass ballads called *Walking Wounded*, which followed Portishead's trip-hop torch songs straight into the cd racks of middle-

class dinner-party hipsters around the country. Some bandwagon-jumping was simply ludicrous – David Bowie saw an opportunity for yet another piece of self-reinvention and produced the staggeringly crass "Little Wonder" despite the fact that most of the drum and bass scenesters who he approached with offers of production and remix work turned him unceremoniously down.

For a while, drum and bass spread and mutated with viral speed, simultaneously infiltrating TV soundbeds experienced by many millions and tiny club/art spaces known to an infinitesimally rarified few. But many central figures turned a blind eye to all this extraneous activity as well as to the glittering prize of a major-label contract. While the major-label album artists were busy using their samplers to simulate real musicians in an attempt recreate the squelchy virtuosity of Lonnie Liston-Smith or

TALVIN SINGH

Herbie Hancock, the underground producers busied themselves with the essence of the music – making the bass more physical and the drums more percussive, questing perpetually after the intensity and the galvanic buzz that only jungle at its finest was able to deliver. For them, musical realism was irrelevant. Samplers were a way of twisting, intensifying, and generally fucking up sound to increase its impact. This approach ushered in the kind of advance made by Dead Dred's "Dread Bass" (Moving Shadow's fiftieth release), that introduced the new sound celebrated in its title, a wall-crawling, slurred boom of a bassline which descended to subsonic levels and was experienced as much physically as aurally. "Dread Bass" pointed to a defiantly non-"intelligent" future dedicated to the delirium provoked by rampant mutant sound. Gradually, jungle atomized its ragga influences, plugged back into the hip-hop attitude that had inspired hardcore in the first place, and terrorized the dancefloor in the form of jump up.

Jump up is perhaps the most straightforward descendent of rave. Despite the constant nods across the Atlantic, its restless, skittering progression from outrageous bassline to outrageous bassline, from drug-friendly chimes to syncopated gunshots, expresses the same nervous energy, the barely contained hilarity, the lurching moodswings and the sweaty-palmed creativity of the hardcore explosion. And although jump up is a harsher, more straightjacketed distillation of that mood, the exuberance of the biomass still beats warmly at its heart. Producers like DJ Hype, Pascal, DJ Zinc, Gang Related, and Aphrodite developed the intricacy of their rhythm programming without abandoning "the funk" and inflated their basslines like sexdolls, blowing them up into huge, marauding swathes of morphing, low-end noise.

And despite its bad-boy touches and Wu-Tang derived menace, jump up remained provocatively physical music. Trace elements of rare groove and the slackest ragga provided the blue-touch paper for the exploding cybernetic inevitability of the rolling drums. DJ Zinc's "Reach Out" is a case in point: It expands and contracts, teases and delivers in a distinctly sexual manner. Aphrodite's "Woman That Rolls" is even more explicit, packed with urgent, spattering rimshots and furiously building climaxes that articulate directionless desire.

Some took their opposition to the jazz-jungle excesses of Bukemites like Alex Reece, Aquasky, and Dave Wallace even further, locking into the extremism of the old dark sound and pushing it towards psychosis. Ed Rush, Trace, and Nico brought the world techstep, a malevolent, seething morass shaped by many hours of late-night programming and the fluttering paranoia brought on by THC-intense Skunk weed. Like the Frankfurt industrial extremists, the techsteppers reprised the warped strings and squirming Belgian hoover sound – but they managed to intensify that mood a hundredfold. If jump up's sonic manipulation was gleeful, techstep's was compulsive as it warped, twisted, and rewired its sound sources into balefully attenuated shapes, boiling them down into a glutinous coagulation of nameless sinister noise. With seething Ed Rush monsters like "Guncheck" and "Skylab," drum and bass had squirmed about as far as it could get from Mercury Music Prize-approved respectability. From this final, corroded outpost, the only way forward was to go back.

It could be argued that techstep marked the end of the line. Drum and bass has since retreated into the sparse, Detroit-inflected, and stiffly mechanical constructions of neurofunk. Tracks like Jonny L's "Piper," Optical's "Grey Odyssey," and Photek's "Ni Ten Ichi Ryu" are sparse, sexless, and strangely rigid, revolving around sterile two-step drum loops and monastically eschewing any kind of play, any kind of exuberance. "I like to create atmospheres and moods by making the music as unatmospheric as possible," Photek has said. "The absence of feeling kind of becomes the feeling." This new frigidity has coincided in London with the rise of Speed Garage, which blends pumping 4/4 beats with junglist basslines and sporadic bursts of rhythmic science. On any given Sunday in East London, I can tune in to twenty or thirty pirate radio stations, but only 1 or 2 are playing breakbeats. Right now, garage rules.

The story is the same in the clubs. It's an inviolable rule of nightlife that heterosexual male clubbers inevitably follow the women, and for many women speed garage's sultry kick was a blessed relief from drum and bass's relentlessly spartan moodiness. And if the fan base is evaporating, the mass market has already lost interest. Goldie's second album, *Saturnz Returns*, was a commercial failure, disappearing from sight almost as soon as it was released, weighed down by a lukewarm critical reception and a sixty-minute-long concept-song called "Mother." 4 Hero's *Two Pages* album fared slightly better in the press and was nominated for a Mercury Music Prize, but sales were still disappointing. Predicting the future is never an easy pastime, and it's difficult to know exactly what the next stages in the development of breakbeat science will bring, but a lengthy spell back in the underground seems inevitable. In a sense, this is where we came in, and one thing is certain – whether the world is watching or not, drum and bass will continue to evolve.

On one level, jungle is sped-up hip-hop without the rap element. But there are other elements that make it so unique. It's a weird, mongrel, composite hybrid of several different kinds of music. The reggae thing is very important. The whole thing is the bass. Bass is sort of physically experienced – it's almost below the level of hearing. The force hits you right in the gut. And in a club, it becomes like an environment that you swim through. You're swimming through this bass environment. **SIMON REYNOLDS** I like the combination of frantic beats and atmospheric sounds because to me that's heaven. You've got the drive of a beat, and you've got these atmospheric soundscapes around it, and the combination of the two is just dynamic. **LTJ BUKEM** When digital equipment came on-line, you had the idea of the virtual studio. You had computers where the studio became graphical, where the virtual studio was in the interface with the screen. And that obviously has given birth to jungle, which is like the digitalization of rhythm. **KODWO ESHUN** The interface between technology and drugs is a running theme through pop history. The whole evolution of the music in the last ten years has been conditioned by ecstasy and by changing drug use. The music in England changed dramatically in the mid-nineties when a lot of people who'd been taking ecstasy for several years started to experience the dark side. The music went very dark, and that was actually one of the pivotal moments when rave music turned into jungle. **SIMON REYNOLDS** For the techno guys, techno is a revolution, and it's really not; there is nothing revolutionary about it. Our noise, our hardcore drum and bass, this is real. We want to shock people with our music, and we're getting shocked with our music. When I hear one of my records I think: "Oh, my God, what have I done?" **PANACEA** Hip-hop mutated into jungle because, I think, Britain wanted to emulate America and we all wanted to be b-boys and homeboys. **DB**

DOC SCOTT

INTERVIEW:
Squarepusher

I was making computer programs on an old Commodore home computer. I was making slices of white noise to simulate drums and playing bass guitar on top of that. I listen to the tapes now and they are really kind of naive. Then I moved into bands and stuff, but I became less and less interested in the band thing. My bass playing was becoming integrated into the electronics, and the barriers that I originally perceived kind of fell away for me. In the end, I found no barrier between electronics and live instrumentation. I found they could work together completely, very close-knit. The possibilities for experimentation are endless. When I started making drum programs on the computer, I hated electronic music as a rule. I thought it was rubbish because I'd only been exposed to rubbish from commercial major labels – that watered-down stuff that gets into the charts. But as I was exposed to acid house in its more original forms, especially the early Warp stuff and early British rave, I was really turned on to electronic music. I was responding to these tracks with the same kind of emotional reaction that I'd get from rock and jazz. The thing I really responded to was the fact that I actually had an emotional reaction to it; LFO tracks really changed me. They had a kind of intensity, almost a brutality about them, that I hadn't experienced before with live instrumental music. The rigid tempo and harsh sounds of the drum machine had a sense of anarchy to them. Robot music. It just seemed like robot music – not dead robots, but really kind of alive. Ultimately, I'm looking for a feeling of aliveness from my music. I listen to so much music, and I want to pay tribute to the stuff I hear. Not that I want to copy it, but the music gives me life and it feeds me ideas and makes me want to write more music. If it took me too long, I wouldn't do it – I never spend five days doing a track 'cause it would drive me up the wall. For me it's about working really quickly, just doing the whole thing and not sitting around listening to it too much. It's keeping the whole thing going on adrenaline; it's an excitement thing. It's like bang bang bang, idea idea idea. I don't want to get bored. The main track on Alroy Road Tracks took me half an hour just 'cause it was good fun, and before you know it, you're finished. I'm using the same setup I had three years ago, though my music has changed a lot. That change owes a lot to the fact that I have kept the same gear in my studio. I am learning to work outside the gear. The combination of just these three bits of gear — the sequencing drum machine, the Akai sampler, and the eight-track machine — represents already endless possibilities to me. People forget how amazing this stuff is and what we can do with it. The Akai stuff is really accurate: It is totally clean and geared for something like the stuff I do. But a lot of the time, I make the sounds dirty using other machines because you can't get real digital noise out of the Akai, and I really like those real fuzzy digital sounds. If I was to ask Akai to do something, I would ask them to let me adjust the bit rate of the sampler so I could control the resolution and make really low-resolution samples. I really like those sounds. I've actually got a little Yamaha sampler — a little keyboard, like a toy. I have made loads of sounds on this just because it has such low-res sound to it. There are always mistakes that I make that turn out to be — it is quite an age-old thing, not only in music, in art and so forth — that kind of happy mistake. I think it is quite important to incorporate it. The chance thing is something that is completely important to me. The chaos, or situation where you don't quite know what is going to happen, is ultimately the most interesting one to me. I hate situations where everything is all planned out. People ask me, "What are you going to do next? What music are you going to write?" I don't have a clue. I don't really know what I am going to do until I've done it. I don't plan anything. It is just boring to set it all out. I like the idea of getting out of bed, getting your breakfast, coming back, and then you are in the studio. You don't have to go down the road, you don't have to get on a bus to get to the studio, you are just there. It's hands-on straight away. You wake up in the middle of the night and do a track. I don't know, that's what kind of revolutionized it for me. Because I come from a situation with bands and stuff, where you have to go into a studio, and it's all really logical and planned, and you have to set the amps up and get all the sounds right. There is so much mucking around, it just takes the life out of it for me. To be able to just actually go, get out of bed and do a track, is the ultimate privilege. All that deliberation kills the adrenaline, and adrenaline is what I'm all about. If I am not excited about a track, then it doesn't get written. It gets changed into a live mix I suppose....

Breakbeats

Discography:

VARIOUS ARTISTS	*Ultimate Breaks and Beats Vols. 1-25*	Street Beat, 1985-1990
VARIOUS ARTISTS	*Kurtis Blow Presents the History of Hip-Hop Vol. 1*	Rhino, 1997
HONEY DRIPPERS	"Impeach the President"	1974
LYN COLLINS	"Think (About It)"	People, 1972
JAMES BROWN	"Give It Up or Turn It a Loose"	Polydor, 1969

Breakbeats have probably existed since jazz pioneers Jelly Roll Morton and Bunk Johnson first started to play with drummers in New Orleans at the turn of the century. But the idea of isolating the part of the record where the rest of the band "gives the drummer some" didn't occur to anyone until Kool DJ Herc first tapped into the New York City power supply at a Bronx block party in the early seventies. Herc was a Jamaican DJ who had emigrated to the U.S. in 1967 and set up his own sound system in the Bronx. When his reggae records failed to move the crowd at the block parties, he turned to funk, but the only part of the records he would play was the short section where all the instrumentalists dropped out except for the percussionists. The "break" was the part of the record that the dancers wanted to hear anyway, so he isolated it by playing two copies of the same record on two turntables: When the break on one turntable finished, he would play it on the other turntable. Herc's breakbeat style of DJing was much in demand, and soon enough, other DJs like Grandmaster Flash,

Afrika Bambaataa, and Grand Wizard Theodore emerged playing a similar style of music, but with greater skill and more technological sophistication. The breakbeat was music's great equalizer – nearly every record, no matter how unsavory its provenance, had two or three seconds that made it worthwhile. Herc's biggest record was a 1973 cover of Jörgen Ingmann's "Apache" by Michael Viner's Incredible Bongo Band that featured the cheesiest organ and horn fills ever recorded on top of a chorus of massed bongos. Apparently, Viner was a friend of the music industry's most notorious right-wing zealot, Mike Curb, and was the director of entertainment for Richard Nixon's second inaugural party. So hip-hop's national anthem, and probably the most famous breakbeat of all time, was not only originally a hit for Cliff Richard & the Shadows, but also the product of a record that was probably designed to appease a family-values crusader like Jerry Falwell. Hip-hop's cult of the break could redeem anything: Breaks by Neanderthal metal acts like Billy Squier, Aerosmith, and Thin Lizzy, and schlock jazz-lite artists like Bob James and Grover Washington, Jr. became the basis of records by everyone from Run DMC to the Wu-Tang Clan. Searching for its own hip-hop, Britain initially settled on the merger of house, rare groove, disco, and hip-hop fomented by Soul II Soul. The loping beat that characterized Soul II Soul hits like "Keep on Moving" and "Back to Life," and later the entire acid jazz movement, was lifted from the Soul Searchers' old-school classic "Ashley's Roach Clip." As British hardcore started to develop out of Hip-House and Belgian Techno in the early nineties, Shut Up and Dance stole beats from Suzanne Vega and Def Jam records, while 4 Hero's "Mr. Kirk's Nightmare" took a snippet from the Isley Brothers' b-boy classic "Get Into Something." In 1993, LTJ Bukem instigated the use of what may be the most-used breakbeat ever. His single "Music" was based around the drum solo from The Winstons' version of the gospel staple "Amen Brother." Previously used by Mantronik in a chopped-to-bits form on "King of the Beats," the "Amen" break was generally too fast for hip-

hop records, but its searing momentum was perfect for a genre exploring the outer reaches of the bpm speed limit. "Amen" has since been used on literally thousands of records, outdoing even the king of the break, James Brown. Of course, Brown's beats, like "Funky Drummer" and "Give It Up or Turn It a Loose," are the cornerstones of the breakbeat phenomenon. Eric B & Rakim's "I Know You Got Soul" heralded the Godfather's second coming in 1987 by sampling his production of Bobby Byrd's song of the same name. As Stetsasonic said, "To tell the truth, James Brown was old 'til Eric and Rak came out with 'I Know You Got Soul.'" Hip-hop was so dependent on his grooves in the late eighties that, according to legend, he hired someone just to listen to every record that came out to see if he had been sampled. In drum and bass, the Godfather's most used break comes from one of his side productions, Lyn Collins' "Think (About It)." Easily identifiable by the high-pitched hiccup in the background (which is Brown saying either "You're bad, sister" or "You're bad, Hank"), "Think" has graced nearly as many records as "Amen." As hip-hop-derived genres, downtempo and big beat are also completely reliant on the break. Portishead's breakthrough was largely on the back of samples of Lalo Schifrin and Isaac Hayes, while the Chemical Brothers and Fatboy Slim owe debts to jazz organist Jimmy McGriff and soulster Edwin Starr. The "Amen" of big beat, though, is the drum break from "Shack Up" by obscure seventies funkateers Banbarra. Two and a half decades after its development, the term "breakbeat" and "funky breaks" have since come to signify a separate genre of (quasi-) funky drum beats with squelchy techno effects on top. "A break" has come to mean any short instrumental passage, drums or otherwise, that can be sampled and chopped up. However you want to define it, the logic of the breakbeat is hip-hop's gift to the world and the most crucial development in popular music since James Brown almost invented the "give the drummer some" interlude with "Cold Sweat" in 1967. ✺ PETER SHAPIRO

Gabba

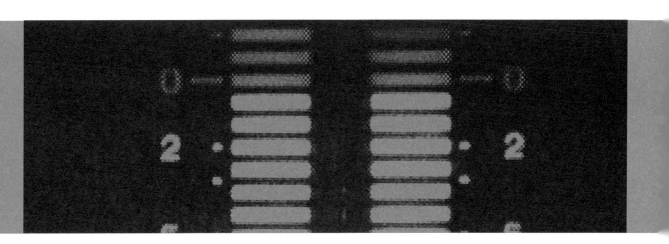

Gabba is where jungle breaks off from hardcore. We can characterize it as a distinction between the kick drum and the breakbeat. The kick drum allows a different relation to the body in that you don't need so much of a bass. So the bass and the kick drum work at the same volume; it's more of a jackhammer approach. In jungle, there are different configurations with the breakbeat and the bass. The bass could run at half the speed of the breaks, or the bass could run at the same speed as the breaks. So you could allow different relations. In Gabba, both the bass and the kick drum fuse together into a jackhammer motion. Gabba therefore becomes much more apocalyptic, much more nihilistic. There's no bass anchoring your heart beat. It kind of becomes heart-attack music. And with no bass, the kick drums get faster and faster until Gabba reaches apocalyptic heights. Gabba's drug-tech interface stopped being ecstasy or speed a long time ago and became any kind of cocktail that is as potent as possible. Hence you get tracks like "Coma Baby," where Gabba kids are using

Tomazopan and using jellies to get themselves into as much of a kind of cabbaged kind of comatose state as possible. Because the music attains such a punishing rate of velocity, reaching bpms of between 180 and 210, 230, it becomes a drilling noise that kind of pummels your head and drills through your cortex. It allows a certain synaptic rearrangement, that is so intense and so strong that it becomes a kind of a terrordome, a war zone. It becomes, How much can you take? How much can you withstand? There's a certain kind of — I wouldn't necessarily call it macho — but Gabba becomes an endurance test. A music you inflict upon yourself. You open yourself to the hardest of the hardcore. Gabba revels in its status a kind of pariah of modern music because Gabba gambles that by the end of the century, when times run out, it will be the music that really expresses that sense of what to do when all the other musics have been used up, when you're at the end of the line. When the apocalypse arrives. When you're at the end of the millennium. Gabba is the only music that will do because it's the only music that expresses that terminal sense of dissatisfaction, that real desire to reach all limits. ✦ KODWO ESHUN

9

Ambient music is like texture, shapes of sounds; it's less involved with melody and har-

mony. Microwave sounds for example, are living, acoustic sounds. **TETSU INOUE**

Ambient music is the place to look for the more interesting philosophies and ideologies

because it's less formularized, and it doesn't require a rhythm. The rhythm is always a

very difficult place to work. **GENESIS P-ORRIDGE**

AMBIENT

BASIC AMBIENT STORY

BY TONY MARCUS

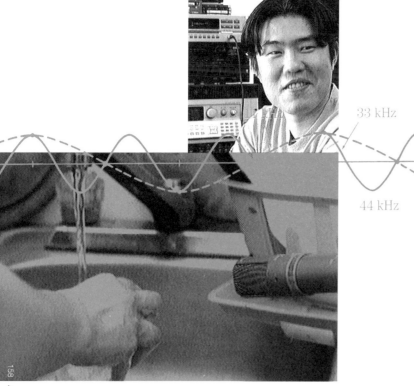

33 kHz

44 kHz

Discography:	BRIAN ENO	*Another Green World*	EG, 1975
	BRIAN ENO	*Discreet Music*	EG, 1975
	BRAIN ENO & JON HASSELL	*Possible Musics: Fourth World*	EG, 1980
	THE ORB	"A Huge Ever-Growing Pulsating Brain That Rules From the Centre of the Ultraworld"	Big Life, 1989
	THE ORB	*The Orb's Adventures Beyond the Ultraworld*	Big Life, 1991
	KLF	*Chill Out*	KLF Communications, 1990
	IRRESISTIBLE FORCE (MIXMASTER MORRIS)	*Flying High*	Rising High, 1992
	APHEX TWIN	*Selected Ambient Works '85-'92*	R&S, 1992
	APHEX TWIN	*Classics*	R&S, 1995

TETSU INOUE

Ambient begins in 1975 with a vision of beauty revealed on a mattress. A physically weak and bedridden Brian Eno is recovering from an accident. "My friend Judy Nylon visited me and brought me a record of eighteenth-century harp music. After she had gone, and with some considerable difficulty, I put on the record. Having laid down, I realized that the amplifier was set at an extremely low level, and that one channel of the stereo had failed completely. Since I hadn't the energy to get up and improve matters, the record played on almost inaudibly. This presented what was for me a new way of hearing music – as part of the ambience of the environment, just as the color of the light and the sound of the rain were parts of that ambience."

He mentioned the rain falling outside his window. The sounds became blurred, cloud-water and harp teasingly meshed into a blueprint towards a new music. Sickness can be a good place for revelation, and Eno was a changed artist. Forever after this he made records that were either wholly or partially ambient – which was a drag for the fans who liked him when his music was brimful of song and rock-noise. His ambient did little more than whisper – just a few decibels of the pale, the weightless, the slow. Was this art or anemia?

"Critics have stated that nothing much happens in my music. But if a painting is hanging on the wall where we live, we don't feel that we're missing something by not paying attention to it...My music and videos do change, but they change slowly. And they change in such a way that it doesn't matter if you miss a bit."

You can't always trust artists. Sometimes they lie. Sometimes their words are part of the art. When Eno described his ambient, he often spoke in haikus and fables. He behaved like the prophet of a new mystery religion (as he should – it's not easy to change the sound of music):

"Ambient music must be able to accommodate many levels of listening attention without enforcing one in particular; it must be as ignorable as it is interesting."

"One of the most important differences between ambient music and nearly any other kind of pop music is that it doesn't have a narrative structure at all, there are no words, and there isn't an attempt to make a story of some kind."

Alex Paterson worked in A&R for Brian Eno's EG Records. Brian Eno, Daniel Lanois, Harold Budd, Jon Hassell, King Crimson, Laraaji, Michael Brook, and Roger Eno recorded for the label. All of them were Eno's disciples – a coterie of ambient composers. Younger than Eno, Patterson was in a gang of his own with Jimmy Cauty (who was published by EG) and Youth (Alex's flatmate and old schoolfriend). The age difference is important: While Eno's gang was approaching their forties, they were in their late-twenties to mid-thirties and music industry insiders – the kind of people who are the real motors (and moneymakers) behind teenage pop and youth subcultures.

The beginnings of their ambient adventure are hidden beneath myth and lack of data. Little has been revealed, but the story (according to both fact and rumor) goes something like this...

Alex and his gang threw great parties and had access to incredible drugs and a killer sound system. Surrounded with the right machinery for art (and infamy), Alex used the turntables to make drug-sensible narratives: His DJ sets included Jamaican dub, hippy electronics, rock ballads, sound effects, and environmental recordings. And, famously, he DJed in the chill-out room at London's acid house Land of Oz club. When he went public with his new aesthetic in 1989 – a mixture of house-related beats and his DJ-styled collage – the record, *A Huge Ever-Growing Pulsating Brain That Rules from the Centre of the Ultraworld (Loving You)*, was emblazoned with the slogan 'Ambient House For The E Generation.' The apprentice had made his move.

His music was Eno through the looking glass. Where

the master's ambience aspired to the state of vapor, Alex's Orb earthed themselves with Japanese kick drums and Jamaican basslines. If Eno was eventless and minimal, then Alex was action packed and – if there is such a word – maximal. Drop the laser on an Orb cd and you will see (because this is wizardry), shazam! - the vast chasms of outer space. Gasp in amazement at a parade of Apollo spacemen, American divas and Hawaiian hula girls. "You've been orbed," explained Alex, "if you're sitting in a room and you get up to look out the window, and you suddenly realize that it was coming from the record."

Magic was always part of the aesthetic. Eno would make music that vanished in front of your eyes – Alex's made things appear. Eventually, he built a whole new world for himself (with a whiz-kid programmer, Thrash, about whom little is known) and released it as a double

album titled The Orb's *Adventures Beyond the Ultraworld*. It was popular with people in prison – *Ultraworld* plus headphones (and probably good prison skag or hash) equaled escape. But most of his fans were followers of the new dance-drug culture, freshly psyche-delicized and looking (like all drug-fucked children) for a leader. Once there was Dr. Leary and now there was Dr. Alex. People began to wonder if DJs were shamans carrying a whole universe beneath their cloaks.

Meanwhile, there was another usurpation. Alex and Jimmy Cauty, it's rumored, once played together in an eleven-hour session or "ambiathon." Tapes from this marathon may (or may not) have provided source material for the KLF record *Chill Out* – a beatless collage that was as suggestive as the titles of its songs ("Pulling Out of Ricardo and the Dusk is Falling Fast,"

APHEX TWIN (POLYGON WINDOW)

"Elvis on the Radio, Steel Guitar in my Soul," "Alone Again with the Dawn Coming Up"). If you put your eye right up close to *Chill Out* you could see a travelogue, a voyage across a fantastic America built only from sound. It was virtual cinema for tripping youth, only more magic, and accompanied by a spell that put a jester's hat on Eno's sober dome.

Ambient house celebrates the sounds we have heard all our lives and never listened to. Ambient house makes love to the wind and talks to the stars. Ambient house was invented by sheep. Ambient house is boring.

– Excerpt from a press release issued by The KLF to accompany *Chill Out*.

Pranksters can play such havoc with aesthetics (especially as there's no "house" in *Chill Out* at all). But whatever KLF's intentions, both *Chill Out* and *Ultraworld*

were taken seriously by their followers. Both records were added to the holy relics, signs, and stigmata of rave. Back when the dance-drug culture was secret (and almost a cult), owning *Chill Out* or *Ultraworld* was the mark of an initiate. After all, you couldn't chill unless you'd been out (and far out) first. These records told bedtime stories to the (still buzzing) rave mind: They whispered the wired to sleep.

Eno invented ambient music, but acid house worked out what to do with it. There's a great logic to this idea, and if you read any generic history of the dance-drug culture you'll find the following sentence, "Chill-out rooms sprang up at clubs and warehouse parties as places for weary dancers to rest for a while before returning to the main room."

The weird thing is they didn't. Chill-out rooms were always the exception and never the norm. Some say it's because drug dealers (often covertly involved in promotion) felt business slacked off as the rhythms vanished. However, it's probably got more to do with the speed at which the seductive myths of Jimmy Cauty and Alex Paterson outran the on-the-ground reality.

Our next wizard was the first to try and catch up. He is also the first true believer. He was the first to quit his job (something boring in computers), turn himself into a

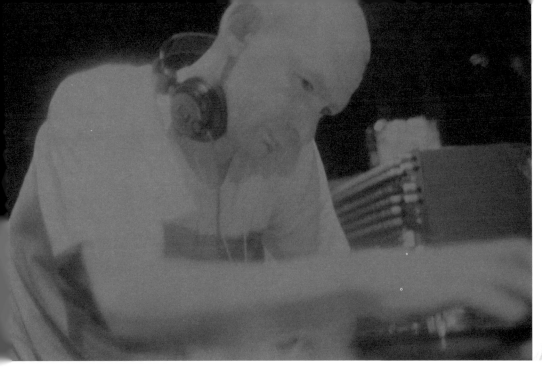

chill-out DJ, and never come back. By the time Mixmaster Morris got around to making his own music, he'd been doing such an intense one-on-one with the aesthetic that he'd magicked himself into a new place. "I think therefore I ambient," he declared.

Where Eno was a noble prophet and Paterson and Cauty obscure (if not in hiding), then Morris became cheerleading, ambient pope. He wanted to build ambient heaven on earth. And he had some great stories about what it could all be like. "If people were competing to make the strangest and weirdest and most spaced-out music instead of the loudest and hardest and fastest, then we'd have a very interesting scene."

That won him some converts. Another tale was "radical beauty: Morris asserting that music should be both daringly experimental and breathlessly exquisite.

He dressed like a conjuror in a silver holographic suit, its fabric turning white light into rainbows – suitable clothing for one who liked to dazzle. His ideas were quirky and so was his music (as a DJ he could shift from New York disco to U.K. techno to German synthdrone in seconds), but he could blind you nevertheless. Radical beauty was aesthetic nonsense until you heard him play records. Then it became real.

He really was an apostle – always bearing witness to the glory of ambient whenever he had decks in front of him. The KLF, meanwhile, abandoned their ambience to make stadium house (and top the U.K. pop charts), while The Orb played large-capacity halls – stadium ambient wannabes. Morris worked closer to the ground. He inspired others to follow him (many with limited success), but created a new world for himself. People treasure his records (as pillow-soft as Eno's, but with Paterson and Cauty's sampladelic drug cinema), and most of the planet got around to asking him to DJ for them. Darker magicians like Crowley would respect his will to power: I think therefore I ambient. The difference between slogan, mantra, and spell is impossibly slender.

The final wizard (to date) was all youth and fire. In fact, he was more Mordred than Merlin, a demon birth. Pure adolescent thrust. A rocket with no brakes. Mixmaster Morris was roughly the same age as Alex Paterson – on the edges of his balding thirties: Aphex Twin was twenty when he started to release records. He had a raver's curtain haircut (the floppy fringe used to hide a drug-mashed visage) and was fast becoming an icon on the hardcore techno scene. His "didjeridoo" (old synthesisers pushed to the point where they emulated the aboriginal "didj") confirmed everything you dared not believe about dancefloors, drugs, tribes, pagans, and cults.

And then he did this amazing, beautiful thing. He turned himself from a monster into an angel in seconds flat. His debut album, *Selected Ambient Works '85-'92*, was a record of electronic ballads – pale, wispy, lonesome, tearful, intimate – a digital Joni Mitchell. Can you imagine the hex he threw over the rave generation? Could you even begin to count all the boys who wanted to be him – awkward and powerful at the same time, ambient and hardcore, tough and tender? What great rocker ever offered anything better?

Tricks and transformations would prove to be his essence. *Ambient Works* often suggested Eno, but Aphex claimed never to have heard his music. Youth was on his side, but he wanted more of it: If you believe the dates on his album, he recorded some of it when he was fourteen. In interviews he discussed his habit of lucid dreaming, of moving between worlds while he made music. The land-

scape of the synesthesiac, he explained, was his, too. So he was a child prodigy, an Eno sound-alike genius, a hardcore demon, rave icon, and ambient cherub. He was suddenly so many things at once – and a voyager between the sleeping and waking worlds (like all drug shamans), too – that he seemed the best thing in town.

Critics compared Aphex to Mozart, Stockhausen, My Bloody Valentine, Velvet Underground, Eno, and Holst. His fans started to look like him; many started to make music that sounded like him. Ambient finally had its first youth cult leader, its own little antichrist. And he really did seem quite wicked at times. A subsequent (and rousingly hardcore) track "Come to Daddy" reveals him vocalizing, "I want your soul." Such an intriguing boy, Aphex, he seemed pretender to both Eno's petal-soft crown and Marilyn Manson's satanic throne. In fact, and perhaps we'd better just whisper the word, all things added up; he was perfectly and brilliantly pop.

Ambient had to wait seventeen years for its first pop star, its first rock 'n' roll pinup. And the combined effect of all this wizardry was to cast a spell over Aphex Twin that nothing could break. He would DJ with sandpaper instead of vinyl, grow a beard that made him ugly, and sing like a twisted, malformed brat of his desire to drink milk from "the milkman's wife's tits." His fans only loved him all the more. He was so avant-garde, so terrifying, so unpredictable. The eternal child, a modern Syd Barrett. Many resent him and find him churlish, they wonder about the balance between talent, hype, and immaturity in his work. But he's still there, still fanaticized, still popular, and still rising. The spell holds.

Beyond our famous magicians there are, of course, the lesser-known stories of ambience. There are the histories and desires that created ambient dub, ambient techno, ambient house, ambient trance, ambient In the images of exotica and easy listening (an as-yet unnamed sub-genre), ambient jungle, and on and on without end. And whenever ambient is discussed, many will claim that it's family-tree stretches back in time to include Terry Riley, LaMonte Young, Eric Satie, John Cage, *musique concrète*, Jamaican dub, Tangerine Dream, and Krautrock. For a brief moment, ambient is the most exciting music around, threatening to swallow all other musics whole. But in the end, the tables are turned, and all other musics absorb ambient instead. By 1994, ambient is almost a dirty word. Maybe our wizards succeeded in that their ideas now move like spirits through many other records. Perhaps that's the best they could have hoped for. What they leave behind continues to entrance the modern world – a confused but intriguing blueprint, a few glittering and dreamlike fragments

I color "silences" in different layers. So if I take off one of the silent layers, I hear another silent layer. And then I take that second layer and I hear a third one, because there is no absolute silence in the world. I am still trying to expand this relation between nothing and something. **KARLHEINZ STOCKHAUSEN** When the music gets harder and harder, people inevitably burn out and try to go in softer, more chilled-out directions. People who had originally been into house music complained that the music was becoming heavy metal techno. I think that's when you had the whole movement towards ambient techno and electronic listening music. **SIMON REYNOLDS**

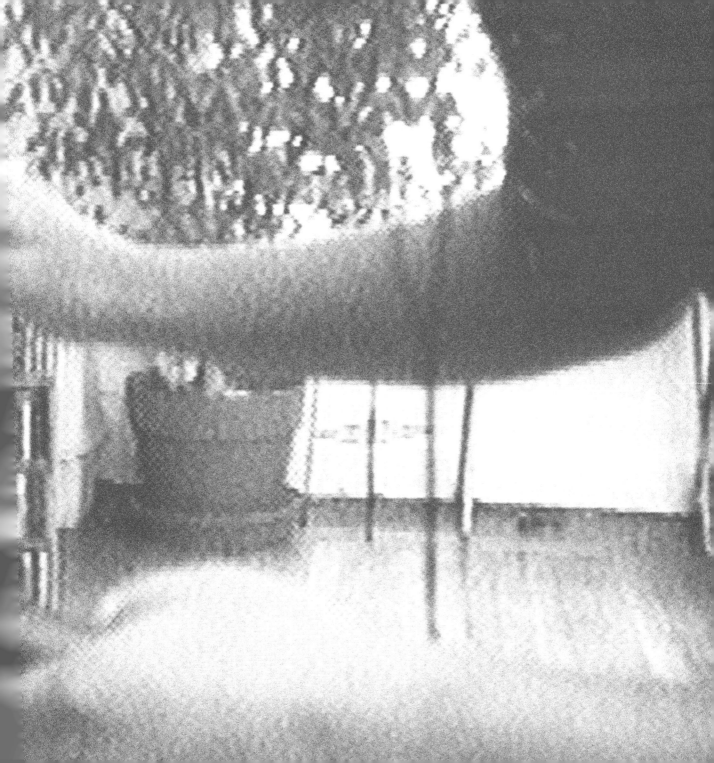

There's the punk rock part of me that says property is theft and everything should be free for everybody and there should be no such thing as copyright. But as someone who has to eat, as a musician, I do kind of enjoy the benefits of selling records and getting publishing royalties. I'm torn between those different things. **MOBY**

10

DOWNTEMPO

LOST IN MUSIC

BY KURT B. REIGHLEY

DJ FOOD

Discography:			
	APHEX TWIN	*Selected Ambient Works '85-'92*	R&S 1992
		Selected Ambient Works Volume II	Warp/Sire/Warner Bros. 1994
		I Care Because You Do	Warp/Sire 1995
	AUTECHRE	*Incunabula*	Warp/Wax Trax!/TVT 1993
		Amber	Warp/Wax Trax!/TVT 1994
		Tri Repetae++	Warp/Wax Trax!/TVT 1995
		Chiastic Slide	Warp 1997
		Autechre	Warp/Nothing 1998
	THE BLACK DOG	*Spanners*	EastWest/Warp 1995
	BOARDS OF CANADA	*Music Has the Right to Children*	Skam/Warp/Matador 1998
	MICROSTORIA	*init ding*	Mille Plateau/Thrill Jockey 1996
		_snd	Mille Plateau/Thrill Jockey 1996
		Reprovisers	Thrill Jockey 1997
	MOUSE ON MARS	*Vulvaland*	Too Pure/American 1994
		Iaora Tahiti	Too Pure/American 1995
		Autoditacker	Thrill Jockey 1997
	OVAL	*Systemisch*	Mille Plateau/Thrill Jockey 1996
		94diskont	Mille Plateau/Thrill Jockey 1996
		Dok	Mille Plateau/Thrill Jockey 1998
	PLAID	*Not For Threes*	Warp/Nothing 1998
	POLYGON WINDOW	*Surfing on Sine Waves*	Warp/Wax Trax!/TVT 1993
	ROBIN RIMBAUD	*The Garden Is Full of Metal*	Sub Rosa 1997
	SCANNER	*Delivery*	Rawkus 1995
		Sound For Spaces	Sub Rosa 1998
	TERRE THAEMLITZ	*Tranquilizer*	Instinct 1994
		Soil	Instinct 1995
		Couture Cosmetique	Caipirinha 1997
	VARIOUS ARTISTS	*Artificial Intelligence*	Warp/Wax Trax!/TVT 1993

Warp Records saved me from becoming a bitter curmudgeon living in a refrigerator box. It's true. In the mid-nineties, pop music nearly got me evicted. Not because I was playing my tunes too loudly and offending my neighbors' delicate ears. Actually, I had scant desire to play records at all. So discouraged was I by the narrow cycles in which the medium repeated and fed on itself that my writing was becoming joyless and flat. Which meant editors lost interest in publishing me, and meeting the rent became a Herculean task. Even when an artist or sound that fundamentally excited me emerged, I would painstakingly compare it against what had gone before. Records that pleased me on a visceral level were ruthlessly broken down to their base elements. I took inventory as new genres quickly deteriorated into another series of clichés.

Now, I could lie and say that the seminal *Artificial Intelligence* compilation on Sheffield's Warp label delighted my discerning critical ears immediately. The truth lies farther off, though. Other colleagues were dropping names like Richard James (Aphex Twin, Polygon Window, The Dice Man), Autechre, and Black Dog, all of whom appeared on the *Artificial Intelligence* disc; I simply investigated. Warp understood that the vitality of house and techno was rapidly diminishing due to the increasing output of interchangeable tracks that simply rearranged codified gestures: Roland TR-808 and TB-303 squalls, hyperspeed piano riffs, wailing divas cut free from long lyrical passages. The U.K. pop charts were dizzy with short-lived hits from rave staples like Moby, Altern-8, Quadrophonia, and Digital Orgasm. "Charly," the chart-topping single by Prodigy, had spawned a mess of hardcore knockoffs that fused children's tv themes with ham-fisted drug references. Warp promised more than a fleeting rush, promoting a stable of career artists who traded in intricate, subtle works that eschewed

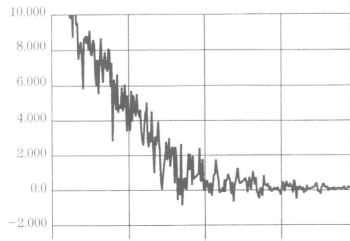

instant gratification.

The idea of tracks composed with contemplative private consumption – and not communal sharing amongst sweaty ravers – in mind delighted my misanthropic side. Here was music born of the techniques and technology of dance culture, yet decidedly anti-dance in execution. In retrospect, promoting "intelligent techno" as post-rave music – for when the conscious mind still craves aural stimulation but the exhausted body has lost the will to dance – missed the point. This music wasn't intended for consumption on the physical plane. The shifting meters and angular rhythms of such offerings discouraged dancing as recreational release. By the very nature of their complexity, the meticulously programmed arrangements of Richard James or Autechre or subsequent luminaries like Luke Vibert (Plug, Wagon Christ)

and Mike Paradinas (µ-Ziq) defy execution in real time by flesh-and-blood players. There was no need to leave the confines of one's own head to appreciate *Artificial Intelligence* to the fullest.

But at first, I hated most of what I heard. "Telefone" by Musicology suggested something previously unimaginable: anemic Kraftwerk. The Dice Man's "Polygon Window" arranged a series of simple gestures with no concern for set structure or harmony. "Crystel" by Autechre, reminded me of a discarded Depèche Mode b-side I'd once owned that featured only metal percussion sounds, albeit minus the underlying pop ditty. The character of these cuts smacked of "minimalism" and "microtonality," concepts I'd already dismissed as arbitrary schools of thought developed by young composers desperate to obscure their failure to master Western classical traditions (without losing their grants).

   Pop music had to follow strict harmonic and structural guidelines before being mass-marketed. Despite stylistic idiosyncrasies, rock 'n' roll, dub reggae, and hip-hop was still easily measured with yardsticks of harmony, context and form. I accepted expressive nuances like blue notes and poor diction as part of the pop lexicon because I could identify how the "true" pitches or words were supposed to sound. Whatever Warp was peddling, it was decidedly not pop music, and thus not for me.

   Autechre's second album, *Amber* (Warp, 1994), proved my undoing. Although the individual sounds the duo of Rob Brown and Sean Booth deployed recalled vintage New Romantic and electro tracks in tandem with their rejection of any traditional order – hummable tunes, toe-tapping rhythms – these timbres underscored how inorganic this music was. Melodies unspooled erratically, as if following free will, while bite-sized figures or percussive patterns lacking discernable meters crisscrossed underneath. I couldn't make heads or tails of this music, let alone distill any of it into evocative prose, but since it refused to slot easily into my system of carefully ordered values, it probably merited exposure. Thus Autechre's poor Rob Brown endured a series of banal, misguided inquiries about the influence of electro and hip-hop on the pair's aesthetic (conveniently overlooking the key role of hip-hop in aligning pop traditions with electronic innovators like Cage, Stockhausen, and Berio).

   Still, *Amber* and its predecessor, *Incunabula* (Warp, 1993), remained in heavy rotation. The absence of familiar structures and sounds in these albums began to taste so refreshing when contrasted with the bland, inter-

changeable offerings that composed the bulk of my listening diet. Select releases by Aphex Twin, Black Dog,
Terre Thaemlitz, and others crept into my collection.
These were titles that were typically promoted to the
general public as "ambient," yet that failed to provoke
the kind of placid reactions embryonic hours whiled
away in chill-out rooms had conditioned me to expect.

Back then, such artists were designated "intelligent
techno" by the press. At around the same time, labels
like Ninja Tune and Mo' Wax were mining similar veins,
albeit with hip-hop, not techno, as ground zero. Artists
like Coldcut, DJ Food, DJ Shadow, and DJ Krush fur-
thered this revolution of the mind by stripping hip-hop of
its puffed-up b-boy adrenaline and insisting that the only
dancing would be done in your head. Nowadays, some
critics lump Autechre and Aphex Twin – plus others like

Oval, Scanner, Boards of Canada, Microstoria, and Plaid
– and their labels (Warp, Mille Plateaux) under the banner "electro-acoustic" music. But aside from being filed
in the same meager section of my specialty record store,
the only common denominators apparent to me between
these artists were the conventions they rejected: traditional harmonic progressions, repetitive melodies, and
easily identified timbres (to say nothing of recognizable
performers and extravagant concerts). In short, all the
essential elements to which my emotional responses
were preprogrammed.

I grew up listening to Broadway cast albums, Disney
soundtracks, and lots of AM radio: Steve and Eydie,
"Tomorrow," and selections from *A Chorus Line*.
Countless hours were passed singing the score of *South
Pacific* and dancing on the sofa. Long before I understood

or questioned why, pleasing music followed certain rules: Playing middle C and G above it on our piano sounded pretty, while middle C against F-sharp did not. Disruptive rhythms were the exclusive property of Leonard Bernstein musicals, and even the complexities of *West Side Story* were revealed eventually. Through a series of naive accidents, classical music became my major in college. My instinctive knowledge of harmony proved woefully insufficient when we began studying advanced theory. But I met the challenge. Like Bernstein before them, even compositions by Varèse and Górecki that did my head in on records made sense (at least theoretically) when studied closely via printed scores. By breaking down symphonies and operas into numeric intervals and harmonic relationships sanctioned by centuries of repetition, compositions I instinctively appreciated dissolved into

something I studiously despised: math.

Still, after graduation, I could discuss Skinny Puppy in terms typically reserved for Schubert and Schoenberg. Since magazines would pay me to do so in print, thus averting a life wasted slinging hash (or worse, singing in regional opera companies), I happily became a pop music critic. With each record or concert review written, I reinforced biases about the importance of following rules of timbre, form, and context while cultivating a rebellious image by championing those who pushed the parameters – but only in the most conservative fashion conceivable.

When I hit that brick wall that almost landed me on the sidewalk, Autechre and their antecedents provided an exciting respite because their records completely eluded my grasp. They beckoned me to explore unknown territory, to take a busman's holiday from my well-traveled beat. Records like Robin Rimbaud's *The Garden Is Full of Metal* (Sub Rosa, 1997) or Microstoria's *_snd* (Mille Plateaux/Thrill Jockey, 1996) transcend short attention spans precisely because they reject, or meticulously subvert, traditions ingrained in the hard drives of kids raised by the radio.

Just in time, too. The era where consumers are limited to a finite number of emotional reactions triggered by fixed cues within a recorded document is drawing to a close. Soon, listeners won't respond to music that remains static; sounds will be arranged by responding to us individually. Software engineered to create original, fluid compositions dictated predominantly by the variable tastes of the user already exists. By eschewing centuries of established Western music traditions, "electro-acoustic" artists are preparing us for the next wave. Their creations manipulate the fundamental components of music in such minute detail as to obliterate all familiar landmarks.

I'm not advocating a complete overthrow of conventional tonality tomorrow. The notion of Madonna trying to reinvent herself as the next Cathy Berberian is profoundly distressing. Still, when an album like Boards of Canada's debut, *Music Has the Right to Children* (Skam/Warp, 1998), lands in my lap and defies me to pigeonhole its polychromatic tones, I smile. You can't sing along to these records, or even pinpoint melodies to whistle, but you can still lose yourself on the sofa, lost once more in glorious sound.

Enticing others to join in this reverie, however, rarely occurs easily, especially in my work. All modes of communication, from smoke signals to digital to "electro-acoustic" music possess some sort of underlying intention. But when a mode of communication is unfamiliar, learning to discern and interpret this intention can be an arduous – and occasionally hilarious – process.

If you've ever contemplated the quiet murmur of computers in an empty office and fantasized they're communicating like whales via songs that elude our ears, the art of Microstoria will transfix you upon first listen. Mechanical clicks and hums and metallic drones like fading bell echoes are fashioned into warm aural arrays that resemble conventional music only in two apparent regards: the results are pleasant to listen to and preserved on compact disc.

I discovered Microstoria in 1996. Unlike in the sound or history of Richard James or Autechre, tangential connections between Microstoria and the rave scene didn't seem to exist; this surpassed "intelligent techno." Since the timbres at play were completely unfamiliar, there were no distracting visual counterparts to contend with. The generator of these alien noises eluded imagination. The ears focused solely on the subtle sonic morphing as frequencies modulated, effects shaded tones, and shifting forms emerged.

Investigation revealed that Microstoria was a project of Germany's Markus Popp, who first attracted attention as Oval by manipulating the surfaces of compact discs with scratches or paint and sampling the subsequent audio outcome, then looping and processing those materials to create disquieting records like *systemisch* and *94diskont*. In collaboration with Jan St. Werner (of Mouse On Mars), Microstoria crafts deceptively complex yet soothing tracks engineered to expose the internal workings of electronic music and to prompt meditation on how organized sound functions in the digital age.

If new music of this stripe confounds you, Popp isn't an ideal candidate to consult for demystification. The very name Microstoria, a term derived from academic theory and referring to historical information divined through the analysis of documents that recount the daily

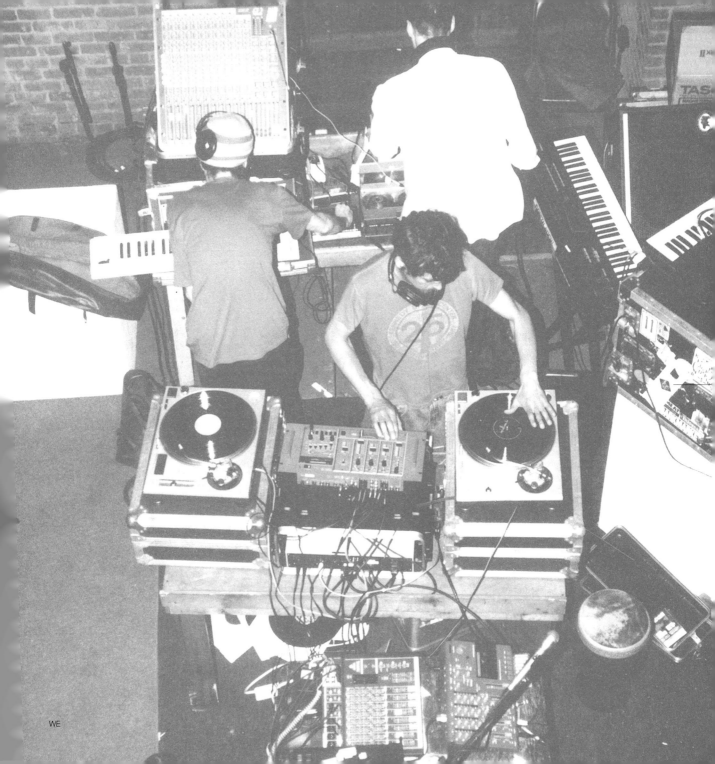

activities of ordinary individuals, should be sufficient warning. When I initiated an e-mail correspondence with him concerning the making of Microstoria's sophomore album, _snd, the twisted syntax of his answers suggested an unfinished chapter sketch from *Alice in Wonderland*.

Deciphering Popp's explanations of the intricate "blend of systems-theory awareness with consumerist criticism" underpinning Popp and St. Werner's works made my head hurt. If Microstoria's creative process was as intuitive as he claimed, the opposing impulses it contained made its genesis impossible to wrestle into the restrictive harness of plain English. Then, slowly, a revelation unfolded. The charm of the group's work lay outside of constrictive linear forms such as written language.

Popp said that rather than "reifying the notion of the artist in charge of technology," both Oval and Microstoria (to varying degrees) saw it "as their obligation to point to other, more problematic factors while working with digital, real-time types of musical interfaces. As soon as one starts working according to digital music media instead of following worn-out concepts like creativity and invention, these interfaces immediately introduce multiple time modes, contingency-on-the-spot, and a complex, challenging workflow."

Listening without associations, however, did indeed seem to be the desired outcome once the duo's handiwork was unleashed. Generating the specific sounds deployed on their records constitutes the chief focus of their production processes. Popp explained how the team, using advanced digital technology, arranged the audio components "not only acoustically, but also in terms of visual orientation," utilizing graphic user interfaces that permitted "structural access to the sampled/processed material in unprecedented detail." "In my opinion, the concept of 'music' itself is almost tragically overshadowed by assumed notions of creativity, authorship, and artistic expression. Every effort in the music field gets judged as mainly stemming from the artist as a creative person," Popp said. In this dawning age of digital music, this misses the point entirely.

I wasn't shocked to subsequently read that Popp has been fine-tuning software that will permit consumers to take any audio source material they choose, then hear it played back after a radical makeover via his various customized processing techniques. Such a tool would eliminate the traditional role of an artist who is

celebrated for creating an individual work or profiled by the press.

Sitting at an outdoor café on New York's Lafayette Street, an elfin man animatedly sorts through booty from a ninety-nine cent store he's just raided. That's my first recollection of Robin Rimbaud, alias Scanner. Based on his thick press kit, reducing Rimbaud to a thumbnail sketch had been simple: the classic "telephone terrorist," straight-up with a twist of black humor, a po'-faced loner who insists that his art eschew any emotional content. Yet here he was finding glee in cheap plastic bric-a-brac.

After months of conditioning myself to empty my mind of all associations when analyzing electronic music not created for the dancefloor (a challenge akin to thinking of nothing during transcendental meditation), Rimbaud gutted that misconception like tuna for sushi

and reduced me to giggles.

As Rimbaud outlined the role of the radio scanner on his imminent Scanner disc, *Delivery* (Rawkus, 1996), on which he integrates conversations plundered from the ether with original electronic compositions, a new appreciation crept over me. So long as a human being arbitrates the content of a work of art, it can't help but include subconscious or deliberate attempts to influence the listener's response. Scanner can't precisely choreograph what sounds will dart across the data stream when he casts his net, but how he manipulates his catch – and what he tosses back – is an inextricable part of the process.

"My work is in part about memory and recording certain moments or spaces in time and capturing them for others to interpret," he later wrote in the liner notes

COLDCUT

to the Scanner anthology *Sound for Spaces* (Sub Rosa, 1998). Rimbaud's recordings and performances acknowledge the mutability of everything that exists as pure data. Nowhere is that more evident than on *The Garden Is Full of Metal*, his 1997 homage to his friend Derek Jarman.

Visionary British artist Derek Jarman, who died of AIDS in 1994, is celebrated for his work as a painter, a filmmaker, a writer, and a designer. But he first entered my consciousness thanks to a U.K. pop phenomenon. Infatuated with the music (and cheekbones and derrière) of Adam Ant, I'd sought out Jarman's 1978 feature *Jubilee*, in which the singer played a small role. Though the absence of a clear narrative, coupled with my ignorance of English history, rendered the film impenetrable to me, Jarman's exploitation of vibrant tableaux and loud

music struck home with my adolescent sensibilities.

Jarman's ability to move between disciplines proved inspirational for many. While in London in 1996, I took in the Jarman retrospective at the Barbican Art Gallery. "Perhaps he wasn't a 'great' painter, in the sense that he didn't redirect the course of visual art," I recorded in my journal. "But he certainly was a brilliant artist, very much in the flow of the creative spirit. There were moments when I was looking at his works, and I could feel my soul opening up, as in that moment when one is aware of taking an especially deep breath."

Coincidentally, the first sound of Rimbaud's audio portrait of Jarman is the subject's labored inhalation on "Open." *The Garden Is Full of Metal* echoes the director's refusal to compartmentalize his art by treating all sonic components as fair game. Rimbaud called the raw materials "sound polaroids." Snapshot recordings of interviews, crunching footsteps on the stones in Jarman's celebrated Dungeness garden, and traffic outside his London flat were woven together with discrete original passages. Rimbaud specifically treated the materials "through modest means, cutting, stretching, and editing tape," so as not to obscure his inspiration. The resulting tracks, crisp with texture, evoked a sense of place without depicting a specific locale, reflecting Jarman's own aesthetic as expressed in his landscape paintings and films like The Garden.

"If only memory responded like a computer, constantly retrievable and recoverable, whereas in reality it is inconsistent and changes focus at the most surreal whim," Rimbaud had lamented earlier in the year to the Wire. Yet with The Garden Is Full of Metal, he created a fluid work that acknowledged how an artist's greatest achievements often transpire in the individual psyche of each observer. While the final document didn't record a specific event, it nodded backward to the physical realm of traditional music (via organizing identifiable sounds), yet set them in an open-ended program shaped by the cut-copy-paste practices of the information age. Neatly bridging this gap between schools of thought, Rimbaud had created a fitting tribute.

How appropriate that my next encounter with Autechre took place at a French restaurant. For five years, I'd fumbled to translate their music into language, even as they moved further into their own private realms. Detailing their discography for a fanzine a year before had proved phenomenally challenging, but engaging in conversation with them – especially since they were native speakers – seemed a fraction less daunting. Sean Booth and Rob Brown answered questions concerning their eponymous fifth album (Warp/Nothing, 1998) in overlapping exchanges peppered with wit. The sentences I was forming with words I barely grasped felt foreign in my mouth, but we actually engaged in a dialogue, not a labored Q&A session.

The fundamental distinctions between the new album and its predecessor, Chiastic Slide (Warp, 1997), hinged on software, Booth explained. "A lot of the melodies, and stuff was from using things that we'd made, rather than things that [other] people had made. We were coming to terms with having a blank sheet of paper in a lot of ways." Now the duo could shape their materials in greater detail than ever before. In the past, they'd maintained a keen focus on hardware and their instruments, keeping one foot firmly in the Old World. "To approach the software side of it was a total breath of fresh air," admitted Brown. "Yet it was something we've been inclined to do for ten, fifteen years already."

"303s and 606s are amazing," added Booth, acknowledging their limitations and associations. "The aesthetic of using those two machines together is totally beautiful. But things get really interesting when you've got the opportunity to create your own environment in which to work, because obviously the aesthetic is completely under your control."

As the partners lapped up bowls of vibrant orange carrot soup, I confessed how much their records meant to me, how charting their evolution had freed me from my rigid world of strict meters and even temperament. They chuckled at the fact that classical theory had long been such a monkey on my back. "That's because we don't know any," snickered Brown.

"Our mate Tom Jenkinson, who records under the name Squarepusher, is self-taught, but pretty well-taught at the same time," Booth told me. "And he reckons the same thing we do: Either you know everything, or you know nothing. There is no in-between. It's in the in-between that people fall over." Until you've assimilated enough of the system to thoroughly subvert it, the benefits are limited. Autechre approached theory from the opposite direction. "We started with nothing and collected things along the way." But even they use numeric representation for pitches and rhythms, he revealed. Math again. "An interval's an interval at the end of the day."

Grasping for validation, I inquired about synesthesia – the subjective sensation of a sense other than the one being stimulated – as a tool for discussing compositions that move beyond Western traditions. Autechre's music begs to be discussed in tactile terms ("a needle skating across a sandpaper slipmat") far more than any other sense. Acknowledging that this is something of a moot point to them, they entertained the topic nonetheless.

"Chords always seem to have some sort of coloration, and rhythm always has some sort of dynamic shape, a curve," admitted Booth. "Curves and straight lines are always apparent. There are very definite parallels." Such as the topographical images on the covers of *Amber* and the *Cichlisuite* EP, or in their visual remixes under the Gescom moniker, altering color, space relations, etc. in graphic works. Like many of their contemporaries – Markus Popp sculpting minute sonic details by honing representative images on his computer screen, Robin Rimbaud evoking a filmmaker's tableaux with environmental sounds – Autechre was redefining how visual and textural elements can function in a "pure" musical context. "We're quite interested in architecture generally," Booth continued. "Actually moving through spaces. The experience of moving through an interesting or well-made space, rather than just being in it and seeing pictures."

"Just turning a still space into a transitional space," added Brown. "Yet it's only transitional because your point of reference is in transition." An obvious parallel, they noted, to their ceaseless fascination with the relationship between time and music.

"The process of something completely changing, all the time, as you move through it," said Sean. "Your sense of it is changing."

It became apparent that there was little point in seeking commandments carved in stone from the men who'd bestowed this music upon me. "We're driven by a childlike fascination and a total curiosity," insisted Booth, struggling not to simplify matters too much. "A love for an aesthetic, without really understanding why."

Perhaps, in the end, that's the ideal position, suggested Brown, offering an illustration. "Take an old electro record, like [Man Parrish's] 'Hip-Hop Be Bop (Don't Stop).' That aesthetic has been with me for years, from not understanding it at all, but just learning it as a presentation of sound. And, fifteen years later, I know exactly what they're doing, and when and why. Well, maybe not why, but how. And that record still spins me out. Now I've got these two ways of viewing it, but I prefer the first one." ✿

I've always used voices in my work. Ever since the earliest age when I was about thirteen or fourteen and used to play around with tape recorders. I always used human voices. I would record my family, my friends on the school bus, and this kind of thing. And as the years went by, I always was looking for a better means of recording voices. I would have a walk-man record people on the underground, on the buses and the street as I walked along. In taxis and so on. And then when I came across the scanner device about five or six years ago, it was a means of entering a very vulnerable intimate space without somebody knowing, achieving the ability to actually find a very clear sound, a very clear signal, and hear people that were not aware they were being listened to so they would talk in a very comfortable and very easy way. I take small samples, small snatches from the atmosphere, from the radio waves around us. As I sit here now, we're surrounded by radio waves. All the sounds, even just me moving my hands, create radio waves. And using the scanner device, it accesses this space, this kind of environmental sound. It plucks them down. What I do, using digital technology, using the sampler, using a computer, is process these sounds. I slow them down, speed them up; I'll reverse them, pitch-change them. I use the most banal, basic sound. I'm not interested in public security in the sense of not being interested in people talking about great financial things. I'm interested in people talking about very interesting but banal simple things. Like. "Would you like to go out for a drink?" Relationship problems. Shopping. These kind of things, situations in the simplest way that we've all been in. Situations that you can empathize with and understand in some way. I like to use really low-tech technology to be quite honest. I like using walkmans. I like using very, very cheap material and bastardizing it in some sense. To abuse it. I don't mean that in such a cruel way. But really to push it to its limits. Tape recorders are wonderful devices. William Burroughs is an example: Back in the late fifties, he recorded all these cut-ups. And they're all just on a basic reel-to-reel recorder. Just with a pair of scissors and some cellutape, he made these wonderful collages of different sounds and different environ-

.

mental voices and so on. And that's what I try to use now. So I try not to let the technology lead me. I try to work the other way around in some sense. Sampling and the recontextualization of sound and image and so on is so important in our culture today: It's something we fail to realize sometimes. I think that the problem with music is that record companies get very heavy about it. And they really feel that they own that piece of music in a sense. And they really become so intrigued and so fascinated by these dollars signs and pound signs it becomes quite disturbing. I myself was caught in a legal situation with an artist a few years ago... I really wish in my heart of hearts that what we could have would be to treat music like a science. You take a bit of research from here, a bit of research from over here. You put it together, and you create something new. We've done that with the sciences for years. A scientist doesn't say, "That was my research. You can't use that," with a development towards resolving a problem with HIV and so on. That's the way it's worked for years. With music it can't be like that. It's like, "We own this sound." For me personally, the work that's interested me over the years has been everything from the work of Duchamp and Dada and so on. I like taking these kind of Dada elements and throwing these quirky voices into this collage soundtrack and seeing what comes out at the end of the day. Copyright is such a major issue. I think we all have rights in our own way. You have your own individual rights. I believe in manners, I believe in good manners. So I think a polite thing would be if somebody samples you, just to send you a copy of the work in question for your records or whatever. Or to maybe ask you about it, if it's a major release. Just to say, "Is this okay with you?" At the same time, I really like the liberating thought of being able to take sound from everywhere, images from everywhere, and creating something new and presenting it. Recontextualizing it and presenting a new work to an audience who can see it in a new way. Basically, I have a very, very small studio. My studio is nothing. It's not like a professional music studio or anything. It's like a mixing desk with a sampler and a couple of effects units. I take very raw material. I take very basic sounds. Where I live at the moment in London, I have, it's like a building site almost, next to me, where they've knocked down the building outside my window. So I've been recording with a microphone out the window and recording that sound. All the building work that's going on. And processing that sound and mixing it into my life environment. I was very liberated by the ideas by John Cage where he talked about you embracing your environment. So if you're trying to work, and you're trying to write or make a film or something, and you hear these sounds in the background, you have to accept the fact that this is part of the situation you're in. It's that environment, whether for good or bad. It's reflective of that situation. And so when I produce my work and in live performances, I've talked about "sound polaroids." I talked about this work being very reflective of that local environment. It's a kind of invisible map of the city. So when I perform in New York, for example, the soundtrack you hear, the voices and the sounds are reflective of that area. And when I perform in Lithuania or Russia or Poland, the sounds I use are the local voices and accents. I think it's important for people to recognize pointers, signals almost, of their own history, their own existence, their own narrative. I like playing with all kinds of sounds. Whether it's taking a sound and processing it and making something quite abstract out of it, making a very rhythmic piece, and so on. I'm also very interested in melancholia. I like very romantic music. So, on a recent record, *Delivery*, what I've tried to do is produce pieces that really move you in a very emotional sense that actually — tacky way to put it — they kind of break your heart in some sense. Using technology and using these machines that people say are very digital, very cold basic data, but producing something that actually moves you in such a physical and emotional way, I think is really important. So I'm trying to give it some kind of life, to humanize it in some way perhaps. Improvisation is really important. It's the work I do. I've released a number of live recordings that are these ideas – these sound polaroids, these invisible maps of the city – and it's really important for me to release this kind of work. I became very interested in performance art when I was a student. I was very intrigued because you weren't a passive viewer just looking at a painting on the wall; you were engaged in a process where the artist was there in person. This was the person who was actually creating the work. It existed for that moment in time only. Photographs could be taken, documentation would exist with text and video and so on, and sound recording... The thing that fascinates me about virtualization of culture, this almost invisible culture, is the fact that when I record, for example, I record at home. I sometimes take digital information off a sampler, I record something into a sampler. When it's in the sampler, I become God very briefly. I'm playing with time, and I can put the sound up. You know, you have an image of the sound, and what intrigues me is the fact that, for that moment in time, you have such power. You can move forward in time and you can go back in time. And where the cursor is, where your mouse is at that very point, is now. It's real time. But then you can go back and you can go forward. But it's digital information, it's zeroes and ones. Then it goes onto a DAT tape, so it's never real; at this point, it's even less real. It's still zeroes and ones. Comes out on compact disc, and in some way, it's never actually existed. It's really funny. So I've released recordings that in fact don't exist. And I love this kind of idea, that these things in a sense are just zeroes and ones. And I get the feeling if you had a decoder set next to a cd player, you could decode it and nothing would exist again. ✺

I don't believe in copyright. I think everything should be free. I don't believe in someone owning a group of notes. If someone stole something that I said I'd written – well, I probably didn't write it anyway. I probably subconsciously transferred it from another memory or another time. I would never sue someone over a sample or even an entire piece of music. It's different when you consider yourself a composer and you think everything springs from your mind – you're using a tired sort of system to do it, where the piano is your instrument, and your mind is the conductor. You're creating composition. People who think that way would be very upset if someone stole an entire piece of music. **BILL LASWELL**

11

The first person to use amplification was Adolph Hitler. Public address systems were developed by the Nazis and are essentially fascist in nature. Hitler was the first person to speak to a million people at once. **MIXMASTER MORRIS** We want to lie down and let the machines get on with it. We want to slack off a bit. We've got the acronym DNA-ROM which stands for "do no art – run our machine." **MATT BLACK (COLDCUT)** Our sampler has a software glitch. If you put the loop position back into minus figures something really weird happens and all the samples kind of get folded up. They sort of all fold into each other and make new sounds. It's really totally bizarre. **AUTECHRE**

TECHNOLOGY

ANALOG FETISHES AND DIGITAL FUTURES

BY MIKE BERK

0.3 mm
Correction

0°
+Azimuth

20°
−Azimuth

0.5 mm

Rotary head
scanning
direction

Guard band

Optional track II

Tape transport direction

Margin
5.051° × 2

SUB
5.05° × 2

ATF
2.296° × 2

PCM
59.63°

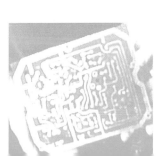

Electronic instruments have been with us for a century now. The unruly early years of electronic music gave rise to a menagerie of bizarre beasts, many designed not only with an ear toward producing new sounds, but with an interest in overcoming traditional modes of instrumental performance. The two-hundred-ton telharmonium transmitted electronic sound over telephone lines while the ribbon controllers of the *ondes martenot* and trautonium gave keyboardists access to the continuous control of pitch and volume enjoyed by vocalists. One of these alternative musical devices, the theremin, played by moving one's hands through the air surrounding a couple of electrostatic antennae, captured the minds of a generation of hobbyists, but most of these instruments disappeared in favor of a few more easily marketable designs. The familiar-sounding (and recognizably keyboard-oriented) Hammond electronic organ locked up the professional market. Massive modular synthesizers, capable of a vast range of audio output but generally triggered by programmed sequencers (recorders of events rather than audio, they were latter-day electronic heirs to the punched-paper rolls that drove player pianos) came to dominate the lab-coated practice of "serious" electronic music.

Meanwhile, the foundations of the recording studio were being established. The recording and playback of sound using a magnetic medium passing over electromagnetic heads was first conceived of in the late 1880s by engineer and theorist Oberlin Smith, and experimental devices, beginning with Valdemar Poulsen's 1898 telegraphone, began to appear around the turn of the century. Commercial models – generally wire recorders that used steel tape as a recording medium – began to emerge at the end of the 1920s. Much of the developmental work on magnetic tape was done in Germany in the late 1930s, and the metal-oxide-coated plastic tape that would become the standard recording medium didn't appear until after World War II. In 1949, stereo recording and the cut-and-splice technique of tape editing emerged, and by the middle of the 1950s, sound-on-sound overdubbing had evolved and the first multitrack recorders began to appear. For composers like *musique concrète* pioneers Pierre Schaeffer and Pierre Henry working with room-filling modular synths and non-instrumental natural sound sources, the arrival of tape made it possible to "perform" electronic works without lugging around tons of gear. The so-called "tape piece" became the prevalent form of electronic music expres-

sion through the 1960s, and along the way, innovators like John Cage and Karlheinz Stockhausen made tape editing and processing art forms in themselves. By the mid-sixties multitrack recording had become widespread. The recording studio existed in more or less its present-day form, and tape editing had become accepted (or at least acknowledged) as part of the creative process of popular music and jazz. This set the stage for dub, ambient, and other mutative studio musics to come.

The synthesizer as we know it today – a keyboard-triggered device designed for use by professional musicians on stage and in commercial recording studios rather than an assemblage of independent modules aimed at academic composers and sound designers working in university labs or specialized research institutes – dates from 1970. That year, electronics innovator and sometime theremin builder Robert Moog released the Minimoog. As the first portable, affordable, and really popular synth, the Minimoog made "synthesist" a viable job description, and the world of popular music was never quite the same again. The Minimoog and its immediate successors from ARP, Sequential Circuits, Oberheim, Korg, Roland, and a host of other companies, established the sound of analog synthesis as *the* sound of synthesis. One or more voltage-controlled oscillators kicked out audio waveforms that were subsequently shaped by a series of modifiers – filters, amplifiers, low-frequency oscillators, ring modulators, and so forth – controlled by the player via a collection of knobs, sliders, switches, buttons, and levers. The sounds they produced were lush, fat, harmonically rich, and curiously organic. The analog synth saw continuous refinement over the course of the seventies. Early monophonic synths (restricted to producing only one note at a time) gave way to polyphonic instruments that could produce chords. Memory units let players catalog their sound dis-

coveries for future use; specialized instruments like analog drum machines emerged; and performance-oriented
sequencers made it possible to recall performances
themselves. Still, the basic sound-generating concept
would endure for more than a decade.

Everything changed in 1983 when Yamaha introduced the DX7, the first commercially viable digital
synthesizer. Digital synthesis dispensed with the maze of
analog circuitry in favor of software algorithms. The new
machines were in many ways clearly superior to their
analog forebears: They significantly increased audio
quality, achieved far more accurate reproductions of
"real" instruments, and promised a near-infinite variety
of sounds. But the increased number of programming
parameters needed to access this power meant the end
of the simple, hands-on interfaces that had made analog

synths so appealing in the first place. Most players
(except for those stalwarts who found the sparkling clarity and resolutely professional high-end sheen of digital
instruments simply "cold") felt that the sacrifice was
worthwhile, and analog synthesis effectively disappeared from the face of the earth. By 1984, the infant
technology of digital sampling was beginning to produce
useful results and MIDI, the newfangled "musical instrument digital interface" that allowed synthesizers to
communicate with each other, was on the cusp of changing the way everything worked, both on stage and in the
studio. You couldn't give away an analog synthesizer –
and that's where the story gets interesting.

EVERYBODY LOVES A 303
The mid-eighties saw piles of analog gear languish-

ing in the back rooms and bargain bins of secondhand music shops across the U.S. and Europe. In and around Detroit and Chicago, a few enterprising young musicians, in pursuit of new sounds but unable to raise the cash for the DX7s then fashionable among proper studio professionals, turned to the few machines that could be had: TR-808s, TR-909s, and TB-303s from the Japanese manufacturer Roland.

Introduced in 1982, the TB-303 Bassline was originally intended as a portable accompanist for practice situations, demo recordings, and solo performances. The 303 is a stripped-down analog synth, optimized for "bass" sounds and thus offering very basic tone-shaping controls that are hitched to a similarly basic on-board sequencer. One punches in a series of notes on the 303's rudimentary keyboard, sets a desired tempo, presses play, and waits for something resembling a bassline to emerge. Given that the programming interface is free of visual aids, the process is fairly counter-intuitive, and it's absolutely impossible to reproduce either the sound or feel of a live bassist. Demand for the unit never emerged, and Roland soon discontinued it.

The TR-808 and TR-909 Rhythm Composers fared somewhat better in their day. They featured an intuitive user interface and a variety of distinctly unrealistic analog drum sounds. The 808, with its deep, resonant bass drum, thin, weightless snare, and ultrasynthetic "cowbell" beep, was one of the first successful, fully programmable drum machines. It was also the first such unit that could store an entire song (verses, choruses, and fills) rather than just patterns. It found its way onto a wide variety of records — everything from Marvin Gaye's "Sexual Healing" to the first couple of Run DMC albums — and provided the pulse for the electro era. The 909, an improvement on the 808 concept, features a more aggressive sound overall: The bass drum has a more tan-

gible, thumpy attack, and the snare is punchier. While both machines had been fairly popular, they fell out of favor as sampling drum machines like the Oberheim DMX and the LinnDrum appeared. These new boxes offered more "realistic" sounds, consigning the 808 and the 909 to the budget bins, where they joined their sibling Bassline.

House and techno had found their electric guitars. In the hands of Marshall Jefferson, Larry Heard, Juan Atkins, Derrick May, and Kevin Saunderson, the supposed faults of these machines became strengths. The difficulty of programming the TB-303 accurately made it a very democratic instrument — a novice had just as good a chance of producing a usable bassline as did an expert musician. Landmark Chicago house records like Phuture's "Acid Tracks" and Sleezy D's "I've Lost Control" - featuring distinctly unbass-like strings of random eighth notes punctuated with accents, a bit of portamento, and some seriously flatulent filter sweeps — made this buzzy, squelchy little box an object of desire once again. Since then, everybody's used one or imitated one (other Roland synths of similar vintage, especially the SH-101 and the MC-202, can be made to behave similarly) at one point or another. Jeff Mills and Richie Hawtin made the 303 essential to second-wave Detroit techno and the European subgenres that followed. Since then, trip-hop godfathers Massive Attack have even found ways to use the 303 effectively for the sort of slow, elegant basslines that its designers might have had in mind in the first place.

In search of futuristic tones, the Belleville Three (Detroit pioneers Juan Atkins, Derrick May, and Kevin Saunderson, so-named after their high school alma mater) had little interest in supposedly realistic drum sounds, and the resolutely synthy outputs of the 808 and 909 fit their needs perfectly. The four-to-the-floor groove and endless snare-roll crescendi ubiquitous in house, techno, and everything that followed come from the 808 and 909. Both machines are so widely used that it would be easier to list records that don't feature them than to even think about the immense catalog of those that do. More recently, a number of audio extremists, including Alec Empire and just about everyone involved in gabba, have discovered that the 909's nasal aggressiveness makes it a potent sonic weapon when combined with distortion from guitar stompboxes or overdriven mixer inputs.

BREAKBEAT SCIENCE

The dominant dance music subgenres of the late 1990s (trip-hop, drum and bass, big beat, and the like) are more easily defined by their studio production processes than by any readily identifiable sound sources. While no single instrument characterizes these genres the way the 303 defined acid house, they depend more heavily on technological progress than any prior post-techno music. While house and techno producers, priced out of their contemporary music technology market, looked back to older tools that had never been fully exploited, musicians involved in the newer genres are heavily invested in the cutting edge. Their radically cut-and-paste-oriented musics are predicated on the existence of studio tools that became available in the late eighties: the sampler and the digital audio workstation.

While analog tape machines record sound by magnetizing particles on a strip of plastic, digital recorders encode audio as a string of ones and zeros on hard disk or in RAM. Sampling, which involves the digital recording of short segments of audio into computer memory for instrument-like processing and playback, had been around in one form or another since the late 1970s, but affordable samplers didn't appear until the mid-eighties, with the introduction of Ensoniq's Mirage sampling key-

board. By today's standards, the recording quality was laughable, but in those days, that was characteristic even of astronomically priced professional machines like the Fairlight. The Mirage was important in that it made sampling a real possibility for struggling musicians. Like the Minimoog two decades earlier, it took a set of innovations, made them available to a broader market, and radically changed the way average musicians thought about creating music. The new science came into its own with the introduction of the quietly revolutionary Akai S1000 in 1988. It was the first reasonably priced sampler that could reproduce cd-quality audio, and it offered usable time-stretching/compression and pitch-shifting tools, along with synthesizer-like editing facilities and automated sample looping functions.

Sounds recorded on the earlier samplers were eas-ily identifiable as samples, given away by the grainy, grungy coloration their eight- and twelve-bit resolution and low sampling frequencies imparted to incoming audio. Sampling at cd specifications made the distinction between sampled sounds and original performances inaudible; with the S1000, producers could finally decide whether or not they wanted to let listeners in on their sampling secrets. It gave them control of the degree of referentiality they wanted to employ; sampled material could be represented in its original form or warped beyond recognition with onboard editing tools. An entire industry grew up solely in order to provide raw material on sample cds – preformatted cd collections of traditional and synthetic instrumental sounds and riffs (often played by well-known studio players, programmers, and jazz artists), breakbeats, sound effects, and wordless vocals.

While early, lo-fi sampling had been adequate only for special effects (the stuttering vocal samples of early hip-hop, for example), by the late eighties sampling technology had begun to dominate the electronic music production. The rise of high-quality sampling made any piece of audio a potential musical instrument. Any sound one could create, record, or borrow from someone else's recorded oeuvre could be incorporated into a sample-based composition. Producers began to work the way DJs did, digging through their record crates in search of source material. Hip-hop turntablism had found its studio counterpart, and producers like Marley Marl began to explore the new medium on groundbreaking discs like Eric B & Rakim's "Eric B is President" and MC Shan's "Kill That Noise." Pioneering audio collagists like Mantronix, along with immediate successors like Coldcut and M/A/R/R/S, began to define a style of sampling – based on funk breakbeats, obscure references, and fantastic *non sequiturs* – that would lay the groundwork for genres like trip-hop and big beat.

Most electronic dance musicians of the early nineties used the sampler mainly as a behind-the-scenes arrangement and production tool. Driven from a hardware sequencer or a software sequencing program like Steinberg's Cubase or Emagic's Logic (generally running on an Atari computer in Europe or on a Macintosh stateside), the sampler was used to build up complex arrangements using just a few electronic instruments or a couple of turntables.

From a technical perspective, this particular discipline may have reached its apotheosis with DJ Shadow's *Endtroducing*. He claims to have done *all* of the production work – tracking, mixing, and mastering – using only an Akai MPC 60II sampling workstation (a device incorporating the Akai sampling engine and a powerful multitrack sequencer). His lone sound source was a Technics turntable fed by an endless record collection. No "instruments," strictly defined, and no "studio." The work of obsessive samplists like Shadow hasn't so much reinvented the studio as a new instrument – dub producers like Lee Perry have been doing that for some thirty years now anyway – as much as it collapsed our concepts of "studio" and "instrument" into one another.

Few producers or remixers were as purist in their approach as Shadow. As computer-based digital audio workstations like Digidesign's Pro Tools began to come down in price (driven by the massive advances in personal computer processing speeds in the mid-nineties), and as the major software sequencer developers began to add audio recording and sample editing functions to their already popular products, further innovations were on the way. MIDI, the communications protocol originally conceived as a way for a single keyboardist to control stacks of sound modules, found its real calling as the organizing principle of the computer music studio, linking software-based sequencers to the hardware universe of keyboard synths, sound modules, and samplers. Digital audio workstations (virtual multitrack recording studios) and sample editing software (stereo editors optimized for working with looped audio and featuring a wide variety of signal processing tools) brought a visual dimension to audio editing. Recorded tracks were displayed as graphical waveforms, making precise editorial work markedly simpler than it had been. Previously, trimming rhythmic loops had involved a fair amount of foresight and calculation: Graphical editing let producers make decisions on the fly and brought on, for better or for worse, a period of increasingly radical (or outlandish) editorial experimentation.

While word-processor-style cut-and-paste editing, complete with "undo" function, is digital recording's most obvious advance over analog, less immediately apparent but no less important is digital's liberation of pitch from duration. In analog recording, raising the pitch of a recorded snippet requires speeding up the tape and therefore shortening the length of the snippet. This becomes a real problem in multitrack recording because audio segments can't be adjusted in pitch without ruining their synchronization with the rest of a project. Conversely, rhythmically offending segments can't be sped up or slowed down without changing their pitch, leading to some potentially sticky harmonization problems.

Taking advantage of the fact that samplers and digital recorders stored audio as infinitely mutable data, engineers set about solving this problem. They came up with time-stretching, time-compression, and pitch-shifting algorithms that were provided as quick-repair tools for difficult mixes. Featured first on high-end professional samplers and recording workstations and aimed at postproduction professionals, these tools were meant to avoid the wholesale rerecording of entire tracks simply to fix a couple of flat notes or missed rhythmic cues. It became possible to compensate for inaccurate singers and tired drummers at mix-down without spending inordinate amounts of money on overdub sessions.

The producers who would go on to develop drum and bass pushed this technology in directions its engineers had never expected. Time-stretching, time-compression, and pitch-shifting were never meant to be foregrounded as audible effects, or even to be aesthetically pleasing. They were engineered to be as inaudible as possible in operation, all the better to convince listeners that their favored diva could really get up into that altissimo range. Drum and bass innovators like Rob Playford, Dego McFarlane, and Rob Haigh dispensed with the divas (well, at least for the most part), and gave

those algorithms the spotlight. Inaugurating a veritable age of enlightenment for breakbeat science, they began experimenting with extreme and explicit pitch-shifting and time-stretching effects, transforming a few simple funk and fusion drum loops into an arsenal of humanly unplayable rhythmic motifs: snare-drum-ascending-a-staircase fills, blurry hyperspeed hi-hat grooves, and stomach-turning sub-bass kicks.

Much of their work depended on software sample editors like ReCycle, a software package developed by Swedish outfit Propellerhead Software (no, not *those* Propellerheads) and marketed by leading sequencer developer Steinberg. ReCycle analyzes a sampled drum loop that can then be chopped up into its component parts, and reassembled, spliced, appended to itself, and otherwise mangled beyond recognition, all with greater speed, precision, and ease than could be accomplished using a hardware sampler alone. It enabled drum and bass producers to piece together their mutant percussion samples into continuously shifting polyrhythmic drumscapes. Pushed beyond their design parameters, pitch-shifting and time-compression operations produced digital noise that gave the drum sounds their characteristic hiss and crisp artificiality. While some popular breakbeats (the Winston's "Amen," for instance) have become clichés, radical digital mutations more often than not transform the source materials beyond easy recognition. Plenty of drum and bass records even employ the supposedly orthodox techno tones of 808s and 909s, but the results rarely resemble anything the Belleville Three might consider kosher.

At the end of the 1990s, the drum and bass commu-

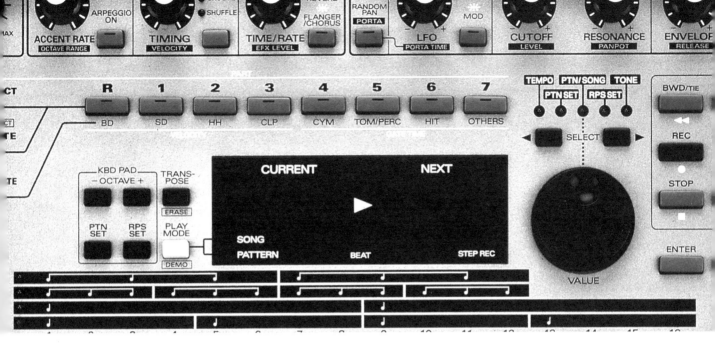

nity has drifted into a dangerous flirtation with traditional studio values, with producers waxing poetic about their Aphex Aural Exciters, SPL Vitalizers, and TC Electronic Finalizers (high-end psychoacoustic processors that impart a polished, professional sheen to finished mixes). While many drum and bass luminaries have flirted with the dubious pleasures of Yellowjackets- and Spyro Gyra-informed fuzak, under this sort of studio pressure, a generalized Steely Dan glassiness threatens the genre itself.

ANALOG FETISHISM AND THE DIGITAL FUTURE

It's worth keeping in mind that electronic instruments are potentially just as uninteresting as electric guitars. No matter how complex and automated they become, synthesizers and samplers simply offer an alter- native set of sound possibilities; whether that potential is realized is ultimately the musician's decision. It's the electronic music studio – instruments, processing gear, and recording and editing equipment – that inaugurates a new sonic paradigm, confounding our standard definitions of what "instruments," "composition," and "recording" are. That's the real legacy of bands like Kraftwerk and their Detroit inheritors. While their pop contemporaries looked only to incorporate electronic sounds into the "realistic" audio contexts of rock and funk bands, they were already experimenting with purely electronic sound worlds in pursuit of a utopian future. They looked forward to a world in which composing was sound design, studios were instruments, and recording had the immediacy of live performance. That they thought about this through 303s, 808s, and 909s was simply an accident of financial necessity. Derrick May used the Yamaha DX100 – a budget digital synth – for those sine-wave bass tones anyway.

By the late nineties, most musicians had forgotten about this, and more than a few of them labored under the spell of an analog fetish, convinced that the *sounds* of the Roland x0x boxes were responsible for making techno and house interesting in the first place. Demand for the 303, 808, and 909 has created a volatile vintage market akin to the trade in beat-up Stratocasters and Fuzz Faces. In a frightening reversal of the conditions that gave birth to techno and house, it's not uncommon to see dealers asking upward of $1000 for any of the big three. Even so, they remain hard to find, and a host of European boutique synthesizer manufacturers, among them Music-And-More, JoMoX, Novation, and Quasimidi, have have moved to fill the gaps with 808, 909, and 303 clones, duplicating the circuitry and sound of the Roland boxes at a somewhat more reasonable price point. While afficionados claim to be able to tell the difference, it's doubtful that it would be apparent from the dancefloor. In any case, fundamentalist attention to supposed "classic" synth sounds is suspect to say the least – especially given that synths were developed in the first place in order to make new and unrecognizable noises.

This sort of fetishism seems antithetical to both the guiding spirit of Detroit techno (which built an imagined future using the cheapest tools at hand) and the low-rent DIY philosophy of the reformed punks who cottoned to the myriad subgenres of the nineties – especially nowadays, when it may even be cheaper to stay on the technological cutting edge than it is to indulge in technological nostalgia. Even for those obsessed with the x0x sound, contemporary technology might be worth considering. ReBirth (from the team that developed ReCycle), provides an 808, a 909, two 303s, a distortion unit, a

delay line, and a mixer for about a quarter the cost of a single battered piece of Roland hardware. ReBirth, by the way, is all-virtual, a software synthesizer running on a Mac or PC, producing analog-sounding output that's difficult to distinguish from the originals.

While this level of replication is certainly a meaningful development and an indicator of the potential usefulness of computer-based instruments, software synthesis promises more than simple analog emulation. Where the first wave of digital synthesis abandoned programming ease in favor of sonic complexity, software synthesis offers potentially unlimited sound-generating possibility and interface design limited only by the imagination. Alternative user interfaces had been part of the electronic instrument's repertoire since the beginning, and the desktop studio has multiplied and democratized the alternatives. Free from real-world hardware design constraints, U&I Software's MetaSynth is "played" via an interface that lets the user draw lines and figures, or import images, that are then interpreted as sound. Some software packages – Clavia's Nord Modular, Seer Systems' Reality, and the academically-oriented sound programming environments SuperCollider, Modalys, and Csound, to name a few – update the infinite variability of modular synthesizers, allowing users to "build" virtual instruments – synths, sequencers, samplers, signal processors, or monstrous hybrids – with the design parameters of their dreams. Musicians ranging from former Roland partisan Taylor Deupree to notorious tinkerers like Richard James and Autechre are already designing such dream instruments and releasing the results for public consumption.

R&D-minded hardware manufacturers have risen to the twin challenges of software synths and the analog revival with so-called "analog modeling" or "virtual analog" keyboards. Instruments like the Clavia Nord Lead, the Roland JP-8000, the Korg Prophecy, and the Yamaha AN1X use physical modeling technology (mathematically approximating the physical characteristics of a circuit) to provide analog-sounding instruments complete with lots of friendly knobs and sliders for real-time control of sound parameters. Of course, these instruments aren't limited to the simple reproduction of analog tones — the Korg in particular is capable of flights of distinctly digital sonic fancy that rival anything patched together on an old ARP.

Still, the future of music technology is likely to be centered on the desktop. Advances in desktop processor speeds and hard disk capacity have made it possible to run all of the elements of a virtual electronic studio — multitrack recorder, signal processors, and sound sources -on a single machine. This makes it likely that the electronic music of the future will conflate composition, recording, sound design, and rhythm programming in new and baffling ways. Today's reasonably powerful Macintoshes and PCs, equipped with a selection of relatively affordable software tools, can already create the sort of audio havoc that was just recently the exclusive province of Bell Labs and IRCAM. For better or for worse, the music of the future has come home. And that's what the Belleville Three had in mind, wasn't it?

Thanks to Taylor Deupree, Marius De Vries, Jim Norman at Roland, Constantine Kotselas at Steinberg, Greg Rule at Keyboard Magazine, *and Paul Miller for their assistance.* 🖎

Discography

CONCRÈTE/TAPE MUSIC

JOHN CAGE — "Imaginary Landscapes" (Hat Hut)

Cage's major works for tape, turntables, prepared piano, and percussion. All of Cage's electronic and tape works are necessary listening, but this makes a fine place to start.

PIERRE HENRY AND PIERRE SCHAEFFER — "Symphonie Pour un Homme Seul" (London)

Their most significant collaboration. Originally assembled as a mix on multiple turntables, for those interested in DJ precedents.

KARLHEINZ STOCKHAUSEN — "Kontakte" (Wergo)

The classic piece for electronics, piano, and percussion. The Wergo release is the definitive 1960 performance, featuring David Tudor, the late dean of new-music interpreters, at the piano. Also worth investigating is the series of archival releases on the Stockhausen-Verlag imprint that includes exhaustive liner notes - and cover art - by the man himself.

EDGARD VARÈSE — "Poème Électronique" (Neuma)

The granddaddy of tape music, originally scored for a massive 400-speaker PA installation at the 1958 Brussels World's Fair. A massively ambitious piece that seeks to incorporate a world of sounds in its *concrète* elements.

IANNIS XENAXIS — "Electronic Music" (EMF)

Engineer-turned-architect-turned-composer Xenakis has pioneered some of the century's most forward-looking approaches to sound and composition, and his electronic work has produced some of the most striking sounds in music. This introductory compilation covers Xenakis' career from 1957 to 1992. 1958's "Concret PH" is based on the sounds produced by a lump of smoldering charcoal. A fine introduction to a maverick's oeuvre.

ELECTROACOUSTICS

ALVIN LUCIER — "I am Sitting in a Room" (Lovely)

A single speaking voice, transformed via room reverb and delay into a textural orchestra.

PAULINE OLIVEROS — "Crone Music" (Lovely)

Oliveros begins with her solo just-intonation accordion and proceeds to alter it beyond recognition with a bank of digital delays, loops, and computer-controlled postprocessing.

DAVID TUDOR	"Neural Synthesis" (Lovely)	Tudor late in his career and behind the controls of a custom-built digital rig instead of his hand-assembled analog noisemakers, but still coaxing the circuits into speaking for themselves.
GEORGE E. LEWIS	"Voyager" (Avant)	A software program that listens to music and improvises on what it hears, written by Lewis and tweaked here and there as it migrated since 1985 from computer platform to computer platform. Lewis improvises on the trombone; Roscoe Mitchell does likewise on saxophones; and Voyager . . . well, it plays along with them. A startling, sensitive dialogue between human and machine.

EARLY ELECTRONIC
INSTRUMENTS:

WENDY CARLOS	*Switched on Bach* (CBS/Sony)	If you want to reexperience the excitement of the Moog synthesizer's moment of arrival in the popular consciousness, this is the way to go.
KRAFTWERK	*Autobahn* (Elektra) or *Trans-Europe Express* (Capitol)	The sounds of the European academic electronic music studios grafted onto a pop framework. The ur-texts for everything that followed.
CLARA ROCKMORE	"The Art of the Theremin" (Delos)	The theremin's greatest virtuoso (and its muse) demonstrates her control over the instrument's intangibles with a program of Rachmaninoff, Ravel, Tchaikovsky, and Stravinsky.

POPULAR ELECTRONICS:

DERRICK MAY	*Innovator* (Transmat)	A fair sampling of Rhythim is Rhythim and Mayday classics, including the seminal "Strings of Life," selected for your listening pleasure by the master himself. A good introduction to the sound of what Techno once was.
PHUTURE	"Acid Tracks" (Trax)	In case you find yourself in need of a field guide to the sounds of the Roland x0x series instruments, here's the primary document of Acid. Nowadays, it's locatable as a bonus track on Phuture 303's 1998 *Alpha & Omega* (A1), which finds them up to the same old tricks more or less.

SAMPLING:

4HERO   "Parallel Universe" (Reinforced)

One of the first big statements of drum and bass as an album-length art form. A beautifully constructed breakbeat edifice, that unfortunately provided the blueprint for the robotized Steely Dan sheen that's hypnotized the majority of breakbeat scientists ever since.

OMNI TRIO   "Music for the Next Millenium" (Sm:)e)

Exemplary time-stretching from Rob Haigh, including the ground-breaking "Renegade Snares."

JOHN OSWALD   "Plexure" (Avant)

Saxophonist/composer Oswald's wide-ranging appropriations and obsessive editorial manipulations have often led him afoul of the copyright laws − after raiding the Michael Jackson catalog for source material, the Gloved One's legal team forced him to destroy all existing copies of the *plunderphonic* cd. While the majority of samplists work with a few loops at a time, Oswald's creations juggle hundreds - or hundreds of thousands − of atom−ized sound-snippets, testing the limits of sampling's possibilities.

PUBLIC ENEMY   *It Takes A Nation of Millions to Hold us Back* (Def Jam)

The Bomb Squad's production aesthetic of impossibly dense sampled reference was as disorienting, or reorienting, as the lyrical innovations of MCs. A sonic promise that's as yet gone unfulfilled.

DJ SHADOW   *Endtroducing* (Mo Wax)

A turntable, a sampler, an endless crate of vinyl. Also worth invest-igating are the "Headz" and "Headz 2" compilations on Mo Wax. For further whimsy, search out a copy of Skylab's "Magenta" (Eye Q).

CARL STONE   "Kamiya Bar" (New Tone)

Stone, one of the Macintosh's most visible virtuosos, reconstructs a virtual Tokyo soundscape from field recordings of an early nineties visit. Those recordings were then subjected to all manner of digital prodding, coaxing, stretching, and shrinking, of course.

GROUND ZERO   "ConsumeRed" (Recommended)

A masterpiece of tension-building from sampling wizard Otomo Yoshihide, who's famously referred to his turntables as his "sec-ond brain." A single reed sample is repeated ad infinitum, subjected along the way to all manner of digital warping.

I think we are going to see a change now that the computer is becoming the default musical tool. When techno started, it was all done on little boxes. Now that people are so familiar with digital editing and computer programs, they will take on a new generation of music software that does things that you couldn't previously do. One of the most exciting software products that I have seen lately is metasynth. It's a program from Barcelona that converts sounds into pictures, pictures into sounds; you make music with Photoshop. Doing graphical transformation on sounds will lead to new areas of sound manipulation. It is about psychedelia, synesthesia. **MIXMASTER MORRIS** I'm always trying to make the machines work randomly. It's difficult — computers are boring. Interface between computer and human is really dull. **JONAH SHARP a.k.a**

SPACETIME CONTINUUM

INTERVIEW:
Robert Moog

Electronics was a hobby of mine when I was a child. I think sound was the most appealing part of being in electronics. It was a visceral pleasure for me to hear all these things coming out of the loudspeaker. Back in the sixties, what was missing in electronic sound was the ability to shape the sound, to change it from the beginning to the end. That sort of shaping becomes a lot about the tone color. If you can't shape a sound, it sounds mechanical, it sounds dead, it sounds very much like an old-fashioned organ. By using electrical voltages to actually change the sound, and then by building other devices that made voltages that changed it in specific ways, you could automatically make new tone colors, new tone colors that you couldn't shape with your hands on a keyboard because they were too fast or too precise. Musicians refer to these things now like VCO, VCF, and VCA. They're part of most electronic musicians' vocabulary, and they understand what they're good for musically. But back then it was a technical concept. VC means voltage controlled. To a musician that means you can make it change by applying a changing voltage to it. Musicians are intelligent people. If they want to build sounds up or construct sounds in certain ways, they can learn techniques for doing it. You don't have to be an engineer to use a synthesizer, but you do have to understand that in order to make the pitch of a sound go up and down regularly, you need a regularly changing voltage to control that pitch. Once you experience connecting a regularly changing controlled voltage to change the pitch, making it go up and down regularly, it becomes a natural thing. It's just as natural as, say, drawing a bow across a string. You develop a feeling for it. You develop an intuition for it; that's different than being an engineer or being a technical person and understanding in great detail and great precision exactly what's going on. I think electronic music is the hot-rodding of the nineties. When I was a kid, cars were the things you hot-rodded. But today it's computers and electronic synthesizers. It just feels good physically to get involved with that stuff. The term "synthesize" means to put together a completed object out of its component parts. A synthesizer is a device that enables you to do that. In a synthesizer there are individual circuits that you connect together; first with patch cords, that was the first way you could do it, and then later with switches or on a computer screen. Each one of these modules did one thing, and one thing only, towards either generating a sound or part of a sound, or shaping it in some way. Or in generating the control voltage that defined the shape. By connecting the various modules or components together, you made a completed sound. So what you were doing to the sound had a hardware counterpart in what you were doing with the instrument itself. At the beginning, I think everybody outside of the electronic music field thought that synthesizers were supposed to imitate traditional instruments. The people who were inside electronic music wanted to used the synthesizer to make completely new sounds. If you listen to the early records, especially *Switched on Bach*, you don't hear anything like traditional sounds. Nonetheless, people just made this assumption that synthesis was about imitation. I think to a certain extent they're still making that assumption, although most musicians today gravitate towards the sounds that synthesizers are particularly good at. The warm, fat, electronic sounds that are so popular in today's dance music, for instance. Wendy Carlos and I knew each other for several years before she did *Switched on Bach*. In fact, I met her for the first time when she was a student of Vladimir Ussachevsky, who was the head of the Columbia/Princeton Electronic Music center in New York City, and she was studying there. Then she had a job as an engineer in a recording studio, and she began to build up her own studio for electronic music composition right in the living room of her apartment. I saw that setup, and I was there several times while *Switched on Bach* was being made. Back in the late sixties, people were generally open to all sorts of new things. *Switched on Bach* was a new sound, and it shed an entirely new musical light on the music of Bach. You could hear the lines distinctly and follow the construction of the piece very easily. That made it musically more accessible and, to a lot of people, more enjoyable. Postwar electronic music really began because of the invention of the tape recorder, which happened was during World War II. What happened in Germany is entirely different from what happened in France after World War II. The French composers at the Paris radio studio took the position that you should use a tape recorder to record natural sounds from the environment and manipulate those. Those were the idea materials for electronic music, whereas the composers at the northwest German radio station in Cologne took the position that you should use absolutely pure electronic sine tones and electronic noise that was 100% controlled and make music out of that. So there are really two different musical approaches to using electronics. In this country, tape music didn't take such a hardline musical position. They used any sound at all — electronically generated as well as natural — and built their music from those. We built our first modular synthesizer in 1964, and from 1964 to about 1970 or '71, that's all we built. A modular synthesizer at that time was typically four feet wide, four feet high. It was a big thing. You couldn't carry it from one place to the other. Besides that, it took a lot of patch cords to connect all the parts together and there were a lot of knobs that you had to set. It took the best part of a half-day sometimes to get just the sound you wanted. As soon as rock musicians began to be interested in using these sounds on stage, they needed something smaller, more convenient and simpler to use. That was the beginning of instruments like the Minimoog. We introduced the Minimoog in 1970. Other manufacturers introduced instruments of similar size, and that was the beginning of the use of synthesizers in rock music. When *Switched on Bach* came out and it became an overnight success, the press naturally assumed that our contribution to the instruments that Carlos used was an integral part of the medium. I guess to a certain extent that's true. For the year or two after Switched on Bach came out, there were dozens and dozens of what we call "Moog records." "Moog Hispania." "Everything you always wanted to know about the Moog." "Country Moog." Just any type of music at all, there was a Moog record for that type of music. They were popular at the time. A lot of them were made. I think that may be a reason that people think of Moog when they think of synthesizers today. It's always been possible for people who are not professional musicians or are not wealthy to make music. There have always been brass bands or dance bands using violins or native instruments of one sort or another. I know my father had a mandolin in his closet, and for him, that was a way he played music. Today, millions of people play the guitar because it's fairly easy to play, it doesn't cost too much, and you can play the sort of music that people like to listen to now. What contemporary technology has added to this is the ability to assemble music in what used to require a very large studio. Now you can do it in you own bedroom or your own family room with a computer and a couple of electronic instruments. So not only do you have the ability to make popular music live, but now you have the ability to make high-quality recorded music on cd, on cassette tape, as part of videos, etc. It's something that anybody with the talent can do. Of course there a lot of people who have the equipment, like to play around with it, but they're not making music. Not because they don't have the equipment, but because they're not musicians. I don't pass judgement on the music that other people listen to, especially people of another generation, or two generations away. I was brought up listening to big band music and I've been told that when that music was first developed in the 1920s, it was considered noisy and vulgar and antihuman. But there we were with new sensibilities, new cultural entities to deal with. I think the same thing is true today. A lot of this techno music is very beautiful, not all, to be sure, maybe not most of it, but a lot of it is really intriguing. We have to listen to it in a different way than we listen to, say, the music of the fifties or the music of the thirties, or even the rock 'n' roll of the seventies. There's an interaction between art and technology: That has always been true. It's not that one dictates the other, but when a technological development comes out that musicians can use, musicians use it in a new way. That in turn inspires further technological development. I can remember when I first began, the voltage control was a brand new piece of technology, but it was also a brand-new musical resource. The two were developed together. Not all of the mainstream is computer-controlled, but it's the same musical mainstream that began in the sixties. The seventies analog synthesizers actually began in the mid-sixties and then became very popular in the seventies. The typical analog synthesizer of that period had a lot of knobs on it. It made these warm, rolling, rich, fat electronic sounds. I think that the fact that it had all these knobs enabled musicians to change the sounds during performance to get exactly the sound they wanted. That made them very popular for the music of that time. In the late seventies and early eighties digital synthesis came out. It was different. Digital synthesizers didn't have a whole bunch of knobs, and they didn't have the same warm, fat sound. However, they had many other features, so musicians rushed off to experiment with these new features. Now they're coming back. This happens over and over again. You explore one area, you pick the big pieces out of that area, and then you realize, "Wait a minute, we're missing something here that we had in the earlier era. Let's go back and do that." I can remember when Keith Emerson first used a modular synthesizer specially made for stage performance. He found a use for the sounds of that modular synthesizer for his song, "Lucky Man." It was a very successful tune. It was the first album that Emerson, Lake and Palmer did. It really got the attention of a lot of top musicians at the time. Keith Emerson had a special gift for sensing how to use a new sound musically. He would spend a half-minute or a minute trying a whole bunch of sounds, and then immediately feel something that would make musical sense, play that, and then that would become part of a tune that he was working on. When we initially developed the synthesizer, we didn't have any specific music in mind. Just because one musician used it to make Bach and another musician used it to make country music or experimental music is no reason for us to think that that's the only way it should be used. A good musical instrument can be used in a lot of ways that aren't discovered right away. Another good example is the electric guitar. When the electric guitar first came out, the developers tried to stay away from distortion. Tried to stay away from overdriving the amplifiers. The musicians who first used that really discovered a new musical resource. That's the screaming, singing, sustained sound of rock guitar, and it wasn't used until some musicians went to where technically they really weren't supposed to be. So I guess I believe that you really can't burn anything out by trying something new, and even if you can burn it out, it can be fixed. Try something new. It's how progress is made in music. 🪶

12

One of the consequences of living through a period like this, which is in fact a revolutionary period, is that the entire structure of society and the processes of change become nonlinear. And nonlinearity I think is defined almost by the statement that "small inputs can have very large consequences." **ALVIN TOFFLER**

EPILOGUE

INTERVIEW: ALVIN TOFFLER

I think there is a revolutionary difference between the kinds of machines that we're producing now, which have intelligence and memory and logic built into them, and industrial machinery, which simply amplified muscle power. Memory and logic are human inputs into the machine. They don't rise from the machine itself, but are built into the machine by human beings – by sometimes very large teams of human beings, concentrating a great deal of intelligence. And these machines amplify the intellectual capabilities of human beings. The question that keeps arising is whether the new technologies can be creative. Or are they simply still, when all is said and done, mechanistic? I believe at a certain point we will in fact be able to mimic creativity, if not in fact produce creative machines. As Alan Turing said, when you mimic something well enough that you can't tell it from the original, it is effectively the original. So I do believe that we will be able to approximate human creativity through the use of intelligent machines that we humans have in fact created and programmed. In an earlier age, before the industrial revolution , most people were peasants. They lived in villages. And the amount of information available in that village was extremely limited. The church in the West served as a kind of primitive mass medium. You got everybody together on Sunday and preached at them and that was a mass message at the level of the village. But by and large, there was very little external communication from the village to the larger world. You had early attempts to create essentially long-distance communications. You had the Persians building "call towers," which I jokingly say were like forerunners of our microwave towers. You would build a tower and put some guy on top who had big lungs so he could shout loud to the next tower, where you had another stentor. You could send a message beyond the village, but the amount of information coming into the village was very limited. A child growing up would very often get the same message from the parents, same message from the church, same message from the neighbors, and the same message from the state (to the degree that the state was present). So the mental universe of the individual was very contained, and in fact within the village, very uniform. The industrial revolution increased the number of media by which information reached the individual and extended the range. You then had the mass media, but you were still trying to send the same message to a very large number of people. When I grew up, and in fact when my daughter grew up, you still had three networks in the U.S. producing television. The result was that on any given midweek morning, there were basically three jokes in circulation from listening to the late shows the night before. Well, we now know that what's happening is that the mass media is demassifying. You're getting multiple channels through which information reaches the individual. We're fracturing the mass mentality of the society. We're creating a demassified culture that goes along with the customization and demassificiation of production, the demassification of distribution channels. The mass society is exploding. This is what my wife and I have written about and called the Third Wave. The second wave of change, the industrial revolution, coming after the first agrarian wave of change, produced a mass society. We are taking that mass society and slicing it and dicing it into an infinite number of units. Those units are called individuals. So what we're getting is a culture and a society based on more fully individualized human beings. That's different from individualist, which carries a connotation of selfishness. Individualized is not the same. It means that each of us, the differences, the genetic differences, the cultural differences, the personality differences, are allowed more space in which to flower. Now, at some point you can reach a point in which everybody is so individualized that we don't speak the same language anymore and we don't have a culture or a social system anymore. But we're still a far piece from arriving at that. And I don't think we will. We're seeing more units of musical production, if you want to call it that. More instruments. More sounds. More audiences, or subaudiences. And more performers. So what you're getting is a breakup of the mass musical scene, which parallels what's happening elsewhere. You still have Disney movies. You still have Mickey Mouse and you still have Bruce Willis breaking glass as mass phenomena. But you also have something that simply didn't exist a generation or more ago. Diversity. You did not have the opportunity to express yourself. You had to own a printing plant in order to publish something. You needed to have your own symphony orchestra. So yes, I think what's happening now is part of this larger social process that we've called demassification of the mass society. Today, the technologies of deception are developing more rapidly than the technologies of verification. Which means we can use a television camera, plus special effects, plus computers, etc. to falsify reality so perfectly that nobody can tell the difference. And the consequence of that eventually could be a society in which nobody believes, everybody knows that seeing is not believing, and nobody believes anything. With the exception of a small minority that decides to believe one thing fanatically. And that's a dangerous social/cultural situation. One of the consequences of living through a period like this, which is in fact a revolutionary period, is that the entire structure of society and the processes of change become nonlinear. And nonlinearity I think is defined almost by the statement that "small inputs can have very large consequences." While large inputs can sometimes have very small consequences. That also means in a political sense that very small groups can, under a given set of circumstances, achieve power. And that is a very threatening idea for anything remotely resembling what we believe to be democracy. So we're going into a period, I think, of high turbulence and considerable danger, along with enormous possibilities. 🐝

The difference between drum and bass and jungle is . . . none, in my mind. I'm sick of all the names. Sick of all the "intelligent techno," "hardstyle," "techstep," etc. **LTJ BUKEM**

INDEXES

GLOSSARY OF TERMS

303

The Roland TB-303 bassline machine was intended as an accompaniment for solo instrumentalists but was picked up by house musicians who experimented with it, discovering that you could tweak the basslines to create weird sounds that drove people crazy on the dancefloor.

4/4 BEAT

A 4/4 beat is a rhythmic pattern that features four beats to a bar. It is the repetitive, regular rhythmic pulse of house and techno. Breakbeats differ in that they use syncopation and are not as regular, not as static.

808

Launched in 1980, the Roland TR-808 drum machine has since become the most important and most used drum machine there is.

909

The Roland TR-909 drum machine is the most utilized drum machine in house music. Made for only one year (from 1983 to 1984), it featured both sampled and synthesized drum sounds a very rare feature.

ACID HOUSE

Acid house originally referred specifically to the house records from Chicago that used the tweaked sounds of a Roland TB-303 bassline machine. Phuture's first album, entitled "Acid Tracks" and recorded in 1987, prompted the use of the acid moniker. The term has now passed into electronic-music parlance and describes tracks that derive their central motif from the 303, the only device capable of making "authentic" acid sounds. Though 303 sounds can be heard everywhere, "acid tracks" tend to refer to instrumental, stripped-down, stark, early Chicago-style tracks fueled by TR-909 kick drums, hi-hats, and snares.

ACID JAZZ

A late eighties/early nineties outgrowth of the British rare-groove movement in which London fashion victims created their own early seventies-infatuated bohemia by copying jazz-funk records of the era note for note. Acid jazz centered around jazz aficionado DJ Giles Peterson and his Acid Jazz and Talkin' Loud labels, which released key records by the likes of Galliano, Brand New Heavies, and the Young Disciples.

AFRO-FUTURISM

A thread of black popular music, beginning with Sun Ra, that reimagines elements from traditional African American culture (such as the transcendence of spirituals) as taking place in outer space rather than heaven. The sound can include use of electronic instruments like the Moog, drum machines, and Roland synthesizers.

ALEATORIC

Music that is random or improvisatory, either in composition or performance (or both).

AMBIENT

Literally, an encompassing atmosphere or environment. In Brian Eno's use of the term, ambient music is music that can be listened to just as easily as it can be ignored.

AMEN BREAK

The most famous breakbeat in jungle music. It originally comes from "Amen Brother" by the Winstons and can be found on volume one of the Ultimate Breaks and Beats series. It was first used in Jungle by LTJ Bukem and has been used literally thousands of times since.

ANALOG

The representation of data as continuously variable physical qualities as opposed to digital, in which data is "digitized" into a series of 1s and 0s.

ANALOG SYNTHESIZER

Uses conventional electronic means of sound reproduction (voltage and resistor regulation of things like sine-wave production). Often said to have a warmer sound than digital synthesizers.

ATONAL

Characterized by the avoidance of traditional tonality, generally by composing without reference to a particular key. A hallmark of "serious" twentieth century music.

BALEARIC

This is a term that refers to a particular moment in British dance music history circa 1989-1993. Many British vacationers would go the Spanish town Ibiza to drink themselves into oblivion. The soundtrack for this sort of activity was termed "Balearic Beat" for the beaches at the edge of the city. Early Balearic champions included Paul Oakenfold, Graham Parks, and Jose Padilla. The music that dominated there was a mixture of Euro-trance (140 bpm and up) with British progressive house from labels such as Tomato, Cowboy, and 23rd Precinct.

BASSLINE

A deceptively simple term that is forced to do a lot of work in describing electronic music. Its simplicity lies in the fact that it refers to the synthesized sound of a bass guitar, though the principle governing it is quite different from that used in "modern rock", where it usually provides a counterpoint to the more foregrounded guitar. The bassline in jungle records conforms more closely to roots reggae, in house to funk, and in techno to German music by Kraftwerk et al.

BEATBOX

This catchall phrase has been used to refer to portable tape and cd players, though in its more common usage it is used to refer to a range of analog and digital instruments that produce percussion and drum sounds such as the Roland Corporation's TB-909 and TR-808. Grandmaster Flash invented his own analog beatbox on the Live Convention records, recorded in 1981 and 1982. Later, artists such as Doug E. Fresh and the Fat Boys pioneered the technique of the "human beatbox" in which an MC would imitate percussion and drum sounds vocally. Exemplary instances of this technique can be found on the Fat Boys' "Jailhouse Rock" and Doug E. Fresh's "The Human Beatbox."

BOOTY

In contemporary electronic music, this term has little to do with its historical meaning – stolen goods – and everything to do with the female posterior. The term is used adjectivally to describe electronic music from Miami, Detroit, the Hagues, and other disparate places. Invariably, "booty music" must contain bass that goes way off the geiger counter and that makes you free your ass (and, as George Clinton would add, your mind will follow). It is preferably played on sound systems loud enough to make your eyes bleed. Unfortunately, the term is often used in a pejorative fashion to refer to black electronic music for the dancefloor and the Pathfinder, though those more racist connotations are being broken down as artists and listeners realize that good electronic music must have, as the late Roger Troutman sang, more bounce to the ounce.

BPM

Beats per minute.

BREAK

This is a heavily used and oft-misunderstood term because it refers to two quite distinct elements within electronic music and DJ culture. For dance DJs, the break is that part of the record where the drums and percussion drop out, leaving space for a segue into the next record. The break is usually visible on the vinyl, making cueing easier. The other, quite different meaning is shorthand for the "breakbeat" which is the drum sound that is either scratched, sped up, or looped for use in making other records. The breakbeat is usually taken from an originally "live" drum sound, though increasingly, "electronic" breakbeats are being utilized. The term is a floating signifier in that it can be taken to mean almost anything you'd like in contemporary electronic music. One can claim that its origins lie in hip-hop culture, when DJs such as Kool Herc would cut up the drum break on records like "Champ" by The Mohawks to replace the sound of a live funky drummer, like Clyde Stubblefield from the JBs.

BREAKBEATS

Hip-hop DJs in the seventies first started the idea of the breakbeat (the part of a record where everything drops out except the drum groove) and extended it by cutting back and forth between two copies of the same record. As the precursor to sampling culture, the cult of the breakbeat was responsible for the idea that anything can be funky.

CAPACITOR

A device giving large capacitance or desired values of capacitance that usually consists of conducting plates or foils separated by thin layers of dielectric (air, paraffin paper, or mica). The plates on the opposite sides of the dielectric layers are an oppositely charged system that is stored in the polarized dielectric; the capacitance is thus proportional to the area and the dielectric constant of the dielectric layer and inversely proportional to its thickness. This is also called a condenser.

CHILL-OUT ROOM

A room at dance clubs that plays music such as ambient or downtempo with a lower bpm and an atmospheric feel.

DETROIT BASS

All talk of origins aside, Detroit bass is the mutant form of classic Detroit techno wedded to the thunderous, woofer-destroying sounds of Miami bass. At the moment, there are two strands of Detroit bass. Firstly, there is the more Miami-influenced tradition of DJ Godfather, Big Daddy Rick, and DJ Assault, whose profane call-and-response records on the Twilight 76 and Data Bass labels are as good an example of "booty music" you're likely to find north of Atlanta. The second strata is that group of artists clustered around the Direct Beat label — Aux 88, DJ D'ijital, and others — and Keith Tucker's Puzzlebox imprint. The latter two labels have closer connections to Kraftwerk and Juan Atkins than to the Poison Clan or the 69 Boyz.

DIGITAL
In digital recording, sounds are translated into binary code (0s and 1s) that can then be played back exactly as is or manipulated by a computer or sampler. In the digital realm, there is no original (all copies are identical), and subsequently, there is no generation loss and no noise is introduced.

DISCO
Genre that grew out of black gay clubs in New York City. Its main hallmarks were lush, orchestrated soul records combined with stiff, mechanized rhythms and European attempts to be funny/funky.

DMX
The Oberheim DMX is yet another in a series of revered analog instruments that lay the foundation for innumerable electronic records from the early to mid-eighties. David Reeves, Jr, a hip-hop artist, named himself Davy DMX in honor of this beatbox and displayed its versatility on the unforgettable "One for the Treble, Ten for the Bass" single (Tuff City/CBS Associated, 1983). The DMX's extensive bassline capabilities made it adaptable to the demands of proto-Miami bass producers such as MC Shy D and MC ADE as well as their descendants: 2 Live Crew, Anquette, Pretty Tony, and Dynamix II.

DOWNTEMPO
Developed out of drum and bass (jungle) music. As the name suggests, it has a slower bpm than most dance music. Often conjures up sonic worlds.

DRUM AND BASS
Another name for jungle.

DRUM MACHINE
Electronic instrument that emulates drum sounds.

DUB
In the seventies Jamaica reggae producers and sound-system operators started exploring the possibilities offered in the recording studio to extend the grooves and sense of space in their records. Dub — as created by people like King Tubby, Lee "Scratch" Perry, Joe Gibbs, and Mikey Dread — was an important precursor to the techniques and sounds employed by many artists today.

EASY LISTENING
A genre of music aimed at polyester-clad leisure class in postwar America and Western Europe. Has made comeback of sorts recently due to legions of irony-trippers.

ECSTASY
The popular term for MDMA, the drug that fuelled the house boom in England.

ELECTRO
Started by Afrika Bambaataa's "Planet Rock" in 1982, electro was a branch of hip-hop that featured drum machines, video-game imagery, and a general funky-robotic feel.

ELECTRO-ACOUSTIC MUSIC
Genre of contemporary classical compositions that combines electronic (often magnetic tape) and acoustic (traditional instruments) music.

ELECTRONIC MUSIC
Music created mostly by electronic instruments or electronic means of manipulating sound.

FUNK
This term really requires a book-length treatise, but suffice it to say that it was used as an adjective to describe the way certain music sounded long before it was codified into the lexicon of musical genres. It would be difficult to identify precisely when rhythm and blues produced that mutant known as funk, but we do certainly know that James Brown had a great deal to do with that moment. On records like "Sex Machine" and "Popcorn", Brown would accentuate the rhythm section of his band over the melodic components, emphasizing the rhythm over the blues. We could go on for

pages, but suffice it to say that George Clinton and Bootsy Collins took the genre into another galaxy that doesn't look at all like this one.

FUSION
The combination of jazz and electronics: Miles Davis, Herbie Hancock, Weldon Irvine, Billy Cobham, and Chick Corea.

GABBA
A variant of techno that is concentrated in the Netherlands, where the bpms exceed 200 and the imagery is brutally violent. Also called "nosebleed techno."

GARAGE
Named in reference to the New York club the Paradise Garage where it was codified by Larry Levan, garage is a form of house music that features diva vocals, skipping hi-hats, gospel piano, and a more disco feel than Chicago house music.

HAPPY HARDCORE
As one wing of hardcore techno mutated into jungle, the other focused on the music's speed and playground feel and celebrated infantilism by creating a genre out of simple, fast rhythms, toy keyboard sounds, and helium vocals.

HARDCORE
The defining sound of the early rave scene, hardcore has evolved to even harder levels of madness

HI-NRG
A branch of disco with a faster tempo, less funkiness, and more mechanization. Pioneered by producers such as Patrick Cowley, Bobby Orlando, and Sylvester.

HIP-HOP
Encompassing graffiti tagging, breakdancing, Djing, and MCing, hip-hop was a culture that developed in Harlem and the Bronx in the seventies. The musical part of hip-hop focused on DJs spinning breakbeats and has slowly mutated to a point where rappers rap over sampled beats.

HIP HOUSE
A combination of hip-hop and house.

HOUSE
When New York disco DJ Frankie Knuckles began augmenting tracks by Donna Summer, Sylvester, and other disco performers with cheap drum machine beats and tape edits at Chicago's Warehouse in the early eighties, house music was born. In 1983, Jesse Saunders released the first house record, On and On.

ILLBIENT
Coined by DJ Spooky to describe music that creates minimal dystopian soundscapes

INTELLIGENT TECHNO
Branch of techno better suited to home headphone listening than to the dancefloor.

INTONARUMORI
Instrument created by Luigi Russolo in the 1910s as a way of creating the industrial sounds that he thought modern music should strive towards.

JAZZ-FUNK
In the late sixties and early seventies, jazz musicians looked back to the roots of their music in bordellos and house parties and injected some funk into an increasingly cerebral music. Related to fusion.

JUMP UP
Subgenre of jungle with prominent Hip-Hop samples, big basslines, and somewhat simplified rhythms aimed squarely at the dancefloor and ruled by producers Aphrodite and DJ Hype.

JUNGLE
In response to the combination of ecstasy and speed, producers in Britain began to meld together hardcore techno, hip-house, and old breakbeat records to create what would eventually be called jungle or drum and bass, the first specifically British form of dance music.

KRAUTROCK
Refers to various eclectic, experimental German groups from the seventies: especially, Can, Neu!, And Faust.

LATIN FREESTYLE
An offshoot of both disco and electro, freestyle is a heavily stylized form of music that talks about romance over stiff, angular electronic beats and is incredibly popular in New York and Miami. Many of today's major House DJs and producers cut their teeth on freestyle records.

LOOP

A section of music that has been taped or sampled and is repeated.

MIAMI BASS

Filthy, dirty, scatological, and also a lot of fun, Miami bass is Detroit techno's closest living relative.

MICROSCOPIC SOUND

A style of experimental music characterized by the use of tiny sound fragments that form rhythms or repetitions. It is often created using the distinct sound of pure-tone software-generated waveforms or random, static-like timbres.

MIDI

Musical Instrument Digital Interface. A means by which electronic instruments communicate with each other and computers.

MINIMALISM

A movement in visual art and music that began in the seventies and is characterized by formal simplicity and the absence of ornamentation. In music (by Terry Riley and Steve Reich), for example, minimalism is marked by minute, shifting changes over time.

MODULATION

The act or process of changing from one tonality to another without a break in the melody or the chord succession.

MOOG SYNTHESIZER

Invented by Robert Moog, this synthesizer was the first important mass-market electronic sound-generating instrument.

MUSIQUE CONCRÈTE

Developed in France in the fifties, musique concrète sought to make music out of natural sounds through studio manipulation.

PITCH

The highness or lowness of a musical tone.

PITCH SHIFT

Changing the pitch of a digitally stored sound without effecting its duration (speed). This was not possible on analog equipment.

PLUNDERPHONICS

A term coined by John Oswald and other sonic outlaws to describe the practice of appropriating (plundering) sound from a variety of mass-media sources.

POST-PUNK

When disgruntled punk musicians were introduced to synthesizers and other electronic toys in the late seventies, an aggressive commentary on postindustial automation was the result.

POST-ROCK

The augmentation of rock's guitar-bass-drum instrumentation with ideas and sounds from electronic music.

RAGGA

Catchall term for the electronic reggae that has predominated Jamaican music since Wayne Smith's 1985 single, "Under Me Sleng Teng."

RARE GROOVE

Like its seventies predecessor, northern soul, rare groove was an exclusively British musical movement from the eighties that saw obsessive record collectors become tastemakers and pretend that hopelessly obscure funk and soul records were better than those of James Brown or the Meters simply because they were rarer.

RAVE

Rave was initially a phenomenon that grew out of England's acid house explosion when the authorities clamped down on London clubs. The acid house parties that were moved out to the countryside of London's suburbs were called raves. As raves grew bigger and more commercial, and as Europeans started to produce their own House records, "rave" began to be identified with a combination of the huge piano riffs of Italian house, diva vocal samples, and Joey Beltram's minimal, steroid techno. When rave records started to feature more and more helium vocals, dodgy drug references, and nods to children tv themes towards the end of 1992, the rave phenomenon died out in Britain's clubbing mainstream.

REGGAE

Although it has now become a catchall term for all Jamaican music, reggae initially referred to a specific beat. When it started to catch on in 1968, reggae was a faster, rougher, more bass-heavy rhythm than its immediate predecessor, rocksteady. At the time, though, Jamaican music was moving in many different directions, and the term "reggae" came to be associated with all of them.

RING MODULATOR
An electronic device that changes the frequency or amplitude of soundwaves. Particularly important in the work of Karlheinz Stockhausen.

SAMPLER
Machine that encodes sounds digitally so that they can be easily accessed for future use. In the hands of hip-hop producers, they've become instruments in their own right.

SEQUENCER
Allows a sequence of sounds to be played back exactly as they were created on any number of electronic instruments.

SYNESTHESIA
A mingling of the senses that may be euphoric or disorienting: Colors may be heard, smells felt, sounds seen.

SYNTHESIZER
An electronic device that produces sound by generating audio waveforms, which are then processed or shaped by a series of modifier stages - (envelope generators, filters, low-frequency oscillators, ring modulators, and so forth).

SYNTH-POP
Synthesized pop songs from the early eighties, often with shimmering surfaces. Glam rock's children.

TAPE SPLICING
The editing of recordings by cutting and taping pieces of magnetic tape. Can be used to create new compositions, as in electro-acoustic music or musique concrète.

TECHNO
Inspired by both Kraftwerk and New York electro, a small network of kids in Detroit made some of the most powerful electronic music ever created. While the Detroit version of techno was both cold and deeply melodic, the rest of the world seemed to hear the music as a series of progressively minimal and aggressive blips and bleeps. The resulting recordings stripped music down to its bare bones: rhythm and texture.

THEREMIN
Electronic musical instrument designed by Leon Theremin

that was the prototype for the earliest synthesizers such as the Moog. Covers a total pitch range from the lowest audible pitch to four octaves above middle C, with a wide selection of tone colors. Looks like a box with an antenna and is operated by one's moving hands around the box.

TIME STRETCHING
A digital technique analogous to pitch shifting. A sample is sped up or slowed down with no consequent shift in pitch.

TRANCE
A variant of techno marked by a relentlessly seductive, hypnotizing beat.

Glossary terms defined by Peter Shapiro and Tim Haslett

ARTIST BIOGRAPHIES

µZIQ
Ambient/weird beat artist. Influenced by his friend Aphex Twin.

2 LIVE CREW
For better or worse, Miami bass' most influential and popular group.

4 HERO
Dego Mcfarlane runs Reinforced label, the most important hardcore/jungle label from between 1992 and 1994, with Mark Mac. Released landmark records by Goldie (Rufige Crew's "Terminator") and Doc Scott (Nasty Habit's "Here Come the Drumz"), as well as their own records as 4 Hero, Tek 9, Manix, and Tom & Jerry. Also records as Nu Era and Jacob's Optical Stairway.

69
see "Carl Craig".

808 STATE
Graham Massey and Company advanced the cause of British house with their stunning Newbuild LP and their lush, reflective hit "Pacific State."

A GUY CALLED GERALD
a.k.a Gerald Simpson. The man who first put British house music on the map with his own "Voodoo Ray" and 808 State's "Pacific State." One of the more creative junglists.

A-TRAK
a.k.a. Alain Macklovitch. Turntablist affiliated with the Invisibl Skratch Piklz and part of the Allies. Seventeen year-old A-Trak is the 1997 Canada and World DMC Champion.

AFRIKA BAMBAATAA
One of the founders of hip-hop and, with Arthur Baker, the creator of electro. Records like "Planet Rock," "Looking For The Perfect Beat," and "Death Mix" marked the beginning of rap music's artistic and commercial success.

ALEC EMPIRE
The founder and principal actor behind Atari Teenage Riot and the Digital Hardcore and Riot Beats labels. Fuses punk attitude and revolutionary politics with jungle beats and feedback.

ALEX PATTERSON
See "The Orb."

ALVIN LUCIER
A composer, Lucier has always avoided synthesis, instead utilizing EEG-amplified brainwaves, galvanic skin sensors, and other unlikely instruments in his sonic investigations.

ALVIN TOFFLER
Futurist author, and great influence on Detroit techno pioneers Juan Atkins, Derrick May, and Kevin Saunderson.

AMON DUUL II
Tripped-out and bombastic, Amon Duul II's kinetic trance-rock made them Germany's equivalent to Hawkwind.

AMON TOBIN
a.k.a. Cujo. Downtempo recording artist who incorporates Brazilian flavor and aspects of jazz and hip-hop into his music.

ANDREA PARKER
Techno and downtempo producer who records for Mo' Wax. Uses lots of strings and other off-beat things.

APHEX TWIN
a.k.a. Richard James. Creates prolific, genre-blurring experimental ambient.

APHRODITE
Author of tunes that will never die like "Some Justice" (classic hardcore made with Mickey Finn, from 1991 or 1992, that sampled Ce Ce Rogers' Chicago house classic "Someday"), "BassLight" (seminal hardstep original from 1994), and "Style From the Darkside", another hardstep classic from 1996.

ARMAND VAN HELDEN
New York City house producer. Records for Strictly Rhythm and Nervous Records. Runs Armed Records.

ARTHUR BAKER
With Afrika Bambaataa, he created electro with his production of "Planet Rock". His electro-funk productions with John Robie on the Streetwise Label dominated the New York dance scene in the early to mid-eighties. Also produced New Order's "Blue Monday," the biggest selling 12" record in British history.

ARTO LINDSAY
One-man bridge connecting the finest music from Brazil with the best of the experimental downtown New York music scene.

ASH RA TEMPEL
Lysergic space-rock unit, Ash Ra Tempel centered around the lyrical lead guitar virtuosity of Manuel Gottsching, Germany's very own Jerry Garcia.

ATARI TEENAGE RIOT
See "Alec Empire."

AUTECHRE
Sean Booth and Rob Brown. Influential British techno duo whose distillation of electro-funk and hip-hop into bleak bleepscapes sends nerdy white boys into paroxysms of delight.

BASS MEKANIK
The man responsible for the extreme low-end frequencies of boom and bass.

BEN NEIL
Downtown New York avant-garde producer and inventor of the mutant trumpet. Has worked with LaMonte Young, DJ Spooky, We, and other denizens of New York's downtown scene.

BILL LASWELL
King of the juxtaposition. Specializes in taking incompatible musical genres and making them work together. Producer of Herbie Hancock's legendary "Rockit" and great deconstruction disco by Material and Nona Hendryx.

BILLY COBHAM
Fusion drummer who played in Miles Davis' band in the early seventies. Pursued a more rock brand of fusion on his own in albums like *Spectrum*.

BLACK RIOT
Alias of Brooklyn's Todd Terry, who set everyone on their head and toes with the shattering staccato "Can You Party", which dissected Public Enemy, T La Rock, and Mr. Fingers with a surgical knife, leaving single syllables on the cutting-room floor.

BOBBY KONDERS
Now a staple of the New York dancehall scene. Konders' "The Poem", which sampled African poet Mutabaruka on the now defunct NuGroove label, was "ambient house" long before anyone coined the term.

BOBBY O
a.k.a Bobby Orlando. The king of Hi-NRG. made disco even more "artificial", by cranking up the beats-per-minute and using more synthesizers.

BOARDS OF CANADA
Scotland's Michael Sandison and Marcus Eoin, alias Boards of Canada, released their debut album *Music Has The Right To Children* in spring of 1998 with a follow-up in 1999.

BRIAN ENO
Musical wanderer and philosopher. After leaving Roxy Music in the early seventies, he came up with the concept of ambient music. Recently developed KOAN, a software program that allows a computer to generate music.

CABARET VOLTAIRE
Very influential electronic band from Sheffield.

CAJMERE
Popular house producer. Started Cajual Records and Relief Records, two of Chicago's premier house labels.

CALVIN BUSH
Journalist for Muzik. Runs the label Fifth Freedom.

CAN
Seminal krautrock band. Members are bassist Holger Czukay, guitarist Michael Karoli, keyboardist Irmin Schmidt, and drummer Jaki Leibezeit.

CARL COX
Britain's best-loved DJ. Involved with the most important clubs of the house boom: Shoom and Spectrum. Allegedly the first to use more than two decks.

CARL CRAIG
Bridge between old- and new-school Detroit innovators.

CARL STONE
Stone's computer-assisted sound design, built around field recordings of the composer's own journeys, aims at creating a virtual travelog, albeit of an alternate reality.

CHEMICAL BROTHERS
Superstar Manchester techno duo. Their second album *Dig Your Own Hole* debuted at number 14 on the Billboard 200, the highest ever at the time.

CHRISTIAN MARCLAY
Pioneering turntable artist and sculptor.

CHROME:
Industrial/psychedelic weirdos from San Francisco.

CLARA ROCKMORE
In the hands of its first and greatest virtuoso performer, the theremin found a singing voice free of the sci-fi associations it would later accumulate.

CLUSTER
Using first processed guitars and then synths, Cluster (Dieter Moebius and Hans-Joachim Roedelius) created mesmerizing and minimal drone-mosaics.

COIL
The electronic project of former Throbbing Gristle member Sleazy Christopherson.

COLDCUT
Kings of the cut-up. Matt Black and Jonathon More were two of the earliest advocates of sampling and have made some of the best sampling records: *Beats and Pieces, Say Kids What Time Is It?*, and their remix of Eric B. & Rakim's "Paid In Full."

COSMIC JOKERS
Germany's counterpart to English hippy buffoons Gong, Cosmic Jokers used the recording studio as their playpen.

CUJO
see "Amon Tobin."

CYBOTRON
a.k.a Juan Atkins.

DAF
Underappreciated German electronic group from the early eighties.

DAFT PUNK
French duo Daft Punk fuses house, funk, electro, and techno.

DANNY TENAGLIA
New York house producer equally adept at screaming-queen garage and hard house.

DARREN EMERSON
Member of Underworld, Britain's popular electronica trio.

DAVE CLARKE
Techno artiste originally from Brighton. Came to prominence with the "Red" series on Bush Records in 1994. Ran his own influential label Magnetic North.

DAVID TUDOR
Right-hand man to John Cage who premiered many of Cage's prepared piano works, and devised pioneering live electronic systems of his own, including the classic Rainforest

DB
DJ responsible for introducing large numbers of American kids to British electronic dance music.

DE LA SOUL
Long Island trio – Posdnous, Pacemaster Mace, Trugoy the Dove – who changed the sound of hip-hop in 1989 with their *3 Feet High and Rising album*.

DEPÈCHE MODE
Enormously successful group that was the brainchild of Vince Clarke, the Stendahl of synth-pop.

DERRICK CARTER
Nifty producer. One of the saviors of Chicago house.

DERRICK MAY
Detroit techno pioneer. Perhaps the greatest DJ ever. Also recorded some of the greatest electronic records, including "Strings Of Life," "Nude Photo," and "The Dance."

DEVO
Two sets of brothers from Ohio who became one of America's most successful New Wave acts.

DEXTER WANSELL
One of the lesser-known names at Philadelphia International, but his records were the label's mid-seventies high points.

DIMITRI FROM PARIS
French DJ and producer who weds kitsch, easy-listening, and trip-hoppy dance beats.

DINOSAUR L.
Nom de disque of Arthur Russell. One of the few avant-gardists who never forsook pleasure.

DJ ASSAULT
Alter ego of pottymouthed Detroit booty/bass/ghetto tech DJ Craig Adams.

DJ FUNK
Nasty-style Chicago house DJ.

DJ KRUSH
Japanese turntablist/collage artist. Brought hip-hop back to its instrumental roots by utilizing minimalist beats, scratching, and sampling.

DJ KRUST
Jungle producer from Bristol who samples hip-hop records. Associated with Roni Size.

DJ MAGIC MIKE
Killer DJ and bass entrepreneur from Orlando.

DJ PIERRE
See "Phuture."

DJ SHADOW
a.k.a Josh Davis. American abstract hip-hop DJ from Davis, California. Early records like "In/Flux" and "What Does Your Soul Look Like?" were incredibly important on the trip-hop scene.

DJ SNEAK
King of the disco cut-up. Records tracks that are minimal enough for techno dancefloors but musical enough for house.

DJ SPOOKY
Downtown New York illbient conceptualist, producer of dystopian soundscapes.

DJ VADIM
Very downtempo trip-hop producer. Records for Ninja Tune and Mille Plateaux, as well as his own Jazz Fudge label.

DOC SCOTT
Jungle producer since the early nineties and cofounder with Goldie of Metalheadz. Helped give birth to the dark jungle of the mid-nineties.

DONNA SUMMER
Disco diva. See "Giorgio Moroder."

DREXCIYA
Mysterious sci-fi-obsessed Detroit electro collective that claim to hail from underwater stomping grounds just south of Atlantis.

DROPPIN' SCIENCE
Danny Breaks, a stalwart of the Romford-based Suburban Base crew, abandoned his Sonz of a Loop Da Loop Era moniker in 1994, going on to produce glittering, state-of-the-art drum and bass as Droppin' Science.

DXT
See "Grandmixer DXT."

DYNAMIX II
Dave Noller and Scott Weiser have been pumping out a more mechanistic version of Miami bass for a decade and a half.

ED RUSH
No U Turn. British tech-step junglist.

E-DANCER
See "Kevin Saunderson."

EDDIE FOWLKES
One of the funkiest Detroit techno producers.

EDGARD VARÈSE
The granddaddy of tape music. *Poème Électronique*, originally scored for a massive 400 speaker PA installation at the 1958 Brussels World's Fair, is a massively ambitious piece that seeks to incorporate a world of sounds in its concrète elements. Along with the Italian futurists, Varèse was the first composer to respond to the modern environment by writing pieces that aimed for speed, rhythmic force, and ferocity. His *Ecuatorial* was one of the first pieces to feature the theremin and the ondes martenot, and his *Poème Électronique* remains one of the landmarks of electronic music.

ELLIOTT SHARP
Invented the vocabulary and syntax of a unique and dynamic music in the interzone between order and chaos using self-designed instruments and computers.

ERIC B & RAKIM
DJ and rapper who revolutionized the sound of hip-hop with their daring use of samples and beats and their influential rapping style.

FARLEY "JACKMASTER" FUNK
In charge of the House label, Farley recorded "Bessie Smith-House Girl" and the hyperparanoid "Jack the Bass," one of the classic Chicago woofer-destroying tunes.

FAUST
Wildly schizo-eclectic krautrock troupe whose work ranges from Dadaist cut-ups to folkadelic ballads to Velvet Underground-style walls of noise.

THE FEARLESS FOUR
Bronx crew who recorded the innovative Kraftwerk-inspired "Rockin' It" and other electro classics in the early eighties.

FRANÇOIS KEVORKIAN
Disco godfather and in-house mixer for the Prelude label. Remixed nearly every Prelude track, which is virtually every great disco song.

FRANKIE BONES
New York techno producer. Sonic Groove.

FRANKIE KNUCKLES
The godfather of house music. Aside from creating the house blueprint with his DJing at the Warehouse in Chicago, Knuckles has also created some of house music's undisputed masterpieces: Jamie Principle's "Your Love" and "Baby Wants To Ride," the Nightwriters' anthem "Let the Music Use You" and Robert Owens' "Tears".

FRONT 242
The kings of Belgian new beat.

FUNKI PORCINI
a.k.a. James Braddell. Downtempo, abstract jazz artist.

FUTURE SOUND OF LONDON
Electronica artists Gary Cobain and Brian Dougan. Came out with the landmark ethno-techno track "Papua New Guinea" in 1992.

GANJA CRU
A loose, hedonistic posse consisting of DJ Hype, Pascal, and Zinc. Massive basslines, scattershot percussion, and rampant, three-dimensional beats make these urban scruffs the undisputed champs of the jump-up sound.

GARY NUMAN
Beginning in the late seventies, Numan mixed synthesizers with drum machines and sci-fi paranoia to create gothic "machine music" with a pop twist.

GENESIS P-ORRIDGE
Founding member of seminal industrial band Throbbing Gristle. Formed Psychic TV with Sleazy Christopherson in 1982. Moving away from TG's grimness, Psychic TV set about re-writing psychedelia until an encounter with house music in Chicago. His explicit fusion of politics and dance music was groundbreaking.

GEORGE CLINTON
Founder and visionary of the Parliament Funkadelic thang that fused funk, rock, comic books, and electronics to forge an eloquent statement of nonessentialist blackness.

GEORGE E. LEWIS
AACM-affiliated trombonist and computer programmer Lewis has made it possible for machines to participate – convincingly – in improvised music.

GEORGE RUSSELL
One of the more interesting thinkers in jazz, Russell's "Electronic Sonata for Souls Loved by Nature" was one of the first intersections between jazz and electronics.

GERALD SIMPSON
See "A Guy Called Gerald."

GIORGIO MORODER
Best known for his disco synthesizer production with Pete Belotte of Donna Summer.

GOLDIE
Goldie's "Terminator" almost single-handedly created dark jungle in 1993. *Timeless* is jungle's biggest-selling album.

GRAND MIXER DXT
Scratcher on Herbie Hancock's "Rockit." Reinvented scratching and DJing.

GRAND WIZARD THEODORE
Hip-hop DJ who invented scratching.

GRANDMASTER FLASH
a.k.a Joseph Sadler. The most important of the first hip-hop djs. Invented turntable techniques like back-spinning and cutting.

GREEN VELVET
a.k.a Cajmere.

GROOVERIDER
The most important DJ in jungle. Was resident DJ along with Fabio at London's Rage Club, which nurtured hardcore and spawned jungle. Runs the Prototype label.

GROUND ZERO
Otomo Yoshihide and his ever-shifting crew of collaborators juxtapose extreme turntablism and sampladelia with a brutal post-prog instrumental attack with intelligence and humor, and without contradiction.

HARDFLOOR
German techno duo responsible for the re-emergence of acid sound.

HARMONIA
A collaboration between ex-Neu! guitarist Michael Rother, Cluster's Dieter Moebius, and Hans-Joachim Roedelius, Harmonia recorded two beatific, synth-infused albums in the mid-seventies.

HEAVEN 17
Former Human Leaguers who attempted to translate Marx for the Korg.

HERBALISER
DJ Ollie Teeba and Jake Wheery. Bass-heavy Ninja Tune recording duo whose style lies somewhere between hip-hop and deep jazz.

HERBIE HANCOCK
Born in 1940, Herbie Hancock was Miles Davis' keyboard player of choice for most of the sixties and is perhaps the most important postwar keyboard player. Hancock's own sextet of the early seventies produced the electric-funk-jazz milestones, *Sextant and Crossings*.

HOLGER CZUKAY
See "Can."

HONEY DRIPPERS
Funk obscurities whose "Impeach the President" features one of hip-hop's favorite drum breaks.

HUMAN LEAGUE
Sheffield's most influential electronic group.

HYPER ON EXPERIENCE
This Moving Shadow-signed duo (Banks and Derriere) produced one of the landmarks in breakbeat evolution with "Lords of the Null Lines." Sadly, other releases failed to make the same impact.

IANNIS XENAKIS
Pioneer of "stochastic" music, in which the rules of probability govern the form the music takes. Used computers to facilitate this process and created scores for both acoustic and electronic instruments.

THE INVISIBL SKRATCH PIKLZ
Perhaps the best scratch DJ troupe around.

IRMIN SCHMIDT
See "Can."

IRRESISTIBLE FORCE
See Mixmaster Morris.

THE J.B.'S
James Brown's backing band after 1970.

JAMES BROWN
Godfather of soul. Hardest working man in show business.

JAMIE PRINCIPLE
The queeny "bad boy" of the early house years. His "Baby Wants to Ride" captured the raunch of Prince and the melancholic strains of early vocal house tracks, such as Mr. Fingers' "Can U Feel It."

JEAN-JACQUES PERREY
As a musical scientist, Perrey has spent a lifetime researching the therapeutic effects of sound. As a scientist-musician he arranged *musique concrète* into rhythmic loops in the sixties, discovering sampling techniques before the invention of sampling technology.

JEFF MILLS
Acknowledged as techno's foremost conceptual musician, Jeff Mills continues to explore new dimensions in techno music through his DJing and compositions.

JESSE SAUNDERS
Saunders founded the legendary Jes 'Say label and in doing so effectively gave birth to house on black wax.

JIMI TENOR
Finnish purveyor of kitsch electronic lounge music.

JM SILK
Duo who recorded a version of Isaac Hayes' "Love Can't Turn Around" that became the most disputed house record in Chicago during a battle to claim ownership over the title "orginator."

JOCELYN ENRIQUEZ
The Filipino singer who is the current queen of freestyle. Joe Gibbs: Legendary reggae and dub producer who, with engineer Errol Thompson, was responsible for some of the best records from reggae's golden age in the seventies.

JOEY BELTRAM
New York techno artist and Black Sabbath fan whose "Energy Flash" and "Mentasm" are the two most important non-Detroit techno songs. Very influential on British hardcore techno.

JOHN CAGE
Probably the most intellectually stimulating modern composer, Cage interrogated fixed ideas of time, space, noise, and what constituted art. *Imaginary Landscape No. 1* was the first piece composed for an electronic reproduction device – the variable-speed turntable.

JOHN OSWALD
Tape editor, samplist, theorist, and political provocateur, Oswald alienates us from the familiar, building his pieces out of thousands of microfragments of songs we know all too well.

JON HASSELL
Coined the term "Fourth World," where music from around the world fuses together in a geographically nonspecific place.

JONAH SHARP
a.k.a. Spacetime Continuum. Ex-pat Brit who purveys lazy ambient in San Francisco runs the Reflective label.

JOSH WINK
Panstylistic DJ and producer from Philadelphia who first came to public attention with house tracks on the Strictly Rhythm label.

JUAN ATKINS
The greatest and the most important of the Detroit techno producers. As Cybotron, he recorded "Clear," the bridge between electro and techno. As Model 500, he has made two of the best techno songs ever: "No UFOs" and "Night Drive Through Babylon."

KARLHEINZ STOCKHAUSEN
The granddaddy of electronic music. Moved from serial compositions to explorations of pure electronic frequencies in the fifties to aleatoric compositions in the sixties and seventies. His masterpieces include *Gesang der Junglinge*, *Kontakte, Telemusik, Kurzwellen* and *Prozession*.

KEVIN SAUNDERSON
Detroit techno artist. One of the Belleville Three (with Derrick May and Juan Atkins).

KEMISTRY & STORM
An influential London-based drum and bass DJ team, Kemistry was tragically killed in a car accident in April 1999.

KID KOALA
a.k.a. Eric San. Scratch DJ from Montreal.

KING TUBBY
a.k.a. Osbourne Ruddock. The monarch of dub.

KLF
Chart-topping popstars, media pranksters, and radical creatives, the Kopyright Liberation Front have succesfully hoaxed/played with high art, commercial music, and mainstream news channels. Also worked under the banner K Foundation, and have most recently been involved in publishing, book readings, projections, and "industrial plant hire."

KOOL KEITH
Rapper with influential Ultramagnetic MCs who later produced eccentric, original solo work as Dr. Octagon, Dr. Dooom, and other alter egos.

KRAFTWERK
German group whose "man-machine" music in the seventies celebrated the pure speed and rush of new technology. Records like *Trans-Europe Express* and *Autobahn* became dancefloor favorites in American discos.

KRUDER & DORFMEISTER
Purveyors of downtempo funk from Vienna.

LARRY LEVAN
Classic house DJ. Used to spin at the famous Paradise Garage in New York City

LAURIE ANDERSON
Downtown New York performance/multimedia artist.

LEE "SCRATCH" PERRY
Jamaica's greatest and most idiosyncratic producer. Produced Bob Marley & The Wailers, Junior Byles, and Junior Murvin. With his band The Upsetters, Perry's early bass-heavy instrumentals helped inaugurate the dub era.

LFO
The 1991 debut "Frequency" by LFO was a groundbreaking underground techno classic that helped establish the reputation of the label Warp.

LISA LISA & CULT JAM
Freestyle's biggest pop stars.

LISETTE MELENDEZ
One of the ruling divas of freestyle.

LTJ BUKEM
Almost single-handedly responsible for atmospheric jungle.

LUC FERRARI
Central figure in the GRM camp, Ferrari's work reactivates location recording, digital synthesis, and environmental sound with a playful sensuality.

LUCIANO BERIO
Born in 1925, Luciano Berio is one of the giants of avant-garde composition. Interested in the human voice and in interrogating the history of music with electronic instruments.

LUIGI RUSSOLO
Italian futurist who wrote the manifesto of "The Art of Noises" just before the outbreak of World War I. Called for a music that embraced the sounds of the new industrialization. Built a series of instruments, including the Intonarumori, to produce these sounds.

LUKE VIBERT
Ambient, weirdbeat, trip-hop, junglist. Makes interesting ambient stuff as Wagon Christ, quirky jungle as Plug, and downtempo hip-hop stuff under his own name.

LYN COLLINS
Singer with the James Brown Revue whose "Think" is one of the three or four most sampled songs of all time.

MAD PROFESSOR
The patron saint of British dub.

MARKUS POPP
Founder of the conceptual techno group Oval that makes music with skipping cds. Also one half of Microstoria.

MARSHALL JEFFERSON
One of the pioneers of Chicago house music. His "Move Your Body" is the unofficial anthem of house music. Also involved with acid house pioneers Phuture.

MARTIN CIRCUS
French one-hit wonder responsible for the all-time classic "Disco Circus."

MC SHY D
Bass' most recognizable MC after 2 Live Crew and the man behind such classics as "Big Booty Girls," "True to the Game," and "I Will Go Off."

MEAT BEAT MANIFESTO
a.k.a. Jack Dangers. Record collector.

MELLE MEL (MELVIN GLOVER)
New York rapper who came to prominence with Grandmaster Flash and the Furious Five, cowrote "The Message," and later worked solo as Grandmaster Melle Mel and collaborated with Quincy Jones.

MICROSTORIA
Oval's Markus Popp and Mouse On Mars' Jan St. Werner (both from Germany) collaborate as Microstoria, an inscrutable union that to date has yielded three full-length albums, including the 1997 remix project *Reprovisers*.

MIKE DEARBORN
Hard house producer from Chicago.

MIKEY DREAD
The clown prince of dub. Producer whose *African Anthem* and *Beyond World War III* albums are landmarks in the use of space and effects.

MILES DAVIS
Born in 1926, Miles Davis has probably been responsible for more innovations than anyone else in jazz. Inaugurated the "cool jazz" era in 1949. His *Kind of Blue* album introduced modal improvisation (based on scales rather than on chord changes) in 1959, while his late-sixties albums bridged the funkier hard-bop style with the intellectual abstracton of free jazz. In the seventies, Davis explored the union of funk rhythms, rock instrumentation, jazz, and electronics, producing some of the most breathtaking records of all-time.

MILTON BABBITT
One of the most serious and important of the American academic classical composers. Pioneer of electro-acoustics and computer-generated methods.

MIXMASTER MORRIS
a.k.a. Irresistible Force. Patron saint of ambient (I think, therefore I ambient).

MOBY
a.k.a. Richard Hall. For years the only electronic artist that the U.S. press would cover. His best record is *Thousand* which is in the Guinness Book of Records as the fastest song in history (1000 Bpm), while "Go" is his biggest hit.

MODEL 500
a.k.a Juan Atkins.

MONEY MARK
Became a household name as the keyboardist for The Beastie Boys, which launched him a successful career as a solo artist. His last two albums are downtempo.

MOODYMANN
Alter ego of Detroit DJ/producer Kenny Dixon, Jr., member of Detroit's late-nineties techno-influenced house scene, owner of KDJ label, coowner of the Three Chairs label.

MORTON SUBOTNICK
One of the United States' premier composers of electronic music and an innovator in works involving instruments and other media, including interactive computer music systems.

MOUSE ON MARS
German electronica duo, Jan St. Werner and Andi Toma, who use both electronics and live instruments to create imaginary soundscapes.

MR. FINGERS
Nearly mythic duo of Larry Heard and vocalist/songwriter Robert Owens recorded some of the most mesmerizing house songs ever recorded, including the sampled beyond recognition "Can U Feel It." The pair also recorded under the name Fingers, Inc.

NEU!
This Düsseldorf duo – guitarist Michael Rother and drummer/vocalist Klaus Dinger – pioneered the silvered, streamlined sound of motorik rock.

NEW ORDER
Former postpunk miserablists who became one of the most successful British bands of the eighties.

NIGHTMARES ON WAX
Group that blended R&B, jazz, hip-hop, film music, and electronics to establish what is commonly referred to as trip-hop.

O. YUKI CONJUGATE
Experimental ambient group. Records for Australia's Extreme.

OLIVIER MESSIAEN
Born in 1908, Olivier Messiaen was one of the most important composers of the twentieth century. Looking for a way out of the traps of neoclassicism and serialism (in which the notes of a scale are arranged in a fixed order that remain constant through the duration of the piece) and for a way to express the divine, Messiaen emphasized rhythm and sought influence from Eastern music (particularly the Indonesian gamelan) and birdsong. Teacher of Pierre Boulez and Karlheinz Stockhausen.

OMNI TRIO
a.k.a Rob Haigh. Omni Trio's finely-poised and string-drenched Volumes 2,3,4 and 5 for Moving Shadow offered infinitely more plangent melodies and complex rhythms than the run-of-the-mill artcore crowd could muster. Later LP projects like Skeleton Keys were similarly acclaimed.

THE ORB
Alex Patterson and Andy Hughes. The godfathers of ambient house.

ORBITAL
a.k.a. Phil and Paul Hartnoll. Perhaps the most popular techno outfit.

OUTKAST
Atlanta duo Big Boi and Dre whose *Aquemini* album mixed thoughtful, serious lyrics with music drenched in Southern feel.

OVAL
See "Marcus Popp."

PANACEA
a.k.a. Mathis Mootz. Really rough techstep junglist from Germany. Records for Force Inc. and Position Chrome.

PAN SONIC
Experimental techno group from Finland led by Miko Vainio. They specialize in making rhythm nothing but texture.

PAPERCLIP PEOPLE
a.k.a. Carl Craig.

PARLIAMENT
Parliament's Mothership Connection made explicit the connection between old spirituals and outer-space fantasies, while their "Flashlight" was the first song to feature a synthesized bassline. See George Clinton.

PATRICK COWLEY
Sylvester's producer and creator of extreme Hi-NRG disco at the end of the seventies and in the early eighties.

PAULINE OLIVEROS
Oliveros' use of signal processing to transform instrumental performance with the Deep Listening Band and as a solo accordionist, has made her one of electro-acoustic music's most consistent innovators.

PEECH BOYS
Studio disco group led by vocalist Bernard Fowler and produced by Larry Levan.

PETE NAMLOOK
Experimental ambient producer and frequent collaborator with other musicians across the world in the attempt to create a worldwide ambient idea.

PHONOSYCOGRAPH
A member of San Francisco's Invisbl Skratch Piklz, DJ Disk made one of the most creative and coherent examples of turntablist art with his 1998 *Ancient Termites* album for Bomb Hip-Hop Records.

PHOTEK
a.k.a.Rupert Parkes. One of the original and best of the junglists.

PHOTON INC.
See "DJ Pierre" and "Phuture."

PHUTURE
Chicago house DJ Pierre and his group (with the production assistance of Marshall Jefferson) turned on a Roland TB-303 and launched the acid revolution.

PIERRE BOULEZ
French composer and conductor. Champion of contemporary classical music.

PIERRE HENRY
Born in 1927, Pierre Henry was one of the prime movers of *Musique Concrète* with Pierre Schaeffer. "Symphonie Pour un Homme Seul" (London) is their most significant collaboration.

PIERRE SCHAEFFER
French composer born in 1910 and responsible for the development of *musique concrète*.

PLAID
Formerly two-thirds of esoteric electronic UK outfit The Black Dog, Ed Handley and Andy Turner's records under the Plaid moniker include *Mbuki Mvuki* (1991) and *Not For Threes* (1997).

PLASTIKMAN
a.k.a Richie Hawtin. Techno geezer from Windsor, Ontario, across the river from Detroit. One of the people responsible for reviving the sound of the Roland TR-303.

POLYGON WINDOW
Polygon Window, best known for the 1993 album *Surfing on Sine Waves*, is yet another manifestation of U.K. multiple-personality-disorder poster boy Richard James (alias Aphex Twin, AFX, Dice Man, etc.).

POPOL VUH
German neopsychedelia at its most kosmiche, Popol Vuh's music ranged from grandiose majesty to meditational calm.

PRINCE JAMMY
Despite his title, producer Prince Jammy was the king of the Jamaican dancehall in the eighties.

PRODIGY
Prodigy has evolved into one of the most popular electronic music acts in the world.

PROTOTYPE 909
America's favorite live techno act.

PSYCHE/BFC
See "Carl Craig."

PSYCHIC TV
See "Genesis P-Orridge".

PUBLIC ENEMY
Long Island group started at Adelphi University by Chuck D and Hank Shocklee; later joined by Flavor Flav to create the most intense, dense mix of complex rhymes, rhetoric, and sound in hip-hop history.

QUAD CITY DJS
The artistes behind the Love Unlimited-sampling "C'mon N' Ride It (the Train)."

RAMMELZEE
Using a unique mix of free-associative rapping and slow, eerie beats on "Beat Bop," graffiti artist Rammelzee proved himself one of the most original artists in hip-hop.

THE RESIDENTS
Anonymous pranksters from Northern California.

RICHARD JAMES
See "Aphex Twin."

ROBERT MOOG
Inventor of the Moog synthesizer and popularizer of the theremin.

ROBERT PEPPERELL
Author of *The Post-Human Condition*. Affiliated with Ninja Tune.

ROBIN RIMBAUD
See "Scanner."

RONI SIZE
Landmark junglist from Bristol.

ROYAL HOUSE
See "Black Riot."

RUN DMC
The most successful and the greatest of hip-hop's superstars. Everything before Run DMC is old school. This Queens trio revolutionized hardcore rap and brought it to the masses.

RUNE LINDBLAD
The Swede's infernal sound collages mixed slash-and-burn tape edits with crosstalk, varispeed disorientation, and the introduction of ethnic samples.

RYUICHI SAKAMOTO
See also "Yellow Magic Orchestra." Avant-garde composer of what he calls new geographic music, which aims at convergence of different styles of music from across the globe. He has also composed scores for various films including *The Last Emperor* and *Merry Christmas, Mr. Lawrence*.

SA-FIRE
Responsible for the freestyle classics "Don't Break My Heart" and "Love Is on Her Mind."

SCANNER
a.k.a. Robin Rimbaud. Scanned cellular telephone conversations for recordings and live sets.

SENSORBAND
Billed as noise terrorists, the three members – Atau Tanaka, Edwin van der Heide and Masami Akita – use interactive instruments, infrared, and ultrasound among other electronically generated sounds to create their music experiments.

SHANNON
Diva responsible for the eternal "Let the Music Play."

SHY FX AND UK APACHE
Producer-and-MC duo whose "Incredible Nuttah" was a fully fledged jungle anthem and hot Top 40 single. Obscurity has since claimed them.

SLEEZY D
See "Marshall Jefferson"

SLIPMATT
Essex native and U.S. house obsessive. Pioneered commercial breakbeat house in the early nineties.

SOULSLINGER
New York-based junglist. Heads the Jungle Sky label.

SPACETIME CONTINUUM
a.k.a. Jonah Sharp.

SQUAREPUSHER
Intricate drum programmer and fusion lover. Also records under his own name, Tom Jenkinson and as the Duke of Harringay.

STACEY PULLEN
One of the new generation of Detroit techno artists who bridges house and techno.

STEREOLAB
With their arcane knowledge of obscure experimental music, their love of the Moog, and their fondness for exotica, Stereolab is perhaps the ultimate rock group of the late twentieth century.

STEVE HURLEY
Working for Rocky Jones' DJ International label, rival to Larry Sherman's Trax empire, Steve "Silk" Hurley produced numerous tracks in house's early years.

STEVE REICH
American minimalist composer. Early works used tape loops moving slowly in and out of phase.

STEVIE WONDER
One of soul music's greatest talents. Introduced the synthesizer into popular black music and created some of the finest moments in the history of electronic music.

SUICIDE
This duo of Martin Rev and Alan Vega was the most successful fusion of electronics and punk sensibilities to date.

SUN RA
Jazz pioneer whose notions of collective improvisation and outer-space mysticism anticipated both free jazz and fusion by years. His linking of Egyptology, astro-metaphysics, and early synthesizers was the beginning of Africanist science fiction, which runs from him through P-Funk and electric Miles Davis to electro, techno, and jungle.

SURGEON
Techno artist from Birmingham.

SVEN VATH
Godfather of trance techno.

SYLVESTER
Gay disco diva and icon who, with Patrick Cowley, created a form of disco that celebrated mechano-eroticism as an alternative to straight bump and grind on songs like "(You Make Me Feel) Mighty Real," "Stars," and "Dance (Disco Heat)."

TALVIN SINGH
Mixes drum and bass with traditional Indian instruments like sitars and tablas.

TEN CITY
Deans of the Chicago soul house scene, Byron Stingily and his comrades have kept the Philly sound of Harold Melvin, Isaac Hayes, et al. at the center of their records. Their music would be taken up in the New Jersey house scene by DJs such as Tony Humphries and in Manhattan by the Paradise Garage's Levan as well as by Frankie Knuckles. For deep-vocal house purists, Ten City and Blaze remain the only true creators.

TEO MACERO
Producer of Miles Davis' electric period records. By splicing up tapes of live and studio performances, he had a huge influence on studio practitioners who came after him.

TERRE THAEMLITZ
Avant-garde composer of electronic music. Brings notions of queer identity into play.

TERRY RILEY
Influenced by psychedelics and Indian ragas, Riley was one of the main movers of minimalism.

TETSU INOUE
Japanese ambient guru. Frequent collaborators include Bill Laswell and Atom Heart.

THE BLACK DOG
Extremely important and original British electronica outfit whose influence came from their use of jazz in their plaintive techno.

THEO PARRISH
Detroit DJ/producer who's a member of the Motor City's late-nineties techno-influenced house scene. Also owner of the Sound Signature label and coowner of the Three Chairs label.

THROBBING GRISTLE
See "Genesis P-Orridge."

TKA
With hits like "Scars of Love" and "Tears May Fall", TKA was freestyle's best group of male heartthrobs.

TO ROCOCO ROT
Using mostly live instruments in their recordings, they brought us full circle by making "real" music that is imitative of electronically produced sounds.

TOD DOCKSTADER
Self-taught tape-loop genius whose long form constructions such as Apocalypse and Quatermass are cited by the likes of Autechre.

TODD TERRY
Amongst the most popular house producers in the world. Perhaps best known for his remixes, Terry has produced for some of the biggest names in the music industry.

TORTOISE
Started by drummer John McEntire and bassist Doug McCombs, this Chicago-based band is the leader of the post-rock movement.

TRANS AM
Washington DC-based post-rock band that merges traditional acoustic instrumentation with synthesizers, processors, and vocal distortion.

UNDERGROUND RESISTANCE
Techno gods led by Mad Mike. UR couch their releases in black cultural nationalist rhetoric and guerilla disguises.

U-ROY
Probably the most important of the Jamaican DJs who would chat over records.

VITTORIO GELMETTI
An almost forgotten Italian tape composer whose low-fidelity homemade constructions sound like an extraterrestrial's perspective of the music and signals emanating from earth.

WAGON CHRIST
See "Luke Vibert."

WALTER/WENDY CARLOS
Pioneer synthesist, best known for "Switched on Bach."

WAYNE SMITH
Ragga vocalist responsible for "Under Mi Sleng Teng," the most important Jamaican record of the eighties.

WELDON IRVINE
Astro-jazz/fusion keyboardist from the mid-seventies who pursued an outer space-inflected mysticism on albums like Time Capsule and Sinbad.

WESTBAM
German techno producer. Emerged from the Low Spirit label in the late eighties.

THE WU-TANG CLAN
Vast collective of Staten Island rappers and producers that includes Method Man, Ghostface Killer, RZA, Raekwon, Ol' Dirty Bastard, Inspectah Deck and GZA and that has carved out an empire through group and solo success.

X-ECUTIONERS
Scratch DJ crew from New York City who count among their members Rob Swift, Roc Raida, and others.

YELLOW MAGIC ORCHESTRA
Haruomi Hosono, Ryuichi Sakamoto, and Yukihiro Takahachi. YMO became one of the pioneers of electronic music by pursuing the links between ethnic trance music and pop.

AUTHOR BIOGRAPHIES

MICHAEL BERK
is a freelance journalist, editor, and musician. His work has appeared in *Option, The San Francisco Bay Guardian*, and *The Los Angeles Reader*. He lives in New York City, where he plays guitar and electronics in several groups.

KODWO ESHUN
is a contributor to *The Wire, i-D, The Face, Mixmag* and author of *More Brilliant Than the Sun*, an exploration of the black science fiction tradition in music. Along with Simon Reynolds, he is the first mainstream journalist to write about jungle and hardcore.

TONY MARCUS
is a contributor to *i-D, The Big Issue, Spin* and *OK!*

KURT B. REIGHLEY
the beloved freelance crackpot, is Editor at Large of *CMJ New Music Monthly*, a regular contributor to *Pulse!* and *Paper*, and a columnist for the Seattle Weekly and Resonance. His examination of the art of the DJ *In the Mix*, will be published by MTV Books in late 1999. As DJ El Toro, he tortures turntables at a variety of Seattle-area hot spots.

SIMON REYNOLDS
is the author of *Generation Ecstasy: Into The World of Techno and Rave Culture*, the paperback edition of which will be published by Routledge in August 1999. In the U.K. and Europe, the book is titled *Energy Flash* and is published by Picador. His previous books include *Blissed Out: The Raptures of Rock* (1990) and *The Sex Revolts: Gender, Rebellion and Rock 'n' Roll* (1995). He is a senior contributing writer for *Spin*, and a freelance contributor to the *Village Voice, The Wire*, and the *New York Times*. He also operates the webzine, "A White Brit Rave Aesthete Thinks Aloud" at http://members.aol.com/blissout/.

MIKE RUBIN
is a senior contributing writer at *Spin* and a regular contributor at the *Village Voice*. For the last dozen years he's been a member of the ruling junta behind *Motorbooty* magazine, an independently published, Detroit-based satirical journal that blends meticulous musical scholarship with irreverent, merciless mockery (and now available on the web at www.motorbooty.com). His work has also appeared in the *New York Times Magazine, GQ*, and *Details*. He lives in Brooklyn, New York.

PETER SHAPIRO
is one of the world's leading authorities on air guitar. He has been a freelance music journalist for such publications as *Spin, The Wire, Urb, Uncut*, and *Music Week* since 1993 and is the author of *The Rough Guide to Drum 'n' Bass* as well as a contributing editor to *The Rough Guide to Rock*.

CHRIS SHARP
by day, runs the press department of XL Recordings, one of the U.K.'s leading independent dance music record labels. He devotes his spare time to writing about music, principally for *The Wire* magazine in the U.K., but more recently for *Spin* in the United States as well. He lives in the East End of London, which is the best place in the world for listening to pirate radio.

DAVID TOOP
is a London-based musician, writer, and sound curator. He has written three books – *Rap Attack* (1984/1991, third edition due 1998), *Ocean of Sound* (1995) and *Exotica* (1999) and released three solo albums – *Screen Ceremonies* (1995), *Pink Noir* (1996) and *Spirit World* (1997). In 1998, he composed music for Acqua Matrix, the outdoor spectacular that closed every night of Lisbon's Expo '98. He has recorded with musicians from many fields, including Prince Far I, Brian Eno, John Zorn, Jon Hassell, Scanner, Evan Parker, Talvin Singh, Bedouin Ascent, and Paul Schutze. He has written for many publications, including *The Wire, The Face, the London Times, the Village Voice, Interview, Vogue, Details, GQ* and *Billboard*.

ROB YOUNG
is the Deputy Editor of *The Wire*, the U.K. based magazine that chronicles developments across a broad spectrum of modern music. In addition to editing and writing for the magazine, he is responsible for developing its website (http://www.dfuse.com/the-wire). Since 1994, he has co-organized leftfield music events and club spaces in London, including Scratch, Transgressions, and Current, and hosted music panels and/or DJed (as The Wire Sound System) at many U.K. and European events and festivals.

INDEX OF SONG/TRACK TITLES

INDEX OF RECORD/LONG WORK TITLES

INDEX OF RECORD LABELS

INDEX OF EQUIPMENT

INDEX OF STYLES

INDEX OF PHOTO CREDITS

Goldie: 111/145 Timeless Record (Iara Lee)
Grandmaster Flash: 95 (Chris Wahl)
Grooverider: 144 left (Carol Taveras)

Herbie Hancock: 52 top (Robert Zuckerman)

Iannis Xenakis: 19 top left (Robbie Busch)

Jesse Saunders: 74 top left (Iara Lee)
John Cage: 16 w/ Toshiro Mayuzumi (courtesy of
 The John Cage Trust)
Josh Wink: 85 top (Iara Lee)
Juan Atkins: 112 (Chris Wahl)
Junior Vasquez: 86 top (Al Perreira)

Karlheinz Stockhausen: 18 (Iara Lee)
Kemistry and Storm: 132 (Chris Wahl)
Kid Koala: 88/89 (Iara Lee)
Kraftwerk: 29 (Marcus Burnett), 32 (Marcus Burnett)
Kruder and Dorfmeister: 187 (Iara Lee)
Krust: 139 (Chris Wahl)

Lee Perry: 50 (Robbie Busch)

Meat Beat Manifesto (a.k.a Jack Dangers): 60 top
 (Jay Blakesburg)
Merzbow: 63 (Robbie Busch)
Miles Davis: 54 w/ Teo Macero (courtesy of Teo Macero)
Mixmaster Mike (Invisibl Skratch Picklz): 97 (Iara Lee)
Mixmaster Morris: 128 (Chris Wahl), 163 (Marcus Burnett)
Money Mark: 170 (Iara Lee)
Morton Subotnick: 10 top left (Jack Mitchell)
Mouse on Mars: 174 (Dinah Frank, courtesy of Too Pure)
Mt. Fuji Rainbow 2000: 118 (Marcus Burnett)

Nightmares on Wax: 179 (W. Mustain)

O. Yuki Conjugate: 163 top right (Iara Lee)
Oval: 181 (Chris Wahl)

Panacea: 134 (Chris Wahl)
Photek: 142 (Marcu Burnett)
Pierre Henry: 22 (Iara Lee), Studio 8/9 (Iara Lee),
 Studio 195 (Iara Lee)
Pierre Schaeffer: 19 top right (S. Lido, photo courtesy
 of INA-GRM)
Plaid: 175 (W. Mustain)
Plastikman (a.k.a Richie Hawtin): 114 left (Chris Wahl)
Public Enemy: 90 top (Al Perreira), 96 (Al Perreira)

Queen Latifah: 101 (Al Perreira)

Ravers: 110 (Robbie Busch), Busted Warehouse Party 124
 (Iara Lee)
Rob Playford: 152 top (Iara Lee)
Robert Moog: 206 (Iara Lee)
Roger Sanchez: 82 top (Iara Lee)
Roni Size: 130/131 (Carl Saytor), 136 (Carl Saytor)
Run DMC: 93 (Al Perreira)
Ryuichi Sakamoto: 114 right (Hiroshi Nomura, courtesy
 of Asphodel Records)

Scanner: 184 (Iara Lee)
Sasha: 86 bottom (Iara Lee)
Sensorband: 62 (Iara Lee)
Squarepusher: 132 (R. Sweeney), 150 (Iara Lee)
Stacey Pullen: 115 across top (Ladybug)
Sun Ra: 56 (Thomas Hunter)
Sylvester: 40 (Phil Bray), 44 (Terry Hinte)

Talvin Singh: 145 (Carol Taveras)
Techno License Plate: 111 (Nancy Mitchell)
Teo Macero: 54 w/ Miles Davis (courtesy of Teo Macero)
Todd Terry: 82 bottom w/ Armand Van Helden
 (Robbie Busch)
Trans Am: 60 (Chris Toliver, courtesy of Thrill
 Jockey Records)

We: 177 (Iara Lee)

X-ecutioners: 90 bottom (Martin Schoeller, courtesy
 of Asphodel Records)

ABOUT THE FILM:
Modulations

WE ARE NOT ENTERTAINERS, WE ARE SOUND SCIENTISTS. – KRAFTWERK

From the makers of *Synthetic Pleasures* comes *Modulations*, a film that captures a moment in history where humans and machines are fusing to create today's most exciting sounds. *Modulations* traces the evolution of electronic music as one of the most profound artistic developments of the twentieth century. By cutting back and forth between avant-garde composers, Kraftwerk's innovative synthesizer drones, Giorgio Moroder's glacial Euro-disco, Afrika Bambaataa's electro-funk and Prodigy's current worldwide superstardom, *Modulations* celebrates, replicates, and illuminates the nomadic drift of the post-human techno sound. The film examines the kids who have turned the turntable into a musical instrument, the disillusioned disco lovers who created acid house out of primitive synthesizers, the Motor City mavericks who saw the drum machine as their escape route out of urban neglect, and a generation of British youth who transformed these blips and bleeps into dancefloor anthems of their own alienation. *Modulations* provides a sense of history and context in which today's electronic music can be understood. It entertains the converted and remixes the mindset of electronica's naysayers. Featuring a stunning collage of interviews, cutting-edge visuals, in-studio footage and live performances, *Modulations* moves at a pace that matches the energy and innovation of the music. Featuring: 2 Bad Mice, 4 Hero, Afrika Bambaataa, Air & Jean Jacques Perrey, Alvin Toffler, Aphrodite, Armand Van Helden, Armando, Arthur Baker, Atari Teenage Riot, Autechre, Babu, Bill Laswell, Boymerang, Bundy Brown, Calvin Bush, Carl Cox, Carl Craig, Christian Marclay, Coldcut & Hex,

Danny Tenaglia, Darren Emerson, David Kristian, Datacide, David Toop, Db, Derrick Carter, Derrick May, Dinosaur L, DJ Atrak, DJ Funk, DJ Petrov, DJ Pierre, DJ Sneak, DJ Spooky, Doc Scott, Donna Summer, DXT, Ed Rush & Nico, Eddie Fowlkes, Eps & DJ Mark, Frankie Bones, Fumiya Tanaka, Future Sound of London, Genesis P-Orridge, Giorgio Moroder, Goldie, Green Velvet, Hardfloor, Holger Czukay/Irmin Schmidt a.k.a. Can, Jesse Saunders, Joey Beltram, John Cage, Jonah Sharp, Juan Atkins, Karlheinz Stockhausen, Ken Ishii, Kevin Saunderson, Kid Koala, Kodwo Eshun, Lee Ranaldo, LFO, LTJ Bukem, Marshall Jefferson, Meat Beat Manifesto, Mike Dearborn, Mixmaster Morris, Moby, Money Mark, Neil Landstrumm, Omni Trio, O Yuki Conjugate, Orbital, Oval, Panacea, Paul Johnson, Photek, Pierre Henry, Prodigy, Prototype 909, Raymond Roker, Rob Playford, Robert Moog, Robert Pepperell, Roni Size, Ryoji Ikeda, Sand, Sasha, Scanner, Sensorband, Simon Reynolds, Sluts'n'strings & 909, Soulslinger & David Quinlan, Squarepusher, Stacey Pullen, Surgeon, Talvin Singh, Taylor Deupree & Savvas Ysatis, Teo Macero, Terre Thaemlitz, Tetsu Inoue, The Invisibl Skratch Piklz, To Rococo Rot, Velocette, Westbam, William S. Burroughs, Workshop, X-Ecutioners DIRECTOR: Iara Lee was born to Korean parents and raised in Brazil. Her career in film began as the producer and programmer of the Sao Paulo International Film Festival, a tenure that lasted from 1984 to 1989. From there Iara relocated to NYC to launch a film production company, Caipirinha Productions. Under the Caipirinha banner, she directed three short films – Prufrock, Neighbors and An Autumn Wind – before embarking on two feature length films – *Synthetic Pleasures* (about all things artificial) and *Modulations* (about the evolution of electronic music). In 1997, Iara launched the Caipirinha Music record label to further promote electronic music and mixed-media projects. Iara's next film project is a narrative feature, a contemporary adaptation of the classic nineteenth century novel Dom Casmurro by famed Brazilian author Machado de Assis. PRODUCER: George Gund is a native of Cleveland who divides his time between San Francisco, New York City, and wherever his involvement in the worlds of ice hockey, basketball, and independent film take him. An enthusiastic patron of the arts and professional and amateur sports, his interests include producing and distributing international films, scouting the eastern and northern hemispheres for emerging hockey talent, and collecting Asian and Native American art. He has produced two films for Caipirinha Productions, *Modulations* - Cinema For The Ear and *Synthetic Pleasures*. Characterized by his bottomless curiosity and his tireless pursuits around the world, George Gund has more stories up his sleeve than any bio can convey. LOCATIONS: Barcelona, Berlin, Budapest, Chicago, Cologne, Dillon/Montana, Frankfurt, Helsinki, Los Angeles, London, Miami, Montreal, Moscow, New York City, Osaka, Paris, Philadelphia, San Francisco, Toronto, Tokyo EVENTS: Billboard Conference (Chicago), CMJ (NYC), Essential Music (Brighton, U.K.), Lollapalooza (USA), Love Parade (Berlin), Popkomm (Cologne), Rainbow 2000 (Mount Fuji, Japan), Siggraph (Los Angeles), Sonar (Barcelona), Winter Music Conference (Miami) VENUES: Alter Planet-Berlin / Anchorage-NYC / Arena-Berlin / Asbury Park Convention Hall-New Jersey / Coney Island High-NYC / Cooler Club-NYC / E-Werk-Berlin / Fondation Cartier-Paris / Groove Society-Montreal / Industry Club-Toronto / Kalkscheune-Berlin / No UFO-Berlin / Paradise-Berlin / Plush 6 Club-NYC / Raveline-Berlin / Roland Factory-Osaka, Japan / Roseland-NYC / Satellite Of Love-Berlin / Sona Club- Montreal / Tresor-Berlin / Tunnel Club-NYC / Turnmills Club-London / Twilo Club-NYC / Vinyl Club-NYC / Westbeth Theatre-NYC / WTF-Berlin / Yaam-Berlin

DIRECTOR'S NOTES ON THE THE MAKING OF '*MODULATIONS*' FILM I'll never forget the first showing of *Modulations*. It was at the Sundance Film Festival. The theatre was filled with a majority of regular film buffs and movie critics. I was nervous. At the end of the screening, I overheard people saying "I thought I hated techno, but this film really opened my mind." I can only hope that this electronic revolution continues and that my contributions can create a positive influence to those willing to listen. I began the documenting process from a tabula rasa, eager to discover and to bring a fresh perspective to the topic, and prepared to consider all genres and different interpretations of the evolution of this so called "disposable" music culture that has turned so unpredictably into a youth culture revolution. The approach was if I could entertain myself while learning, possibly the audience would experience the same thing. I had a mission. Though the film was developed in collaboration with many writers, I must thank Peter Shapiro, the consulting writer for the film and editor of this book: He was the film's encyclopedia. Together we made huge lists of different questions to ask the more than six hundred musicians we wanted to interview. Eventually we then to narrow this mass interrogation down to a manageable size without dismissing the artists' individual contributions to their respective genres. We spent the entire year of 1997 globetrotting, interviewing musicians, going to their studios, and shooting live gigs and different events. The experience was amazing, but tremendously exhausting. During the day we would conduct interviews, then move into the evening by going to film the events until the early hours of the morning. We were constantly on the move, carrying heavy equipment from country to country, haggling with customs, and enduring the grind of sweaty nightclubs (fun, but with a camera and crew most difficult!). Despite the insanity of the process, we always found it possible to have a good laugh at the end of the day. Every shoot brought a new adventure. We covered more than forty cities around the world. One very memorable experience was the shoot at Mt. Fuji, Japan for the Rainbow 2000 rave. A typhoon had struck, yet the storm did not stop the kids from partying. What a sight; pouring rain and punishing winds...The DJ's covered the stage with plastic, and we covered our cameras in garbage bags. One of my favorite shots in the movie was taken there. We wanted to get an overview of the kids dancing in the mud yet there was no crane. Marcus Burnett, our cameraman, came up with a brilliant idea that cost a healthy repair bill but we got the shot. He threw the camera in the air for an elevated effect!! All in the name of filmmaking...Another normal procedure was to stay up all night in order to get the prime two-minute shot of an artist performing at an event. A great moment was in New York, with Danny Tenaglia holding us from 12A.M. until 6A.M. for the best shot. Needless to say it WAS the best shot. We also had to resort to some virtual filmmaking. There were many times that we wanted to be or needed to be in two places at the same time in order to get footage of two events going on simultaneously, or so that we could conduct interviews that we had been attempting forever and had finally gotten set up at the last minute. We would search for cameramen via the internet, e-mail the questions, and have them conduct the interviews and courier the footage to New York. That was how we got Derrick May, LTJ Bukem, and Giorgio Moroder on the same weekend! Due to their rare public disclosures, the Future Sound of London interview was conducted via isdn line. By the end of the year, we had accumulated over 300 hours of film, started the editing process, and begunthe rights clearance of the 93 tracks that appeared in the film. With the film out to the world and now on video I'm constantly asked where the other innovators/heroes of electronic music are. Everything was done to bring innovators and purveyors to the film, but for those who want to learn more, here is a book for your further enjoyment. My obsessive desire to investigate the evolution of this music has become a continual mission. Today, through Caipirinha Music, I continue to attempt to convey what I feel about the music: Utter fascination with these continually evolving and risk-taking frequencies that break boundaries and move music forward towards a new era. In ten years, we shall be able to look back and see if we seeded the ground well enough to build a cultural legacy. – Iara Lee

THE **MODULATIONS** SOUNDTRACK IS AVAILABLE ON CAIPIRINHA MUSIC

Track list:

1. Donna Summer	I FEEL LOVE
2. Afrika Bambaataa	PLANET ROCK
3. Juan Atkins / Model 500	NO UFO'S - REMIX
4. LFO	SIMON FROM SYDNEY
5. Derrick May	STRINGS OF LIFE
6. Jesse Saunders	YEAH
7. Aphrodite	AMAZON 2 – KING OF THE BEATS
8. Panacea	STORMBRINGER
9. Goldie & Rob Playford	THE SHADOW
10. Ryoji Ikeda	LUXUS 1-3
11. Coldcut	ATOMIC MOOG 2000
12. To Rococo Rot	KRITISCHE MASSE 1

THE **EARLY MODULATIONS: VINTAGE VOLTS** COMPILATION IS AVAILABLE ON CAIPIRINHA MUSIC

1. Vladimir Ussachevsky/Otto Leuning	INCANTATION
2. Max Matthews	BICYCLE BUILT FOR TWO
3. Pierre Schaeffer	ÉTUDE AUX CHEMINS DE FER
4. Iannis Xenakis	CONCRET PH
5. John Cage	IMAGINARY LANDSCAPE NO. 1
6. Vittorio Gelmetti	TRENI D'ONDA A MODULAZIONE D'INTENSITÀ
7. Vladimir Ussachevsky	PIECE FOR TAPE RECORDER
8. Luc Ferrari	TÊTE ET QEUE DU DRAGON
9. Morton Subotnick	SILVER APPLES OF THE MOON

ABOUT CAIPIRINHA PRODUCTIONS Caipirinha Productions is an independent art/culture company with activities in just about every facet of communication, including film, electronic music, fashion, architecture, and the written word. Our first film, *Synthetic Pleasures*, explores the ways in which technology affects global society, investigating such cutting-edge technologies as controlled environments, virtual reality, cybersex, nootropics, and plastic beauty. *Modulations*, our second film, is an exploration of electronic music and its impact on 20th century pop culture. Our philosophy is not only to discover new talents, but to promote collaborations between countries in all forms of media and to cultivate strange and unusual musical experiments. The Caipirinha Music record label is a genre-defying melting pot of a record label. Since its launch in 1997, the label has released a combination of full albums, concept compilations, and soundtracks to both of our films. We are interested in exploring the synergies among different art forms in order, ultimately, to elevate and reinvent today's culture. www.caipirinha.com

A CAIPIRINHA (PRONOUNCED KY-PEE-REEN-YA) IS A POTENT BRAZILIAN COCKTAIL.
1 large or two small limes
2 heaping tablespoons of sugar
3 ounces of cachaça (Brazilian sugarcane brandy)
Crushed ice
First cut the lime into eight wedges. Put the pieces into a 10-oz. drinking glass. Sprinkle the sugar on the lime. Crush the sugar into the lime with a wooden pestle. Pour the cachaça over the lime. Shake or stir well. Add ice. If you use vodka instead of cachaça, it's a caipiroska; with rum, it's a caipírissima.

CAIPIRINHA PRODUCTIONS
WORKING TOWARDS A BETTER FUTURE!
REINVENTING CULTURE
FILM*MUSIC*COCKTAILS

GRATITUDE:

12k Music, 31 Records, 7 PM Management - Matt Jagger/ Phil Fajer, 83 West Records ADA-All the reps, Adrienne Orlando, Alex Berberich, Alex Figliolia Watermain & Sewer Contracting, Alex Ostroy, Alexis Maryon, Alma Melendez Amitav Koul, Andreas Troeger, Andrei Khabad, Antonio Arroyo, Aphrodite Recordings, Archive Films, Artbeats Software, Ash Records, Asphodel - Erik Gilbert, Sarah Mackenzie, Astralwerks, Atau Tanaka, Aurelia Apostle-Tobiass, Avery Lozada, Axel Baumann, Axiom - Bill Murphy, Babu, BBC Worldwide Americas, Inc., Beggars Banquet - Lesley Bleakley, Ben Perowsky, Bennett Management - Robert Bennett, Big Briar - Bob Moog, Binbun Furusawa, Bionic Dots,Black Flag Recordings - Sasha (Lady Bug), BMG Music Publishing, Bomb Hip-Hop Records, Boymerang Publishing, Breakbeat Science, Brian Bumbery, Brian Long, Buddha Music - Michael Perlstein, Burnt Friedman, C.F. Peters Corp., Cajual Records - Cajmere, Can Oral/Cem Oral/Kerosene, Canal Street Communications - Norene Maciwoda, Carl Craig, Carl Saytor, Carla Leighton, Caroline Records - Allison Tarnofsky, CCI Recordings, Cductive - Tom Ryan/ JC Gaviria, Channel Zero - Stephen Marshall, Chantal Passamonte, Cheap Records, Chris Bierlein, Chris Cunningham, Chris Wahl, Christian Marclay, Christina Puschmann, Christopher North, Chrome Records, City Slang World, Columbia Pictures, Comatonse Recordings, Complete Music, Christian Fleming, Curious Pics - Meredith Brown, Daisyworld - Eichii Azuma, Damion Clayton, Dan Roe, Daniel Kessler, Danny Blume/Chris Kelley, Danny Tenaglia/Kevin Mchugh, David Kristian, David Read, David Toop, Defiant Records, Deluxe Music Management - Claire, Designers Republic, Dietrich Schoeneman, Digital Hardcore - Miwa Okumura, Digital Hardcore Recordings - Peter Lawton, DMC Canada - Chris Kendall, Donna Summer, Doron Gura, Dynamic Tension Records, Earache Records, Earth Program - Joel Jordan, Echo & Feedback Music Newsletter,EK Promotions - Ethan & Kerry Morehart, Electrogroove, EMI Virgin Music, Inc., Emil Somogyi, Jr, Eric Watson, European American Music Distributors Corporation, Evidence Records - Jerry Gordon, Eye Q Entertainment, Fantasy Records - Terry Hinte, Fast Back Management - Cathy Cohn, Flyer Mag - Florian/Hosi/Daniel, Fondation Cartier, Paris, Formula - Sioux/ Jo, Freedom Management - Martyn Barter, Freibank - Klaus Meck, Funk Entertainment - Charles Chambers, Gary Beer, Gavin King, Gee Street, Genesis P-Orridge, Georgia Rucker, Gerald Rosenblatt, Giant Step - Jonathan/ Maurice/Gamall, Gisela Gumper, Good Looking Records- Sally Gross, Good Machine - Anthony Bregman, Gotta Move Productionz - Maidai Stocksberg, Grand Royal - Gena Rankin, Natalie Carlson, Green Frog Productions, Grey Multimedia - Sandra Chaikin, Ken Grey, Groove Essentials - Wayne Briggs, Ground Control - Terry Martin, Hat Hut Records, Hexstatic - Tracie Storey, Stuart Hill, Higher Ground - Rich, Hildegard Schmidt, Hope Carr, Hot Jams, Chicago, Il-Morrow Music, Industry Club, Toronto - Ronnie, Gavin, Invisibl Skratch Piklz, Ion Records, Irv Rudley, Isabel Urpi,Isabel Warnier & Bernadette Mangin (Pierre Henry's office), Jack Leitenberg, James and Rob Capria, James Lebrecht, Jason Jordan, JD Frantz, Jeremy Lowrence, John Cage Trust - Laura Kuhn, John Parker - Rees, Jon Berry, Judge Al Bradley, Jumpin' and Pumpin', Just Say Productions - Jesse Saunders, Karla Calderon, Katharine Mcquerrey, Katie King, Keith Blankinship, Ken Ishii, Kent Zuber, Kid Koala, Kim's Video - Yong Man Kim, Kinetic Art & Business, America - Norika Sora, Clare de Graw, Kitty-Yo - Antje Greie, Klangbad - Cornelia Paul, Koji Asano, Konkrete Jungle - Mac, L'il Joe Records - Joe Weinberg, Demetris Dawson, Ladomat - Tausher, Larry Stanley, Laurie Anderson, Lea & Solicitors - Stephen Lea, Lee Caruso, Lee Ranaldo, Leosong Copyright Services, Linda Toffler, Lollapalooza, Love Parade - Pia Hohnhaus, Lulie Gund, Malka Katzav, Marcus Burnett, Marcus Schmickler, Margarita Ochoa, Marita Hallfors, Mark Jan Wlodarkiewicz, Mark Kidel, Mark Newman - The Orb, Mark Perlson, MCA Music Limited - Simon Goffee, Mego Label, Merce Cunningham Foundation, Mercury

Records - Sue Marcus, Metroplex Records, Michael Holman, Midi Management - Mike Champion, Mike Pantino, Mille Plateaux - Achim Szepanski, Bernd Lennartz, Mixer Mag - Darren Ressler, Mixmaster Morris, Mo Wax - Andy Holmes, Moonquake Music, Moving Shadow Records - Julia, Scott Garrod, Mr. & Mrs. Macklovitch, Music & Arts Management - Steve Cohen, Music Mine - Hideki Amano, Nam June Paik, Nano - Rota Publishing Bmi,Nasty Little Man - Matt Sweeney, NBC News Archives - Rob Wright, Neal Page, Neil Harris, Nicholas Godin, Nicole Blackman Public Relations, Ninja Tune - Jeff and Philipa, Alastair Nicholson, No U Turn Records - Beverley Price, Steve Linden, Noodles Recordings, Omar Vargas, Oren Silverstein, Orlando Puerta, Oschatz/Popp, Other Music - Tom Cappodano, Parallel Recordings, Patricia Bates, Paul D. Miller, Paul Gilbert, Paul Yates, Paula Heredia, Pauline Oliveiros Foundation, Peace Magazine - Harris Rosen, Peter Kempter, Peter Romani, Pirkko Tiiknen, Planet E - Hannah Sawtell, Play It Again Sam, Plex/OHM/D'Vox - Rick Garrido, Steve Castro, Plus 8 - Clarke Warner, Pointblank - John Wright, Polygram Film & TV Music, Polygram Special Products - Gary Miller, R&S Records, Rachael Phillipps, Rainbow 2000 - Mr. Ochi, Rather Interesting, Ravers - Kristen Lubina, KD Dougherty, Alfio Giuliano, David Luna, Linda, Real Time, Regal Records, Reinforced Records, Relief Records, Rhapsody Films, Rhonda Mitrani, Rob Holden, Robert Leaton, Rogue Music - Michael Miguel And Ed Sullivan, Roland Corporation - Haruo Shoji, Kaz Tanaka- Japan, Roland USA - Jim Norman, Ryoji Ikeda, Sanlar, Scandinavia Records, Shakin Baker - Arthur Baker, Sharon Gallagher, Sioux Free (Big Briar), Sire Records, Six Flags Great Adventure Amusement Park, Skid, Skratch Music Publishing, Sonar - Georgia Taglietti, Sonic Groove-NYC, Sonicnet - Sara Gibson, Soundlab - Beth Coleman & Howard Goldkrand, Source 360 - Anne Hollande, Source/Virgin France, Steve Cauley, Steve Doughton, Steve Hoppe, Steve Tartakoff, Stockhausen Verlag - Suzanne Stevens, Streetsound - Chris Torella, Strictly Rhythm - Bari, Sub Rosa Records, Sundance Institute - Geoffrey Gilmore, Nicole Guillemet, Sundance Institute - Robert Redford, Surgeon (Tony Childs) - Dynamic Tension,Talking Loud, Taylor Deupree, Teo Macero, Terre Thaemlitz, Theresa Radka, Thrill Jockey - Bettina Richards, Howard, Tip Toe Productions, Tomato Design, Tommy Boy Records - Ana Sobrino, Too Pure - Susanna Grant, Torema Records - Keiko Suzuki, Fumiya Tanaka, Transmat - Derrick Ortencio, Derrick May, Trax Records, Triage Radio, Twilo - Mike Bindra, Twisted America Records, Ty Bertrand, Undercover, Unipix Entertainment and Transatlantic Films, Universal Edition, Upright Songs, Urb Mag - Raymond Roker, Urban Takeover, Us National Archives And Record Administration, Utopia Club, Las Vegas, Verve Records - Theodora Kuslan, Victor Schiffman, Warlock Records, Warner Chappell, Warp Records - Greg Eden, Rachel Thomas, Westbeth Theatre - John Weiss, Westbury Music, Will Flower, Waste Management Of New York, William Morris - Matt Bialer, Eric Zohn, William Neal, XL Recordings - Kathy Doherty, Chris Sharp, XLR8R Mag - Andrew Smith and the rest of the gang, XSV Music, Yin-Sight Management - Laura Gavoor, YMA - Toshio Kajiwara, Yuki Watanabe and Associates, Zachary Mortensen. . . . **AND TO ALL THE EDUCATORS, INNOVATORS, CLUBBERS, RAVERS + EVERYONE WHO SUPPORTED CAIPIRINHA AND *MODULATIONS.***